The Art of Living

Extemporaneous talks given by
Osho in Mumbai, India

OSHO

The Art of Living

MACMILLAN

First published in the Indian subcontinent 2016 by Macmillan
This updated edition published 2024 by Macmillan
an imprint of Pan Macmillan Publishing India Private Limited
707 Kailash Building
26 K. G. Marg, New Delhi 110001
www.panmacmillan.co.in

Pan Macmillan, The Smithson, 6 Briset Street, Farringdon, London EC1M 5NR
Associated companies throughout the world
www.panmacmillan.com

ISBN 978-93-82616-64-1

The material in this book is a translation of a series of original OSHO Talks, *Jyon Ki Tyon Dhari Deenhi Chadariya*, given to a live audience. The complete text archive can be found at www.osho.com/library

9 8

Typeset in Adobe Garamond Pro by R. Ajith Kumar, New Delhi
Printed and bound in India by Replika Press Pvt. Ltd.

MIX
Paper | Supporting responsible forestry
FSC www.fsc.org FSC™ C016779

Contents

Preface

If you don't take the lamp of awareness with you, you are going to create a hell around you. Light your lamp wherever you go. Wherever you go, whatsoever you do, always do it in the inner light, with awareness.

And don't be worried about moralities, concepts about what is good and what is bad. Good follows your inner light just like a shadow. Take care of the inner light.

That's what meditation is all about: to become more alert. Live the same life, just change your alertness, make it more intense. Eat the same food, walk the same path, live in the same house, be with the same woman and the children, but be totally different from your inside. Be alert! Walk the same path but with awareness. If you become aware, suddenly the path is no longer the same because you are no longer the same. If you are aware, the same food is not the same because you are not the same, the same woman is not the same because you are not the same. Everything changes with your inner change.

If somebody changes his within, the without changes totally. My definition of the world is that you must be living in a deep inner darkness – hence the world. If you light your inner lamp, suddenly the world disappears and there is only godliness. The world and godliness are not two things but two perceptions of the same energy. If you are unaware, the energy appears to you to be as the world, samsara; if you are alert, the same energy appears as godliness. The whole thing depends on your inner awareness or unawareness. That is the only change, the only transformation, the only revolution that has to be made.

Ancient Music in the Pines
Osho

A Note about Language

Spoken Words: Osho's books are not "written" but rather are transcribed from recordings of his talks. These talks are extemporaneous, without reference to notes other than copies of questions, stories or scriptures he has been asked to comment upon, or jokes he might use to drive home a particular point. He has asked his editors to preserve that quality of the spoken word in his printed books.

Pronouns: When hearing him speak, it is quite clear to the listener that generally when Osho talks about "man" he is referring to "human beings." His use of "he" as a default pronoun simply serves an ease and flow of speaking – in no way does it imply that "she" (or "they") is being dismissed or disregarded.

Osho's unique vantage point is good to keep in mind:

A meditator is neither a man nor a woman,
because meditation has nothing to do with your body;
neither does it have anything to do with your mind.
In meditation you are simply and purely consciousness.
And consciousness is neither male nor female.

~Osho

1

Nonviolence

My beloved ones.

Non-violence, *non-possessiveness*, *non theft*, *non-desire*, *non-unawareness* are all negative words: they express negatively. This is very significant, and must be understood. In fact, the discipline of seeking can only be negative.

Attainment will be positive: what will be attained is already the case, and what we have to lose is only what is not really there. If darkness is dispelled, light is attained. If untruth is lost, truth is attained.

It is necessary to bear one more point in mind: the negative word indicates that nonviolence is our intrinsic nature. It cannot be attained; it is already the case. Violence is acquired, it is not our nature. It has been achieved, it is an accomplishment. To become violent we have to do something. Violence is our achievement; we have sought it, we have created it. Nonviolence cannot be an achievement. If violence disappears, what remains will be nonviolence.

Hence the disciplines of seeking are negative. We have picked up something which is not worth having and we have to drop it. No one is violent by nature – they cannot be because no one can desire unhappiness, and violence only leads you to unhappiness.

Violence is incidental; it is not in the stream of life. Even a violent person cannot be violent twenty-four hours a day. Yet a nonviolent person can be in nonviolence twenty-four hours a day. Even a violent person has to be nonviolent sometimes. Actually, even if he is committing violence, he does it so that he can be nonviolent with others; that's why he is doing it. A man cannot be a thief twenty-four hours a day. And even if someone is stealing, he does it so that he can be without stealing for a while. The thief's goal is non-theft, and a violent person's goal is nonviolence. So all these words are negative.

In the language of religiousness there are two positive words, otherwise all words are negative. I have omitted both of them from the discussion so far. One is the word *satya*, truth, which is positive; and the other is the word *brahmacharya*, godlike behavior, which is also positive.

So first it is important to bear in mind that the five words I have chosen, which I am calling the five great virtues, are negative. When those five are fulfilled, what will be attained inside will be truth, and what will be manifest on the outside will be godlike behavior.

When these five virtues are fulfilled, truth will become the soul and godlike behavior will become the behavior. They are both positive words. Truth means what will be known on the inside, and godlike behavior means what will be lived on the outside. *Brahmacharya* means godlike behavior. Only a person who has become godlike can have godlike behavior. Truth means becoming godlike; the meaning of truth *is* godliness. And the behavior of one who has become godlike is brahmacharya. His behavior will become godlike. In the language of religiousness, only these two words are positive, otherwise the entire language of religiousness is negative. In the next five days, we will discuss these five negations. Today we start with the first negation: nonviolence.

If you understand correctly, there can be no discussion of nonviolence. We can only discuss violence and the disappearance of violence. Remember, the meaning of nonviolence is only this: the nonbeing of violence, the non-presence, the absence of violence.

Look at it like this. Ask a doctor what the definition of health is: How do you define it? So many sciences about health have been developed, but none gives the definition of health. If you ask what the definition of health is, the doctor will say it is where there is no illness. But that is about illness; it is not speaking about health. It is the absence of illness. There can be a definition of illness, of what illness is, but there can be no definition of health: What is health? At the most, we can say that when someone is not ill, he is healthy.

Religiousness is supreme health! That is why there can be no definition of religiousness. All definitions are of non-religiousness. In these five days, we will not discuss religiousness. We will discuss non-religiousness.

If through thinking, through awareness, non-religiousness is dropped, what remains is non-thinking, and its name is religiousness. That is why wherever there is a discussion about religiousness, useless debates happen. A discussion can only be about non-religiousness. A discussion about religiousness cannot happen at all. A discussion can only be about illness, not about health. Health can be known, health can be lived, one can become healthy – but there can be no discussion about it. Religiousness can be known, religiousness can be lived, one can be in religiousness, but there can be no discussion about it. That is why all religious scriptures actually discuss non-religiousness. No one discusses religiousness.

So let us discuss the first non-religiousness – violence. The virtue we are discussing today is for the violent. Understand that underlying whatever we discuss today will be the belief that we are violent – otherwise this discussion would have no meaning. Anyway, we *are* violent. There may be differences in our violence... Violence has so many layers, so many subtleties, that often what we call nonviolence and understand as nonviolence is only a very subtle form of violence. And it can also be that what we call violence is also a gross form of nonviolence. Life is very complicated.

For example, I call Gandhi's nonviolence a subtle form of violence, and I call Krishna's violence a gross form of nonviolence.

This will be understood when we discuss it. Only the violent need to discuss nonviolence; that is why it is also relevant to understand that the idea of nonviolence came into this world from violent communities.

The twenty-four tirthankaras of the Jainas were kshatriyas, warriors. They were a tribe of violent people. There was not even one brahmin among them. There was not even one vaishya, one merchant among them. Buddha was also a kshatriya. The concept of nonviolence has come into the world from these violent groups. The idea of nonviolence was born in this world where violence was thick and prolific.

Actually, it was only the violent who were forced to consider nonviolence. To those who were engrossed in violence twenty-four hours a day, it became clear that violence was not their innermost reality. If a warrior has a sword in his hand and in his mind, it will not take him long to realize, "Violence is all pain and misery. It cannot be the meaning of life, it cannot bring bliss."

The virtue we are discussing today is for the violent. However, those who consider themselves nonviolent should also meditate on today's virtue. I will discuss with the assumption that we who are assembled here together are the violent. And when I talk to you about the many forms of violence, you will be able to understand which kind of violent person you are.

The first condition toward being nonviolent is to recognize your violence in the right way – because one who recognizes his violence cannot remain violent. The trick, the technique to remain violent, is to see your violence as nonviolence. So untruth comes in the garb of truth, and violence comes in the garb of nonviolence. An illusion is created.

I have heard a story; it is a Syrian tale…

When God created the deities of beauty and ugliness, they descended to earth. Their clothes were covered in dust and grime, so they put them on the bank of a lake and went in to bathe.

Naturally, the goddess of beauty did not even think that her clothes could be switched. Actually, beauty is not aware of her clothes, she is not even aware of her body. Only ugliness is aware of her body, only ugliness is worried about her clothes. Ugliness finds ways to hide herself by arranging her body and her clothes.

The goddess of beauty went far into the lake to bathe and then the goddess of ugliness took her chance. She came out, dressed herself in the clothes of the goddess of beauty, and ran away. When the goddess of beauty came out, she was very surprised. Her clothes were not there. She was standing naked; the people in the village had started moving about and the path had become busy. Out of desperation, and as the goddess of ugliness had taken her clothes and run away, she had to wear the clothes of ugliness.

The story says that ever since that time she is searching for the goddess of ugliness, but she has still not found her. Ugliness is still wearing the clothes of beauty, and the goddess of beauty is still garbed in the clothes of ugliness.

Actually, whenever untruth is expressed, it has to borrow the facade of truth. If untruth wants to express itself, then it has to adopt the ways of truth. Violence also has to become nonviolence to be able to exist. So the first thing that is necessary in the pursuit of nonviolence is to understand the facades of violence. Its nonviolent facades are especially important to recognize. Directly, violence cannot deceive anyone at all. All the sins of the world are incapable of deceiving directly. Evil can only deceive in the guise of virtue.

This is the story of the grandeur of virtue. Even if evil wins, it is because it has put on the facade of virtue. It is the quality of virtue that always wins, even if it is being used as a facade of evil. Evil never wins; evil is a defeat in itself. Violence cannot win – but violence has not disappeared from the world because we have found many nonviolent ways to be violent. So we must first try to understand the many faces of violence.

The first form of violence – the first dimension, its first rule – is very deep; let us start from there. The first violence begins whenever you consider another as "the other." As soon I say that you are the other, I have become violent toward you. Actually it is impossible to be nonviolent with another. We can only be nonviolent with ourselves; such is nature. We can only be nonviolent with ourselves; we simply cannot be nonviolent with another. The question itself does not arise – because violence begins with the very perception of the other as the other. It is very subtle; it is very deep.

Sartre's dictum is: the other is hell; whoever is the other is hell. I am in agreement with Sartre's statement up to a point. His understanding is deep. He is correct in saying that the other is hell, but his understanding is incomplete. The other is not hell. *Seeing* the other as "the other" is hell. That is why whatever few moments of bliss we experience, we get only when we accept the other as our own self. This is what we call love.

If, in some moment, I consider someone to be my own self, then in that moment the stream that flows between him and me is one of nonviolence; it cannot remain one of violence. That moment of seeing someone as my own self is a moment of love. But the one that I consider to be my own self remains the other deep inside. Calling someone else my own self is a recognition of the fact that he is another, but that I consider him to be one with me.

Hence somewhere in the depths of what we call love there is violence. That is why the flame of love, the fire of love, keeps waxing and waning. Sometimes the other becomes the other; sometimes he is one with me. In twenty-four hours, this change may happen several times. When someone goes a little too far and appears as the other, then violence comes in between. When someone comes a little closer and begins to appear as my own self, then the violence diminishes. But the one I call my own is also the other. A wife is the other, however much she is mine. A son is the other, however much he is mine. A husband is also the other. The feeling of the other is always present, even when calling someone my own. That is why love cannot be completely nonviolent. Love has its own ways of violence.

Love commits violence in its own way; it commits violence lovingly. A wife tortures her husband in a loving manner. A husband tortures his wife in a loving manner. A father tortures his son in a loving manner. And when the torture is loving, it becomes very self-assured; then to torture becomes easy because violence puts on the mask of nonviolence. A teacher tortures a student and says, "I am torturing you for your own good."

When we torture someone else for their own benefit, torturing is very easy. It becomes glorified and virtuous. So remember: when torturing others, our faces are without masks, but when torturing those we call our own, our faces are never clear, they are masked. And the greatest violence committed in the world is not against others; it is against those we call our own.

The truth is that before making anyone an enemy, first it is essential to make him a friend. To make someone a friend, it is not a necessary condition to first make him an enemy; there is no condition at all. But to make an enemy, it is necessary to first make him a friend. Without making him a friend, you cannot make him an enemy. Yes, you can make him a friend without making him an enemy, but friendship always precedes enmity.

The most profound pretense of nonviolence occurs when we are being violent toward those we call our own. So, one who wants to become aware of his own violence will first have to become aware of the violence that he has toward those he calls his own.

As I have said, in certain moments when we are very close, the other appears to be our own self. This moving toward and moving away is very fluid. It keeps changing all the time. We are never in love with someone for twenty-four hours a day. There are only moments of love. There are no hours of love; there are no days of love. There are no years of love, only moments. But from those moments the illusion of permanence arises; then violence begins. If I love someone, then it is a matter of the moment. I may also love him in the next moment, but this is not a certainty. If I have promised to keep loving him in the next moment too, if we have moved apart and violence has come between us when the next moment comes, that violence will take the facade, the appearance of love. That is why all the institutions in the world that were created to possess the other are violent. No institution has committed more violence than the institution called the family, but its violence is very subtle.

So when a sannyasin, a seeker, had to leave his family, it was for a reason – to go beyond this subtle violence. There was no other reason. There is only one reason: the subtle web of violence among those we call our own. It is difficult to fight the family because they are being violent for our own good. And society is just an extended version of the family, so the amount of violence committed by society is incalculable. The reality is that society has nearly killed the individual.

So be aware that when you relate with someone as a member of society, you are being violent. If you relate with someone as a Jaina, then you are violent. If you relate as a Hindu, then you are violent. If you relate as a Mohammedan, then you are violent. Because now you are not behaving like an individual, you are behaving like society. As long as the individual is unable to become nonviolent, then the possibility of society being nonviolent is very remote. Society can never be nonviolent; hence the greatest violence in the world has been committed by societies, not by individuals.

If you tell a Mohammedan to burn down a temple on his own, as an individual, he will think twenty times about it because this violence is clearly visible. But put him in a crowd of ten thousand Mohammedans and he will not think even once – because a crowd of ten thousand is a society. Now the violence is not so clear; in fact now it can be said that he may set fire to the temple for the sake of religion. A Hindu may do exactly the same thing to a mosque. All the societies of the world are doing the same thing to each other.

Society means a crowd, a group of those we call our own. And it will be difficult to banish violence from the world unless we stop this insistence on creating a crowd which we call our own. The meaning of "our own crowd" is that this crowd will forever stand against another crowd. That is why all the institutions in the world are violent. No institution in the world can be nonviolent; there is no possibility at the present time, it could take millions of years. When the whole of humanity is transformed, then perhaps there could just sometimes be a gathering of nonviolent people.

Right now, all gatherings are of violent people, even the family. A family is a unit created against other people. A family is a biological unit. It is a biological unit against other biological units. Society is a communal unit against other societies. A state is a political unit against other states. All these units are violent. Man will be nonviolent only when he commits completely to being an individual.

Hence Mahavira cannot be called a Jaina, and the ones who call him that do him an injustice. Mahavira cannot be part of any society. Krishna cannot be called a Hindu, and calling Jesus a Christian is complete insanity. They are individuals; they are their own unit. They are not ready to join any other unit.

Sannyas is a refusal to join all such units, such crowds. Actually, sannyas is a declaration of the fact that society is violent, and that by standing with society one will have to be violent. This is the facade, the face of those we call our own people, and it represents the subtlest form of violence.

Even what we call love is not yet nonviolence. Someone who I call my own is also not me; he too is the other. Nonviolence begins the day there *is* no other. Not that the other belongs to me, the other simply does not exist.

But what is the reason for the other appearing to be the other? You would think that the other must exist – after all, he appears as the other. But it is not necessarily true that something is what it appears to be. In the dark, even a rope may look like a snake. It is only in the light that we come to know that it is not.

Seen with naked eyes, a stone appears solid. Seen with the penetrating eyes of science, the solidity disappears. The stone is no longer substantial. Actually, the stone is no longer a stone at all, it is no longer material at all, it does not even remain as matter – it is only energy. No, it is not at all how it appears to be. How it appears to be is only an indication of our capability to see. Is it visible because it is the other? No, the reason for the visibility of the other is not its existence. The reason for the visibility of the other is quite astonishing. It is necessary to understand this. Without understanding it, you will not be able to understand the real depth of violence.

The other is visible to you because as yet, you are not. You might not understand this immediately. You are not; you do not know yourself at all. And this nonexistence of yourself, this not knowing of yourself, this ignorance of yourself, you have turned into perceiving the other. You see the other because you don't know how to see yourself. But you will have to see yourself eventually.

There are only two possibilities of seeing: either other-directed – looking toward the other – or inner-directed, looking toward the inner. The arrow is either directed inward or outward. Seeing another or seeing oneself – these are the two alternatives, these are the two dimensions of seeing. Because we fail to see ourselves, because we have never seen ourselves, we go on seeing the other. The very existence of the other is born out of our ignorance of ourselves. In fact, these are the two dimensions of meditation.

A young man playing on the hockey field injures his leg; he is bleeding. Thousands of spectators can see that his leg is bleeding, only he himself does not know. What has happened to him? Isn't he conscious? He is fully conscious because he is able to see even the slightest movement of the ball. Is he unconscious? He is not at all unconscious because the slightest movement, the slightest stirring of the other players is visible to him. He is not unconscious because he is able to run and is in full control of his body. But his leg is bleeding. Why is it not visible to him? Why is this not getting through to him?

His entire attention is other-directed. In this moment, his consciousness is one-dimensional. It is pointed in an outward direction. He is engrossed in the game. He is engrossed with such intensity that not even a fragment of consciousness remains that can go inward. His whole consciousness is directed outward. Then the game stops and he sits down clutching his leg, crying, "I'm badly injured; how come I didn't notice it?"

Where was he for half an hour? He was there for that half hour, but he was focused on the other. Now he has returned to himself. Now he is aware that he has an injured leg; he is in pain, he is suffering. Now his attention goes to his body. But deep down, he is still other-directed. His attention has gone to his body but that too is "the other." It is still only the exterior. He is aware that there is pain in his leg – but he is still not aware of the one who is aware that there is pain in his leg. He still has no awareness of himself at all. A deeper journey inside is possible, and he is standing in the middle.

The other is outside, I am inside, and between the two is my body. My journey – either toward the other or toward my own body – keeps moving between the two. My consciousness goes on moving back and forth between these two. I know the other, or I know my body, which is also the other.

Actually our bodies and our relationships are just like the banks of a river; between my body and your body the river of consciousness goes on flowing. By "your" body I do not mean you; just as "my" refers only to my body, so "your" means only your body. Neither do I have any interest in your consciousness, nor do I know anything about your consciousness. If one does not know one's own consciousness, how can he know about the other's consciousness?

I know my body and I know your body, and it would be correct to say that the relationship between our two bodies is one of violence. There can be no relationship of nonviolence between two bodies; it will always be one of violence. It can be of good violence, it can be of bad violence; it can be of harmful violence, it can be of harmless violence. But it is difficult to decide when something harmless becomes dangerous, or when something dangerous becomes harmless.

A man is pressing someone to his chest in love; it is a completely harmless form of violence. Actually, he is taking pleasure in pressing another's body against his own. But if it gets a little stronger, if he presses a little harder, fear will arise. If he does not let go, if he presses even harder and the other starts suffocating, then what was love will suddenly turn into hatred; it will become violence.

There are lovers whom we call sadists, torturers of each other. Unless they torture the other, their love is not satisfied. In love we all torture each other. What we call a kiss is a way of torturing, but soft, mild. Violence is there, but it is mild. But if it gets stronger, becomes biting, then the violence increases a little. And some lovers bite too! Even up to this point it is okay, but when tearing and cutting begins... The writers of the scriptures on love have even accepted clawing your lover with your nails as a method of lovemaking.

In India, experts on the *Kama Sutra* say that unless you scratch your lover with your nails, love will not arise inside. But scratching with your nails? Then what is the harm in scratching with an instrument? It can amplify it! It does amplify the sensation, because when scratching with your nails becomes a daily habit, then the novelty is lost. Then you will have to use an instrument.

The man after whom the word *sadism* was coined, de Sade, used to keep a whip with him and a five-fingered needle, and stones. He kept other instruments of love in his bag also. When he would make love to someone, after shutting and locking the door, he would take out his whip. First he would beat the other person's body. When his lover's whole body had become bloody from the whip, he would pierce it with needles – and all this was love.

You would say, "This is not my kind of love," but he just went a little further. The difference is only of degree; there is no qualitative difference, no difference in the nature of it. There is only a quantitative difference, of degrees, of proportion. Actually whatever relationship we have with the other's body will be one of violence, more or less. There is not much difference.

Many lovers have squeezed the lover's throat in moments of love – they have killed them! There have been trials. The courts could not understand what kind of love this was. But the courts should understand that this is a more advanced form of love, the relationship has become a little more intimate. All lovers squeeze each other's throats. Some squeeze by hand, some squeeze with the mind, some squeeze with other techniques. But squeezing the lover has been our way – one way or another.

Whether it is stabbing with a knife or kissing and embracing, there is no fundamental difference in the relationship that exists between two bodies. You will be surprised to know that the joy that some people get from stabbing another's body with a knife is derived from the idea of sexual penetration. Have you ever thought about it? The pleasure of putting a knife into someone's body, or the pleasure of shooting a bullet into someone's body has arisen out of sexual perversion.

Actually sexual pleasure is also the pleasure of entering another's body. If a person's mind has become a little perverted then he can seek other ways of penetration. Call him perverted or inventive; he has become innovative. He can say that entering another person's body through the vagina is also done by animals; what is man's achievement in it? So man seeks other techniques by which he can enter another's body. Those who look into it deeply say that the joy of murdering somebody is perverted sex. They say that the pleasure of killing another is the pleasure of entering the other.

Have you noticed? Sometimes if small children see an insect moving, they will injure it and watch; if they find a flower, they will tear it up. Can you imagine that for some men the same curiosity is being played out by tearing someone apart and watching? Could you also say that science is violent, deep down? It is an attempt to tear things up and look. But it is acceptable. If you are killing a frog outdoors, people will say you are doing something bad. But if you are dissecting the frog on the laboratory table, no one will call it bad. It could be that the scientist is getting the same kind of pleasure from it. It would take a lot of time to understand the consciousness of a scientist, but we can see that he has given his violent behavior a scientific direction, which is acceptable.

We can give violent behavior many directions. Sometimes we have directed it into sacrificial offerings, giving violence a religious aspect. Someone wants to kill an animal, but killing is evil, it is a sin – so let's make killing a virtue! We want to have the pleasure of killing, so we kill for sacrificial offerings; we kill on the sacred grounds of a deity, then it becomes virtuous.

But now this has become madness. Now that we know there are no sacred grounds belonging to the deities, now that we know there is no place to make sacrificial offerings, where can we kill?

If you want to kill, then kill honestly; say that you want to kill! Why do you involve the gods in it? Why bring the gods into it?

There is a story in Ramakrishna's life about a man who always came to him. Every year during the festival of Kali, he would have hundreds of goats killed. Then the killing of goats stopped, and the man stopped celebrating. Two years passed. He did not come to Ramakrishna for a long time. Then suddenly he came.

Ramakrishna said, "Have you abandoned your devotion to Kali? You don't kill goats anymore?"

The man said, "I don't have any teeth anymore, so what is the point of killing goats?"

So Ramakrishna said, "Were you killing the goats because of your teeth?"

He said, "When my teeth fell out there was no pleasure in it anymore. It was difficult to eat meat, but somehow under the name of Kali I could do it."

The old sacred religious grounds have disappeared. Today's religion is science. That is why on the sacred grounds of science, violence occurs; many kinds of violence occur. Science devises thousands of ways to torture but we don't protest. In earlier times, we did not protest against religious sacrifices because at that time they were acceptable. In the same way, the sacred grounds of science are acceptable today.

If you go into a scientist's laboratory, you will be very surprised. So many rats are being killed. So many frogs are being cut up. So many animals are being hung upside down. So many animals are being made unconscious. So many animals are being dissected. All this is happening, but the scientist is quite sure that he is not committing violence. He thinks that he is doing it to discover happiness for mankind. Now violence is covered up with a facade of nonviolence and so it is okay.

When you love someone, consider whether your inner violence has not assumed the face of love. If it has, then it is the most dangerous face because it is very difficult to be aware of. You will continue to feel that you are being loving.

Another person is "the other" as long as I do not know myself. I call this the foundation stone of violence. The meaning of violence is other-oriented consciousness, a consciousness based on the other. A consciousness based on oneself becomes nonviolence; a consciousness based on the other becomes violence.

But we only know the other. Whenever we look, we only see the other. And even if we think of ourselves sometimes, it is always through the other. We think about ourselves according to what others think about us. Even if I have a face, then it is a face given by you, the other. I will always be careful that your mind does not form a bad impression of me. Otherwise my image will be destroyed – because I don't have an authentic image of myself. It is as if I have created my image from newspaper clippings. I have created an image of myself by hearing what you say, and collecting your opinions about me.

If even one of these opinion-givers slips away – a guru's devotee starts calling him names, a disciple turns into an enemy, a friend is no longer a friend, a son disowns his father – then the father's image starts crumbling, the guru's image starts to disintegrate and he begins to panic: "Now I'm finished!" All this happens because they don't have an authentic image of themselves. Their images are created by others.

A father is not aware of being a father, he is only aware of someone being his son. He is a father because someone is his son. If the son refuses to remain his son, his fatherhood is threatened. A husband is not aware of being a husband, he is a husband only in the context of someone being his wife. If the wife begins to take the slightest of liberties, his status as husband is shaken. We are all dependent on others. And someone who is dependent on others will always have to keep looking to others.

We see others in our dreams, we see others while awake. Even if we sit for meditation, we meditate upon others; we meditate on Mahavira, we meditate on Buddha, we meditate on Krishna. Even there, others are present. Meditation in which others are present is violent. Meditation in which only you remain may perhaps lead you to nonviolence.

The other is, therefore I am unable to see rightly. Since I do not see myself, my consciousness is focused on the other. The day I see myself, you will cease to be seen as the other.

But when Mahavira avoids stepping on an ant while walking, don't be under the illusion that his reason is the same as yours when you avoid stepping on an ant. When you avoid an ant, you are only avoiding an ant, but when Mahavira avoids an ant, he avoids stepping on his own self. There is a fundamental difference between these two. Mahavira's avoidance is nonviolence; your avoidance is still violence. To you, the other exists; your concern is that the ant may be killed. And why are you worried that the ant may be killed?

Your only worry is that you would become a sinner by killing an ant. This is other-oriented consciousness – you may sin by killing an ant, you may go to hell for killing an ant, you may lose all your virtues for killing an ant, you may lose your place in heaven because you killed an ant. You are not concerned about the ant, your concern is always with yourself, but it is oriented toward the ant. Your mind is focused on the ant; you are avoiding the ant itself.

No, you don't feel the way Mahavira feels. Mahavira's avoiding of the ant is a different matter altogether. He is not avoiding the ant at all. If we ask Mahavira why he is avoiding it, he would say, "How can I step on myself?" No, this is not avoidance. The reality is that it is not possible to step on oneself.

One day, Ramakrishna was crossing the Ganges in a boat. Suddenly he started shouting aloud, "Don't beat me, don't beat me! Why are you beating me?"

People were sitting around him and no one was beating him. They were all his devotees; they would touch his feet, massage his feet, no one ever beat him. Everyone asked, "What are you talking about? Who is beating you?" Ramakrishna went on shouting; he bared his back and they saw wounds from a whipping on his back. Blood was oozing. Everyone was puzzled and nervous. They all asked Ramakrishna, "What has happened? Who whipped you?"

Ramakrishna said, "Look! There! They are beating me."

On the other bank, some boatmen were whipping a man and the whip marks that appeared on his back had also appeared on Ramakrishna's back, the exact identical marks. When people disembarked and gathered around the scene and started to compare the marks, it became difficult to see who had received the original whipping. Ramakrishna was wounded more deeply than the other man; the marks were the same, but the wounds were deeper – because the man being whipped may have been resisting it from within but Ramakrishna accepted it totally. That caused the deeper wounds.

Do you understand the implication of the phrase, "Don't beat me," as it was uttered by Ramakrishna?

We have a word: *sympathy*. But this is not sympathy. Sympathy arises in the heart of a man of violence. He says, "Don't beat him, don't beat the other." *Sympathy* means the feeling of pity. But pity is always for someone else. This is empathy, not sympathy. Ramakrishna does not say, "Don't beat him," he says, "Don't beat *me*." The other has disappeared for him.

In fact, our whole distance from the other is only of the body. There is no gap in consciousness. On the level of consciousness, there are not two persons. If we protect the other, it is never nonviolence. When we save the other, it is still violence. When only "I" remain, and no other remains to be protected, on that day nonviolence is born.

Therefore, in the context of nonviolence, it is necessary to understand this deep violence and to understand how to drop it, how to let go of the other. Sartre is right in saying, "The other is hell," but it would be better to make a little amendment to his statement: the other is not hell, "otherness" is hell. If otherness can be dropped, then even another person is not the other.

Mahavira's nonviolence has not been understood because we, the violent, give even Mahavira's nonviolence a violent meaning. We say, "Do not hurt others." But remember, as long as the other is there, violence will continue. Then it makes no difference whether you push a real knife into someone's chest, or a knife that is made out of an idea that you call "the other."

Are you aware that when you are sitting in a room and someone else enters, you are no longer the same as you were before he came in? The other has come and violence has begun – his eyes, his presence are there. He is not beating you, he is not hurting you, he is saying very nice things such as "How are you doing?" but the way he looks…

As soon as another person comes in, he has made you the other. As soon as someone else comes into the room, you have made him the other too. Violence has begun. Now his eyes, his inspection, his looking, his sitting, his being, his presence are violent. Now you are afraid; we only become afraid when there is violence. Now you have to sit carefully.

In your bathroom, you are a different kind of person than in your sitting room because in your sitting room there is a possibility of violence. In the sitting room we tolerate the violence of others; it is where we greet others, where we invite others. So we decorate the room in a nonviolent manner. We decorate it in such a way that another person's violence becomes as small as possible; the decoration lessens the other person's violence. Our faces are all smiles in the sitting room because smiling is a defense against the other's violence. We say nice words, we observe etiquette, we observe civility. These are all arrangements, security measures to reduce another person's violence.

If you curse, then the other person's violence will have a chance to become stronger. You say, "So compassionate of you to come! The guest is God. Come grace us." You are reducing the other's violence; he will find it hard to be violent. The other is also reducing your violence. That is why when two men meet for the first time, there is great etiquette. After three or four hours, the etiquette falls away. After three or four days, it is finished. After three or four months, they start cursing each other – even though they say they are cursing each other with love, they are doing it out of friendship. When they first meet they say "you" respectfully, and when they meet after two or three months they say "you" casually. What happens in three months? Actually, the violence of both has now become settled, organized. Now it is not necessary to take so many safety precautions.

Thus the presence of the other becomes violence. Not only for you: your presence is also violence for the other.

There is a surprising incident in Mahavira's life. Mahavira wanted to take sannyas, so he asked his mother, "Should I go and take sannyas?"

His mother said, "Do not say this in front of me again. While I am alive you cannot take sannyas. It would be a great sorrow for me." Mahavira withdrew.

His mother must have wondered, because sannyasins are not usually so passive that they withdraw so quickly. If Mahavira had a violent manner, he would have remained obstinate. He would have said, "No, I am going to take sannyas. This material world is all an illusion. Who is 'mine'? Who is my family, and who is a stranger? It is all a lie! I am going to take sannyas. Who are you to stop me? What kind of bondage is this?"

But no, Mahavira left quietly. His mother must have been surprised. What kind of sannyasin says just once "I want to take sannyas," and then withdraws when his mother, or his father, or his wife says "No, I will be very sad"? Can such a man ever be a sannyasin? He can never *become* one, it is not even necessary; such a man is already a sannyasin.

His mother died. His father died. As Mahavira was coming back from the cremation ground, he said to his elder brother, "I discussed it with our mother and father, and they said that as long as they were alive, I should not take sannyas; they would be sad. Can I take sannyas now?" As they were returning from the cremation ground!

The brother said, "Have you gone mad? Mother is gone, father is gone, we have become orphans, and you also want to leave? I would not be able to bear such sorrow." Mahavira became silent.

He did not raise the subject of sannyas again. He must have been an amazing sannyasin. Such a small sorrow inflicted on the other must have seemed insignificant to him, but what kind of enlightenment could happen if he would have to cause someone sorrow? He stayed.

But a strange thing occurred in that house. Such an occurrence has probably never happened anywhere else on earth. After a year or two, the people in the house began to wonder, "Is Mahavira there or not?" It became unclear. He was in the house – he was getting up, sitting down, coming, going, eating, drinking, sleeping – but the people of the house began to doubt whether he was there or not. His presence became like an absence. His being became like nonbeing.

Actually, if we lose awareness of the other, then it will start to be difficult to sense his presence. We have to make our presence felt, and we make it felt in a thousand ways. If a husband comes into the house, he makes it known that he has come with the sound of his footsteps. He makes it known with his eyes: "I am here – and who I am should be clear." A teacher comes into the classroom and makes it known: "I am here." A guru comes into the midst of his disciples and in every way makes it understood: "Know that I am here."

Mahavira became like an absence. He would neither see anyone, nor would he be seen by anyone: that is how absent he became. He started living in the house quietly, passing through it quietly. He did not cause anyone any hindrance nor was he hindered by anyone. In a way he entered what is called a living death. The people of the house had a meeting one day and everyone said, "Now it is futile to stop him becoming a sannyasin because he is simply not there. Who are we stopping?"

Can the wind be trapped by making a fist? You can stop a stone: you can hold a stone back by making a fist because it is a stone; it is there with great strength. The stone says, "I am." But if you stop the wind by making a fist, then what was there will escape because the wind is simply not. It is not in the same category as a stone. The wind does not say… So you cannot throw the wind and hit someone. You can hit someone by throwing a stone. The wind's character is very nonviolent. The stone's character is very violent.

Mahavira became like the wind, so the people of the house said, "Now we are making fists pointlessly; he has already gone. The more we clench our fists, the more he slips out. We should not try to stop him. Now he is simply not there; now to stop him is just pointless. It was appropriate to stop him as long as he was staying or not staying. If he does either one, then there is some meaning in stopping him. Now he is just not there."

They said to Mahavira, "Now if you want to go, you can go."

And he said, "Now it is too late; I have already gone. Now I am not here."

The first deep wound of violence comes from two points, which need to be understood. Does "the other" exist? As long as the other exists, violence will continue, and because of the other, you will create a false "I," a false ego, which is not you. But you will have to create it to interact with the other.

The ego is a temporary identity. We have no idea who we are, but we say, "I am." Even someone who does not know who he is says, "I am." This is too much. You can only claim to be when you know the reality of being.

I do not know who I am, but I say that I am. From where has this "I" come? Where is it born? If this "I" is born out of my knowledge, then it is a very strange thing, because anyone who has come to know himself stops saying "I." Those who have found themselves say, "We are not." Those who have found themselves have lost themselves.

Those who have not found themselves say, "I am." From where does this "I" come? It has not come from inside us. We should call it a social by-product. Society has created it. To interact with others, we have had to find two words, "I am." It is as if we have found a name. A child is born without a name, nameless; then we give him a name – Rama, Krishna – we give him any name. That name does not come from inside the child; society gives it to him. Then he remains Rama his whole life. He will fight for this name; if someone curses the name, he will fight.

Ramateertha was in America. Some people cursed him and he came back home laughing. When his friends found out that he had been cursed, they were very angry. Seeing Ramateertha laughing, they asked him, "Are you crazy? Why are you laughing? Curses have been said against you."

Ramateertha said, "If someone had cursed me, I would have answered. Those people were cursing Rama. What is my relationship with Rama? I might not have had this name; I might have had another name, or a third name. Someone curses *A*, *B*, *C*, or *D*; what have I got to do with it? When they were cursing Rama, I was also enjoying myself inside: 'Rama, see what curses are being thrown at you; are you having fun? If you become Rama you are bound to be cursed. They gave you the name, which they are cursing.' But I was outside all of it. The name is from them; the curse is also theirs. They were only playing with themselves."

Some people play such games. Some people play cards by themselves. They make moves from both sides. They should be in a madhouse, but they are considered to be very intelligent people.

Society plays a double game – it gives you the name and the curses too. It praises and condemns, shows respect and insults. This is the double game of society. And man gets deeply trapped in this double game. The other is false and this "I" of mine is also false. These two falsities live together. The day the "I" drops, "the other" also drops.

When the "I" and the "you" are dropped, what remains is nonviolence. So as long as we can say "You," violence will continue. As long as we can say "I"... I am not saying not to use the word *I*, we have to use it. Mahavira also uses it, but then it is just a word, a linguistic trick, then it is a play of language. Then it is not identification. Then *I* is just a useful word. Many words can be useful without having any connection with our identity.

Understand that the turmoil that has been created between "you" and "I" is violence. There can only be turmoil between these two existing falsities. Yes, sometimes this turmoil can be loving, sometimes it can be unloving. Sometimes it can become love, sometimes hate – that is a different matter. But as long as "I am" and as long as "you are," there is violence. This is the primary and most subtle form of violence. Then there are many other forms of violence that go on developing out of it. I will not go into a detailed account of them because if the original source of violence is understood, an infinite variety of forms follows. It is difficult to go into details.

Nonviolence is one. Violence has countless forms and many dimensions but it emerges from one source, the source of "you" and "I," or one can say, the source of self-ignorance.

If you ask Mahavira what nonviolence is, he will say, "Self-realization." If you ask Mahavira, "What is violence?" then he will say, "Self-ignorance." Not knowing oneself is violence.

This is a very strange thing. Our understanding is that causing unhappiness to another is violence, and that giving happiness to another is nonviolence. But be aware: whether we give happiness or unhappiness to another, in both cases unhappiness is the only result. All aspirations for giving are futile because it is not possible to give happiness to another. It is only possible to give happiness to yourself.

When you are no longer you, you are no longer the other, and only then can joy flow toward you from me. As long as I try to give you joy, I can only give you unhappiness. But we do not realize this.

Have you ever thought that all those to whom you gave happiness received only unhappiness? People complain every day that others do not return the happiness that they offer them. You may be giving happiness, but what reaches the other is unhappiness. Others offer happiness too, but what reaches you is unhappiness. This is a great misunderstanding. What we give does not reach, it has never reached.

That is why we do not get nearly as angry with those who make us miserable as with those who give us happiness, because at least the exchange is clean: they are giving us unhappiness. People talk about giving us happiness but only unhappiness reaches us. When you start to love a woman and you marry her, you will try to give her every kind of happiness, but only unhappiness will reach her.

Which husband has ever given happiness to his wife? Which wife has ever given any joy to her husband? But you may think that you are giving happiness and getting unhappiness in return – and the same misconception is happening to the other person; they are thinking the same thing.

The entire inner duality of man's life is born out of this attempt to bring happiness, and the state of unhappiness which results from trying. Everyone gives happiness, and what reaches is always unhappiness. Actually, we cannot even bring happiness to the other; we just cannot be nonviolent toward the other. But it is an impossibility: there is no way to be nonviolent with the other. Even if we hit the other with a flower, when it hits it will become a stone.

A mystic, Mansoor, was being crucified. People were throwing stones at him, throwing live embers at him. Mansoor was hanging on the cross and people were throwing things.

Another mystic called Junnaid was present. He too was a Sufi. There was a big crowd and everybody was throwing something or other. There was sorrow in Junnaid's heart: Mansoor's death was not right, but he did not have the courage to say so.

Everyone was throwing something. If Junnaid did not throw anything, people might stone him too: "Why are you just standing there?" So Junnaid hit him with a flower. He didn't think it would hurt Mansoor. Mansoor would understand that he had thrown a flower, and the crowd would know that he had thrown something; he was not standing there empty-handed.

But although Mansoor was able to bear the people's stones, he could not bear Junnaid's flower. As soon as Junnaid's flower hit him, Mansoor started weeping profusely. Up to that point he had been laughing.

Junnaid was frightened; he said, "I threw a flower and you are crying. You had withstood so many stones."

Mansoor said, "But you threw a flower and hit me! Hitting causes sorrow. If someone throws stones, it is clear. But a flower? You are hitting me and hiding at the same time. You also want to hit me, and you don't want to admit it. The wound went deep, Junnaid. They are ignorant, they can be forgiven, but you hit me too!"

Junnaid said, "But I have only thrown a flower."

Mansoor said, "Throw anything and a wound is inflicted."

Actually we only throw things when someone else is there, otherwise at whom will we throw them?

Remember, offering flowers before a deity's statue is also violence because we are accepting "the other." The real devotee does not offer flowers to a statue of God. The devotee sets off on a search and finds nothing but godliness. He finds it in a flower and also finds it in a stone; he finds it in the one who offers, and in the one to whom it is offered. And he asks, "What is there to give? Who is there to offer it to? And on whose behalf is it offered? Who is there to offer, so how can anything be offered?"

When someone attains nonviolence, the other disappears. When does that happen? When someone knows himself, then the other disappears. Before that, the other remains and several kinds of violence go on being created. When we walk, it is violence; when we get up, it is violence; when we sit down, it is violence; when we talk, it is violence; when we look, it is violence.

So don't think stopping very gross violence will make any difference. It is good not to eat meat, but don't have any misconceptions: it is wrong to think that this is nonviolence. You can only say that a little violence has been stopped. But be careful that this violence does not emerge from somewhere else.

It will emerge – it will look for a way – because violence has not disappeared. It cannot disappear, not in this way. Even if one has given up eating meat… A meat eater who is just as good a person may appear; the vegetarian may not even appear to be as good. This is a very strange thing; it is sad but true. Generally, someone who drinks alcohol, smokes cigarettes, and eats everything will appear to be a little gentler. Someone who doesn't smoke or eat meat, who doesn't eat certain things, someone who chooses to live in a certain way and not another, will become arrogant and hard. The violence which is not released collects and begins to build up inside him.

That is why people we would usually call good men do not prove to be so good. It is an unfortunate state of affairs. A bad person may sometimes prove to be very good, and good people often prove to be bad. Anyway, it is difficult to be friends with a good man; it is only possible with a bad person. For friendship, a little gentleness of heart is required, and a good man does not have this in him anymore. That is why it is very difficult to be friends with saints. Even two saints find it difficult to be friends; what to say about all the others?

You can be a disciple of a saint or you can be an enemy, but you cannot be a friend. Friendship is lost to a saint; he becomes hard. The hand he might have extended in friendship is gone. Good people will often be found in a society that lives naturally, which does not differentiate much between good and evil. It is difficult to find good people in societies which live unnaturally, and which differentiate a lot between good and evil; if evil is no longer there on the outside, it accumulates inside.

It is difficult to find angrier people than holy men. A Durvasa, the ancient sage known for his short temper, can only be born among holy men. He cannot be born anywhere else.

I have thought about this many times, and it came to me that if Hitler had smoked a few cigarettes, eaten a little meat, stayed awake at odd hours, gone to a dance hall and danced a little, then maybe millions of people in the world would have been saved from being killed. But Hitler did not smoke cigarettes, did not eat meat; he did not even drink tea – he was a strict vegetarian, a puritan, a purist. He would sleep according to a routine; he would get up before dawn according to a routine. He was a man of strict principles; he was disciplined in all matters. And all that energy accumulated.

Often it seems to me that if your so-called good men could indulge in a few of what we can call innocent foolishnesses, they would become soft and simple. But good men always aspire to do good. Being good is one thing, doing good is a totally different thing. No one ever becomes good by doing good. From being good, good deeds can arise, but that is a very different thing. We always start from the wrong end.

We say that Mahavira did not eat meat and we decide not to eat it so that we will become saintly like Mahavira. This is a misconception, a false argument; somewhere the calculation has become inaccurate. Eating meat was impossible for Mahavira because he had attained something, a higher state of being. One cannot become Mahavira by not eating meat. If you can become like Mahavira by not eating meat, then being Mahavira means nothing; his worth becomes equal to that of meat, no more than that. It is not such a cheap matter. Religiousness is not so cheap that if we do not eat this or that we will become religious, if we don't drink we will become religious, if we don't drink water at night – like certain religious orders prescribe – we will become religious.

I am not telling you to drink. I am not saying drink water at night; you will not become religious by drinking or not drinking. It is good if you don't drink, but don't make the mistake of thinking that you have become religious, that you have become nonviolent. This is very dangerous: you do something very cheap and create a very costly belief; you do nothing and think you have attained everything. You collect stones and pebbles and think you have acquired diamonds.

This misconception about nonviolence has gone very deep. Our nonviolence is acquired through superficial behavior, not from our depths, not spiritually. If nonviolence is acquired through behavior, it is dangerous. And when someone acquires nonviolence through behavior, then he goes on being violent in subtle ways.

One more point in this connection and then I will finish my talk. When violence becomes subtle, it becomes unrecognizable. I can oppress you in many ways. Hitler would oppress you by putting a knife to your chest. A saint would not put a knife to your chest, he would put a knife to his own chest. I can threaten to kill you if you don't listen to me, or I can oppress you by saying that I will die if you don't listen to me. But oppression and coercion are happening. Good people oppress in a good way, evil people oppress in a bad way. But evil people are at least sincere, the situation is clear: they know that there is a knife in their hands. Good people know that there is a garland in their hands – but you can strangle someone with a garland too. They are not aware of this oppression.

If violence is subtle, it takes two forms. On one hand, it assumes a mask of nonviolence toward the other – and it does the work of violence. If violence becomes even subtler, then one starts to torture oneself. What is strange is that while a nonviolent person cannot even torture another, violence can actually become self-torture as well. So violence becomes self-torture in the end.

As I said, there are basically only two kinds of people. There is a third kind of person who appears only sometimes: a Mahavira, a Krishna, a Buddha, a Jesus appears… But in general, there are two kinds of people: people who torture others and people who torture themselves, sadists and masochists. As I said about de Sade, if he loved someone he would torture them. There was another man, Masoch, who would only torture himself. If he did not whip himself ten or twenty times after getting up in the morning, he would not feel fresh.

So the people who whip themselves have become the sannyasins of the world. People who lie on thorns or who wear shoes of thorns or inflict wounds on themselves have become sannyasins. What kind of people are they? Is this sannyas? Is this religiousness?

If a man starves someone else we call him irreligious, and if a man starves himself he acquires a following! It is really astonishing. If torturing someone else is irreligious, how can torturing oneself be religious? If torturing is irreligious, then what difference does it make who is being tortured? Yes, if you torture another, then the other can at least protect himself; if you torture yourself, there is no protection. It is very easy to torture yourself, but there are thousands of obstacles to torturing another person: there is the society, there is the law, there are the police, the courts. Until now there is no law against torturing yourself, neither is there any difficulty with the police, the courts. There should be because people who torture themselves are evil, and in a just world there would be a court for them too.

And be aware that someone who tortures himself will certainly torture others in every way. How can he spare others if he does not spare himself? This is impossible, absolutely impossible. If I starve myself and acquire a following, I will make every attempt to keep you hungry too. I will not rest until you have your following too. So when violence becomes deeper and subtler it becomes masochistic, it becomes self-torture.

Have you seen Mahavira's statue? Does this man look like he has tortured himself? Have you seen this man's body? Have you seen this man's grandeur? Have you seen this man's beauty? Does it look like he has tortured himself? Either the stories are false or the statue is false. This man has not tortured himself. No one's statue, as I understand it, is as beautiful as Mahavira's. I always think that Mahavira's beauty was the reason behind his becoming naked. Actually an ugly person cannot be naked. An ugly person will always look after his clothes carefully. No one hides beauty behind clothes; only ugliness is hidden behind clothes.

Whatever parts of the body are beautiful we keep outside our clothing. Whatever parts of the body are ugly we hide inside. Mahavira seems to have only beautiful body parts. Such a well-proportioned body is rarely seen. I feel that all the stories of self-torture could not have happened to this man. Otherwise the statue does not seem real and should be changed.

I agree that the statue is real and the stories are false. Actually, masochists have written those stories. They have been written by people who were impelled to torture themselves. They have twisted the stories, they are turning Mahavira's bliss into sorrow, and turning his ecstasy into sacrifice. They are even calling Mahavira's accomplishment, his supreme accomplishment, a sacrifice. In my view,

Mahavira renounced the palace because a greater palace had become visible to him. In their eyes, he only renounced the palace, no greater treasure was visible. I know that Mahavira renounced gold because it became mud to him, but gold of a more supreme nature was attained instead.

If Mahavira does not eat food for a day, it is not starvation, it is fasting. Starvation means to die of hunger. Fasting means being in such bliss that one does not even know of hunger. That is a very different matter, totally different. You hear the word *fasting.* In that very word, bread and food, eating and drinking, are not expressed. They are just not there in that word. The meaning of fasting is being closer and closer to the inner, nearer to oneself. *Fasting* means just that: being with oneself. When a man is deep within himself, then he is unable to be with the body. Hence he forgets the body's hunger and thirst. A man only realizes hunger and thirst when he is close to the body. When the awareness is deep inside, awareness of the body is forgotten. Fasting means the inner journey of awareness.

But the masochist will turn fasting into starvation. He will say that unless one remains hungry, the soul cannot be found. What connection can there be between staying hungry and finding your soul? Does the soul love hunger?

There is no relationship between staying hungry and finding the soul. Yes, in the moment when you find the soul, you may remain hungry. Have you ever noticed – if you haven't, do it now – on a day when you are blissful you will not be able to eat much. If your beloved comes to your house and you are very blissful, then your food intake will be smaller. You are so filled with bliss, it is so fulfilling that there is no room for food inside.

The bliss that Mahavira has known is the supreme bliss; it fills you up so much inside, it fulfills you so much that no space remains empty.

Sad people eat more food. Just watch: on a day when you are sad, you will eat more food because you are so empty inside. So the sadder you are, the more food you start to eat.

Actually, in childhood... A child realizes for the first time that there is a relationship between happiness and food. When a mother really loves a child she gives him milk, and he also receives bliss from that love. If the child is completely sure that when he wants milk he will get it, he does not drink a lot. The mother worries that he is not drinking enough. He does not drink more because he knows that whenever he wants, he will get it. But if the person giving the milk is a nurse... And many mothers are just nurses; they may have carried the child in their womb but that makes no difference. If a mother is unhappy with nursing and forcefully weans the child off her milk, then the child will start drinking more because he is not sure of the future. The child becomes worried, is filled with anxiety. That is why the greater the anxiety, the more food is eaten. Anxious people start to eat more.

Anxious people become empty; anxiety is a kind of emptiness, it makes everything empty inside. Then a person starts to eat more. Eating more is just a declaration of the fact that someone is sad. Eating less is a declaration that someone is happy.

Bliss is an advanced matter; when someone is filled with bliss, then months can pass without eating. Remember, Mahavira spent months fasting, he did not eat for months. I wouldn't say he could not eat, I would say he was so fulfilled.

But if a month had passed, even in such bliss there should be some damage to Mahavira's body from the lack of food. It is ironic that whatever damage the body would suffer from a lack of food, just as much damage could be caused just by the idea that no food is available. The absence of food does not cause as much damage as the thought that it is not available. Deep inside, the damage to the body is because of the state of mind.

A few days ago, I heard a story about a woman named Pyari Bai in Bengal. She did not eat for thirty years, for thirty whole years, and there was no damage to her body. The story about Mahavira is ancient, so there is no way of carrying out medical tests on him. But every kind of medical investigation was carried out on this Pyari

Bai. She did not eat for thirty years; no grain of rice entered her stomach. All her intestines shriveled and dried up, but her health was not affected. What happened? Did a miracle happen? A miracle happened. What happened to her? Medical science found it difficult to understand it.

Actually she was so blissful – and we cannot even imagine that bliss can also become food. We only know one thing – that food is bliss, but we don't realize that bliss can also become food. We only know one side, that food becomes bliss. There is also another side. Everything is interchangeable. If water can become ice, then ice can become water. If energy can become matter, then matter can become energy. If food can become bliss, then bliss can become food. It happened: Pyari Bai fasted for thirty years and proved that if a hungry Mahavira only ate for a total of three hundred and sixty-five days in twelve years, it was not starvation. Otherwise the body would have disappeared. Bliss became food.

Recently there was a similar case with a woman in Europe. On her, even more experiments were possible. She was supremely healthy, extraordinarily healthy – and she did not eat for years. What happened? She was not a devotee of Krishna like Pyari Bai, she was a Christian.

An event even more significant than Pyari Bai's occurred in her life. Every Friday, the day that Christ was crucified, blood would start flowing from her hands without causing any injury. She had become so completely in empathy with Jesus that instead of quoting him she would say, "While I was being crucified I said, 'Forgive them all because they are innocent and they know not what they do.'" So every Friday, the day Jesus was crucified, her hands would spread out, her eyes would close and from the uncut palms of her hands, blood would start to flow. Stigmata would appear. In the night, the wounds would disappear and the bleeding would stop. The next day her hands would be completely fine. And hundreds of times, blood flowed from her hands and she stopped eating.

And then there was a big dilemma: she did not lose weight! What was happening?

I want to say something very precious to you. It is this: there are a few truths, a few secrets, through which even bliss becomes food. But that is fasting; that is not starvation.

Nonviolence neither tortures the other nor oneself. Nonviolence just does not torture; only violence tortures. Violence has everyday forms, violence has different kinds of forms; violence has good forms, violence has bad forms. If we become alert to them all, then maybe the search for nonviolence can happen.

On each of the next four days, I would like to explore one of these virtues with you and on the fifth day I will talk about how you can enter them. Nonviolence, non-possessiveness, non-theft, and non-desire are the four goals, and the fifth virtue, "non-unawareness," is the path to reach these goals. What will be found is truth. What will blossom in life, the flowering that will happen, is brahmacharya.

I am grateful that you listened to me with such love and silence. Now to end, I bow down to the godliness that dwells in you all. Please accept my *pranam*, my offering of respect.

2

Non-Possessiveness

My beloved ones.

To understand the second great virtue, *aparigrah* or non-possessiveness, it is essential to understand *parigrah*, or possessiveness. There are great misconceptions about possessiveness. Possessiveness is not about having things, it refers to the feeling of ownership over things. *Parigrah* means possessiveness. It has nothing to do with how many things you have. It all depends on the attitude with which you relate to those things, in what way you are connected to them. And we are not only possessive about things, we are also possessive about people.

Yesterday I said a few things to you about violence. Possessiveness is nothing but another dimension of violence. Only a violent person is possessive. As soon as I claim ownership of someone or something, I have immediately moved into deep violence. Without being violent, it is impossible to be an owner. Ownership *is* violence. Ownership of things is widespread, but we even hold ownership over human beings.

Pati, the husband, is the owner of the wife. The very meaning of the word *pati* is owner. In India the husband is also called *swami* and that word too means owner. Possessiveness means a desire for ownership. A father may be the owner of his son, a teacher may be the owner of his disciple – but wherever there is ownership there is possessiveness, and wherever there is possessiveness the relationship becomes violent. Without being violent toward someone, one cannot be his owner; without making someone a slave, one cannot be his owner. Without imposing slavery, it is impossible to be possessive.

Why is there such a desire in man's heart to possess? Why is there such a desire to possess someone? Why is there such interest in being the owner of someone? It is an interesting phenomenon – it is because we are not masters of ourselves. In someone who becomes his own master, this idea of ownership disappears. But we are not our own masters, and throughout life we compensate for this lack by possessing others.

Even if one becomes the owner of the whole earth, this lack cannot be compensated for because the bliss which comes with being the master of oneself is altogether unique, and becoming a master of others brings nothing but misery. To be the master of oneself is bliss, to be the master of others is always suffering. Hence, the greater the ownership, the greater the misery. In becoming the possessors and owners of others, we spend our whole lives trying to compensate for that one lack: not being our own masters, not being emperors to our own selves.

It is like someone trying to quench his thirst with fire; the thirst goes on increasing. Thirst cannot be quenched with fire. Likewise, mastery of oneself cannot be attained by becoming a master of others. Rather – and the interesting point is – the more we become a master of others, the more we become a slave of the enslaved.

Ownership is actually a double slavery. The one whose master we become certainly becomes our slave but we also become *his* slave. The master is also the slave of his slave. However much the husband becomes the master over his wife, he becomes her slave too. And however great an empire the emperor might own, he becomes a complete slave to it. He also becomes a slave to fear because those we make dependent upon us become afraid, and then opposition and rebellion against us begin. They also want to make *us* dependent.

I have heard…

A man was taking a cow tied with a rope toward the forest and a sannyasin was passing on the road. The man was dragging the cow toward the forest.

The sannyasin stopped and said to the people of the village, "I want to ask a question. Is this cow tied to the man or is the man tied to the cow?"

The people of the village said, "It is clear and simple that the cow is tied to the man."

Then the sannyasin asked, "If the cow runs away will the man run after her or not?"

They said, "He would have to run."

The sannyasin said, "The cow is tied with a very visible rope and the man is tied with a very invisible rope. He cannot leave the cow. There is a rope around the cow's neck, which is very clear and can be seen. The cow has a rope around this man's neck too, which is clear but cannot be seen."

This is the only difference between master and slave – one's slavery is visible and the other's slavery is invisible. Other than that, there is no difference. The one we enslave makes us a slave too. The possessor becomes the possessed. Non-possessiveness arises by searching with the question, "How do I become my own master?"

I have heard…

A mystic was dying. He had a little money and said to his disciples, "I want to give this money to the poorest man of the village." So all the poor people of the village gathered the next day, but he did not accept any of them as poor. He told each one, "No, you are not; no, you are not. The really poor one has not come yet."

When in the afternoon the emperor passed by in his chariot, the mystic threw the bag of money at the emperor's chariot. The emperor also knew that the poorest man of all was going to get the mystic's money, so he laughed and said, "Have you gone crazy, throwing money at the richest man? You had sent for the poorest man."

The mystic said, "Those who have fewer things have less slavery, and their poverty is also less. You have more things, so your slavery is greater and your poverty too. And, the strange thing is that those who have very little may have abandoned any hope for more, but for those who have a lot, their hope of finding more is still without measure. I do not know a poorer man than you on this earth, so I give this money to you."

Maybe that mystic's words were true after all. People who are under the illusion that others are slaves are only slaves themselves. The really poor are those who want to destroy their inner poverty with external wealth. And the really dependent are those who, by making others dependent, remain lost in the illusion of their own independence. No one can be independent after making another dependent. Possessiveness is the name of this illusion.

I want to be independent so I think, "Let me make someone dependent on me, then I will become independent." But the dependence is two-sided; the chains tighten on both sides. Prisoners in jail are not the only ones imprisoned. The sentry standing outside the jail is just as much a prisoner. One is imprisoned outside the wall; the other is imprisoned inside the wall. Neither can the one inside the wall escape, nor can the one outside the wall escape. And the strangest thing is that the one inside the wall may even attempt to escape, but the one outside will not even try. He thinks he is independent.

I have heard…

A band of outlaws kidnapped a politician. His car was passing through the forest, and they stopped the car and captured him. But those outlaws were strange people. The politician was very frightened, but the bandits said, "Don't be afraid, because we are the same type of people."

The politician said, "I don't understand."

They said, "In many ways we are very much in harmony with each other. The police move ahead of you, the police come after us. There is not much difference. You are tied to the police from the front; we are tied from the back. And watch out, if the police are ahead of you, it is difficult to escape. If the police are behind us, at least we can run."

It is one of life's extraordinary secrets that whoever we imprison, imprisons us too. In order to imprison someone, we will also have to be imprisoned. There is a great depth to possessiveness. It is important to understand its subtle aspects, so that the enormity of it can also be understood from the outside.

The possessive person first tries to forget the idea that he is dependent, to forget that he is limited, that he is not his own master. But it cannot be forgotten. If I am not the master then I do not exist, and however much distraction I create to forget this, even in the distraction, deep inside me I know that I am not the master.

Alexander knew that he was not the master; Hitler also knew it. And the more one knows that one is not the master, the more one continues to expand and strengthen external possessiveness. But however strong the external possessiveness becomes… Perhaps one forgets for a while but again and again the memory returns that one is not the master. So why are we not the master inside? We don't even know what is inside, so being the master of it is quite impossible.

Swami Ramateertha went to America and the American president went to meet him. The president found Rama's words very strange. The language was different. The language had to be different: the language that Ramateertha speaks is the language of another world. He always used to call himself "Emperor Rama."

The American president said, "I don't understand, what do you mean by 'Emperor Rama,' what is the meaning of that? You seem to have nothing. You don't have anything except this loincloth. How can you be an emperor?"

So Rama said, "Actually this loincloth is something of a hindrance to my being an emperor. That's why I make the declaration a little softly. I am not bound to anything, just this loincloth remains. But I am an emperor because I have no needs, I have no requirements, I have no desires. There is just this loincloth which binds me a little. And why does it bind me? I have bound it myself; that's why we are both bound. The loincloth has become bound to me, and I have become bound to the loincloth."

Certainly, Mahavira can call himself an emperor. Mahavira's brother must have wondered why his younger brother had forsaken the kingdom and gone away. He must have thought, "What a lunatic! He doesn't understand anything." Mahavira handed over the entire kingdom, all the wealth, into the hands of his elder brother and became naked and destitute. But very few people were able to understand that Mahavira became an emperor, and the elder brother remained a slave.

Being an emperor begins with this: "What I am is sufficient; it is enough to be myself. I don't need anything, I don't have to complete anything. There is no deprivation making me empty; nothing is lacking." Being an emperor is an inner fulfillment. Everything just is; hence there is no lack. But an outside emperor has nothing. He has much outside that is visible in all directions, but he is not inside with himself. Inside, there is emptiness, a vacuum.

Inside, we are all empty. We fill this emptiness with furniture, we fill it with a house, we fill it with wealth. We fill it with fame, position, and prestige. Then when all the position and prestige has been gathered, when the whole pile of wealth has been collected, we find that the inner emptiness is still there. But it was not as visible before as it is now; now there is a contrast – outside there are piles of wealth, but inside the emptiness appears even clearer. A poor man is unable to see his inner poverty as clearly as a wealthy man.

In my view, this is the one and only benefit of wealth, that inner poverty becomes more visible. That's why I am always in favor of wealth because without it, inner poverty never becomes visible. Like white lines which emerge and become visible on a blackboard, inner poverty becomes visible and distinct against the wealth gathered outside. Everything happens outside and nothing at all happens inside. Possessiveness exists just to fill the emptiness which is inside.

Someone may be thinking, "If I forsake these external things, will the inner emptiness disappear?" This is the real question – but if the inner emptiness has not disappeared before, when these external possessions existed, then how can it disappear when they are not there, when they have been dropped?

But the heart of man remains surrounded by some fundamental misconceptions. First he thinks that he can fill the void by collecting things. Then when he sees that external possessions have been accumulated, but fulfillment has not happened, he thinks, "I will fill the void by forsaking the outer world." But he is crazy. If it could not be filled with objects, then how will it be filled by removing them?

So understand that non-possessiveness does not mean forsaking external things, it means attaining inner fulfillment. And when there is inner fulfillment, the race to possess things externally just goes away.

That's why I said that the meaning of possessiveness is not the things themselves, it is the possessive attitude. Janak, the enlightened king, could live in a palace, but he was not possessive. He had many possessions, but he was not possessive. A sannyasin may appear to own nothing but he can be possessive – it often happens. He has made the second mistake; he has made the mistake of discarding possessions.

What will happen by dropping possessions? The inner emptiness can become invisible, but it remains the same. Nothing is left on the outside so the outer is empty; the inside is also empty but the contrast is no longer there, and everything ceases to be visible. But inner emptiness cannot disappear through external emptiness. Internal fulfillment is required; a positive birth of self-realization is required internally. Only then will the external hold on things disappear; otherwise it cannot go away.

There was a mystic, Diogenes. He was passing through the forest, naked. Perhaps he was the only man of Mahavira's caliber who lived in the West. Diogenes was naked just like Mahavira and he was just as ecstatic, just as blissful, just as healthy. He was passing through the forest. Some men were going to the market to sell slaves. They saw Diogenes – alone, naked, healthy, beautiful, powerful. They thought, "If we could capture this man, he would fetch a good price." But they were worried that they would not be able to capture him even though there were eight of them! He was very strong. What if there was trouble? But they were eight, so they gave it a try.

They gathered their strength and attacked Diogenes, but Diogenes did not respond to the attack – or you could say he responded, but in his own style. He stood in the middle with closed eyes and said to them, "Tell me, what do you want?" He did not fight at all. They were all trembling with fear. He said, "Don't be afraid, I will not harm you." How can one who has stopped harming himself cause harm to another? "Speak, what are your intentions?"

They were very afraid. They would not have been so scared if he had responded to their attack. They even had difficulty saying, "We have come to make you a slave." They started looking at each other.

Diogenes said, "Don't worry, speak. Whatever you say will happen."

They lowered their eyes and said, "We are very ashamed, but we have come to make you a slave."

Diogenes said, "Wonderful! Okay, so I become a slave. Now what are your intentions?"

Those people looked at Diogenes and said, "You will become a slave? You won't protest?"

Diogenes said. "I am a master of myself. I can also choose to be a slave, there is no conflict. Now where do I have to go?"

So they said, "Allow us to put chains around your hands."

Diogenes said, "You idiots, there is no need for chains. I am coming with you anyway, wherever you want. Let's go!"

They reached the market and a crowd gathered. Such a beautiful slave must seldom have come to be sold. Diogenes was put on the platform and the auctioneer said, "Those who want to buy this slave should start bidding."

Diogenes said, "Be quiet, you fool, ask them who has come with whom? Have they come behind me or have I come behind them? Who is tied to whom? Am I tied to them or are they tied to me? And do not use the word *slave*. I am my own master. Wait, I will announce myself." So Diogenes stood up on the platform and said, "If someone wants to buy a master, then a master has come to be sold."

The crowd was astonished: "Master?"

Diogenes replied, "I am my own master."

This self-possession is a positive achievement. If it happens, then the external hold drops. The external hold is only there because there is no grasp of the inner. We keep holding on to the outer, and we start destroying whoever we hold on to on the outside.

The violence of possessiveness is just that: if you hold on to someone you begin to destroy them. Without destroying them you cannot possess them, so you will have to destroy them. If a master holds on to a disciple he will start destroying him. A disciple cannot be made a disciple while alive, it is necessary to destroy him. So he will be destroyed by discipline, rules, limits. His independence will be destroyed. When he becomes a corpse, then he can become a disciple. A husband will start destroying his wife; a wife will destroy her husband. A friend will start destroying another friend, because only when he has been completely destroyed is he sure that the other will not run away, will not become independent.

But internally there is a great problem with that. When we destroy someone and become their master, the pleasure of being the master disappears. This is the contradiction. Without destroying, one cannot be the master, and as soon as the other is destroyed, the pleasure is gone. There is no pleasure in being a master of the dead.

Hence the heart moves from one wife to the second; from the second it moves to the third; from one house to the second, from the second to the third. And from one master to the second; from one disciple to the second. Whoever you have become the owner of becomes insignificant. Because as soon as you become the owner, they become lifeless and there is no great pleasure in owning something lifeless. There is no pleasure in it at all. One needs to be the owner of someone who is alive.

There is another paradox in ownership. The paradox is that ownership kills, and after the killing comes misery. Happiness is lost. A wife does not give as much happiness as a lover, but there is an immediate desire to make the beloved a wife. Ownership of a beloved is uncertain; ownership of a wife is very clear. But on becoming a wife, she dies instantly, and as soon as she dies she becomes insignificant.

So whoever we possess becomes insignificant. We forget them; they cease to mean anything anymore. People who go on collecting and destroying others slowly get bored with them. They have to work to destroy them – then after all the work, there is no reward.

Possessive people who are also clever or shrewd, abandon people and build collections of objects instead. They don't have to take the trouble to destroy them, they are already dead. Hence people who have become fed up with others become engrossed in accumulating wealth and status. It is more convenient.

If you bring a chair into a house, it arrives already dead. You have absolute control over where it should be kept. If you want to keep it or you don't want to keep it, you are the absolute owner. There is no responsibility, no difficulty over destroying it. And when you bring a person into the house, you want to make him into a chair too. Until he becomes a chair, you are anxious. Then when he becomes a chair, the anxiety begins again.

That's why clever, possessive people work hard collecting objects, and those who are not so clever work hard collecting people – but both are ignorant. We can neither fill ourselves with people, nor can we fill ourselves with objects. Our hands remain empty. There is only one place to fill, and we can fill it only with ourselves. There is no other fulfillment. There is just no other fulfillment in this world, there never has been. We can fill only with ourselves – but we don't know anything about ourselves.

How to find out about this self? And how will an attitude of non-possessiveness be helpful in knowing this self? I would like to ask you to look deeply into it whatever you possess. Have you been fulfilled by it a little, even just a fraction? Has whatever you possess fulfilled you even an inch?

Everyone has something or other. If this something has fulfilled you even a little, you become engrossed in expanding it. If it has fulfilled you a little, then it will be able to fulfill you more, and even more, and more. But if it has not fulfilled you at all, you will come to understand that however much this "something" increases, it will not be able to fulfill you. Our past experience is that possession could not fulfill us. But the wish for the future is always there, that maybe we will get something more and be fulfilled.

I have heard that in a village, a man's third wife died and he married for the fourth time. The people of the village wanted to give him a gift, but they were tired of giving him gifts. He had married three times, and each time the gifts were smaller. When he married for the fourth time, he was much older and the people were fed up with choosing gifts for him. So, they gave him a board on which was written: "The triumph of hope over experience."

Even the experience of three wives was not able to deter him from a fourth. The whole village knew that as long as his wife was alive, he would moan about her in the village. Then, when his wife would die, he would cry over her death.

Hope always wins over experience. The mind of a possessive man is always tied to hope. You will only attain a non-possessive attitude when experience wins over hope. Your past, your experience, is enough to tell you that even after attaining everything, nothing has been gained. People become presidents, and sitting on their chairs suddenly discover that they have reached high office but nothing has been attained.

What you need to attain is the dimension of being, and what you live in is the dimension of having. What you acquire are things, but what you truly have to attain is the soul. Things can never become your soul. And this deluded race goes on, not only for one lifetime but endlessly, for lives and lives.

Actually we keep on forgetting our past experiences. Not only have we forgotten our past life experiences, we have even forgotten or ignored the realities of *this* life. We forever deny our experiences, and imagine that something different from what has happened so far can happen in the future. But even the experience of many lifetimes does not keep us from the idea that we will bring fulfillment to our souls by possessing more things. Having cannot become being – it is impossible.

Sometimes it happens that even wishing the impossible can be pleasurable. You want to do what cannot be done. Many times you get this urge simply because it cannot be done. Now the excitement of landing on the moon is gone, but for thousands of years man longed for it. The ambition to reach the moon was very attractive because it seemed impossible. It seemed so impossible that those who dreamed of reaching the moon were considered crazy.

In English the word for a mad person, *lunatic*, means moonstruck. It comes from *luna*. A man in whose brain the moon reigns, who wants to reach the moon, is called a lunatic. In Hindi too, the word for a crazy person, *chandmara*, means moonstruck, someone who is assailed by the moon, who is stricken by the impossible.

But we are all moonstruck, we are all lunatics in the sense that we all go on wishing for the impossible. What is the greatest impossibility in this world, the most impossible? Now we can reach the moon, so it is not right to call those longing to reach the moon lunatics. The matter is finished; this word should be changed. *Moonstruck* is no longer a synonym for crazy. Now intelligent people have reached the moon, they might reach Mars, and after that maybe they will reach a star. All that is difficult but not impossible.

According to me, there is just one impossibility in this world: that objects can become the soul, that having can become being. This is an impossibility and will certainly remain so.

That's why Mahavira, Buddha, and Jesus call the people who are obsessed with possessions mad. They are engrossed in tasks that just cannot be done. The only attraction might be in attempting the impossible. But untruths do not become truths just by attraction. The truth about possession is that it is, in itself, impossible.

I have heard…

Diogenes once asked Alexander the Great, "Have you ever thought about what you will do when you have conquered the world?"

It is said that Alexander became sad on hearing this and said, "I didn't think of it, but you are right. There is no other world. If I conquer this one, then what will I do? I will be totally unemployed."

Seeing that there was no second world, Alexander became very sad. Why? Because if he conquered the whole world, where would he be? At least for the moment it was just a dream, so it was okay.

Have you ever thought about what would happen if all your desires were fulfilled? If someday an arrangement could be made that heaven existed in this world, as it does in fairy tales? If ever we could make a wishing tree so that every man would become a

Mahavira, and under the wishing tree whatever he desired would become instantly available? "Of course, then the whole world would become non-possessive. There would be no more possessiveness." You would be surprised: the moment you get something, it becomes worthless. You are standing again in the same place you were before fulfilling your desire. That same attitude is directed toward something else. You are a hunger, an attitude, an emptiness, a void. Man is like a horizon; after each desire is fulfilled, again something else comes in front of him.

The earth appears to touch the sky: "Keep walking, it seems as if it is just near – maybe ten miles further, maybe twenty miles. We will reach it sooner or later." We arrive and find that the sky has moved twenty miles away. It could not move if it was there. There is no connection between your walking and the sky moving. The sky never touches the earth, it only appears to touch. The earth is round and that's why the sky appears to touch it – but it doesn't touch the earth anywhere.

Man's desires move in a circle. So it looks as if a hope will become a fulfillment, but that never happens. Man's desires are spherical like the earth. The sky of hope stretches in all four directions, so it seems as if it is just ten miles away. We expect to arrive very soon, and our hope will become fulfillment – so whatever we have desired will be achieved and we will be fulfilled. But after walking ten miles, we see that the horizon has moved away. The sky has moved forward; it is now touching the earth further ahead. We move forward again. All our life – and for many lives – we keep moving forward.

The joke is that we don't even realize that the sky that appeared to touch the earth ten miles back again appears to touch it ten miles ahead. Is it possible that the sky never touches the earth at all? Or is the sky scared of us, running ahead and changing where it touches the earth? That cannot be possible.

Another even bigger joke is that those who are ten miles ahead of us are also running. The people who are located just where we think the sky touches the earth are also running further ahead. And those who are even ahead of them, where *they* feel that the sky touches the earth, are running too. When the whole earth is running, it should not be difficult for those with the slightest perception to figure out that the sky does not touch the earth anywhere. It is just an appearance; the sky just seems to touch the earth. Hope doesn't reach fulfillment anywhere. Desire is not fulfilled anywhere, lust is not satisfied anywhere; it only seems to reach, seems to happen. And man keeps on running.

So as far as possessiveness is concerned, it is important to have a thorough look at our past experience. But we are adept at deceiving ourselves. We are not as good at deceiving others as we are at deceiving ourselves. It is very difficult to deceive another because the other is present. But self-deception is very easy; we go on deceiving ourselves constantly.

I think that if I get one rupee, I will be happy. A rupee comes into my hand but I'm not at all happy. I think that if I get another rupee… But it does not occur to me that the second rupee is a copy of the first one. I get the second rupee, I get the third. The third rupee is also a copy of the second; it has the same face on it. I get the fourth, too. I go on getting them, and getting them. One day I realize that I'm lost – just rupees and more rupees. But millions of rupees later the sky seems to be touching in the same way as with that first rupee. The distance is the same as it was with the desire for one rupee; millions of rupees later the same hope remains.

That's why we are sometimes astonished when a millionaire goes crazy over even one rupee! A millionaire is as crazy about one rupee as someone who does not even have one because the distance for both stays the same forever. The distance between hope and fulfillment is the same. How much we have makes no difference. That which is ahead of us and is not ours keeps us running.

A millionaire is often even more miserable because his experience tells him that even after a million rupees have been collected, he will not be fulfilled. His whole life has been wasted. Now he might hold on to each rupee as tightly as possible – because life is wasting away, life is passing by. When he had one rupee, he was also alive. The energy was there, the strength was there; but now even that is finished. Now he has a million rupees but his life energy has become weak. So a man becomes more possessive as he ages; he starts clutching his possessions more tightly because there is very little life left. The more that can be grasped and the faster it can be done, the sooner the journey can be completed.

I have heard…

Alice has arrived in Wonderland and is in trouble. She is just standing there hungry and thirsty. It has been a long journey from earth to the land of the fairies. Then she sees the queen of the fairies standing under a tree and calling to her. Her voice can be heard – voices are very deceptive, they can be heard. Her hand can be seen – hands are very deceptive, they can be seen. And around the queen there is a pile of sweetmeats, a pile of flowers and fruit. Hungry, Alice starts to run. It is morning, the sun is rising. She runs and runs. Morning becomes afternoon and the sun is overhead, but the distance remains the same.

Alice is a young girl, she stops to think. If she were older she would not even stop to think. What is the matter? The morning is past, and while running it has turned into afternoon and the queen who appeared to be so near is still just as far away. There has been no change, the distance is the same! So she yells and asks, "Queen, what is this land of yours? While running, morning has become afternoon but the distance is not getting any shorter."

The queen says, "You are running a little too slowly, that's why the distance does not get any shorter. Run a little faster! You are putting too little effort into your running, you are not fast enough."

That makes sense to Alice. It makes sense to older people. It even makes sense to older people, so it is understandable that it makes sense to her. It makes sense to her that of course, the distance is not getting shorter because her speed is too slow. So she runs faster.

Then, at dusk, the sun begins to set but the distance is still just the same. Again she yells and asks, "Now it is beginning to get dark."

The queen says, "You are too slow."

The girl runs even faster. Now it is getting considerably darker and it is becoming difficult to see the queen. So she yells in the dark and asks, "What kind of land is this?" Night has descended and she loses all hope of reaching.

The queen's laughter can be heard and she says, "Crazy girl, maybe you don't know that everywhere on earth – the earth you come from – in that place too, no one ever reaches where they want to reach. The distance always remains the same as at the beginning."

From the day you are born until the day you die, the distance is the same. There is only one difference. On the day you are born, the sun comes out; and on the day you die, the sun sets and darkness descends. On the day you are born, there are hopes; on the day you die, there is frustration, there is defeat. On the day you are born, there are hopes, there are longings, there is the strength to run; on the day you die, the heart is tired, there is defeat, you are broken. But even then it cannot be assumed that a dying man becomes non-possessive. Even a dying man wishes he had a little more strength, a few more days left so he could run, he could reach.

There is a story…

An emperor was nearing death; he had reached one hundred. Death came close and said to him, "I have come to take you. Get ready."

Death comes close to everyone and says, "Get ready." We don't listen but that is another matter; we are deaf to it but that is another matter.

The emperor said, "My time may have come, but I have still not been able to enjoy anything. All my hopes are still fresh and yet none of my desires have been fulfilled. How can I go now?"

But Death said, "I will just have to take someone else. If one of your sons is ready to die in your place, then I can take him. He can give his years to you."

The emperor called his sons. He had many queens and many sons, a hundred sons. He asked all those sons, "I have not fulfilled anything yet, so who among you will give me his years?"

But those sons were also human and when a dying hundred-year-old man wants to stay alive, why shouldn't his fifty-year-old son also want to stay alive? Why shouldn't his eighty-year-old son want to stay alive? And why shouldn't his twenty-year-old son want to stay alive? Ninety-nine sons remained silent and sat down. The youngest son stood up; he was about fifteen or sixteen. He said, "Take my years."

Death tried to stop him, "You fool, what are you doing?"

The son said, "If my father could not fulfill anything in a hundred years, neither will I be able to. I will give him my time and go. Maybe in two hundred years he can fulfill something."

The emperor said, "So I have another hundred years. And one of my sons might be ready when I need more years. I see that now out of ninety-nine sons, no one is ready – maybe just one of my sons will be ready then."

The youngest son said to Death, "At least I know that none of my hopes have remained unfulfilled because I have no hopes at all yet. So at least I will be able to die with joy. My father is dying with great frustration. Have some compassion on me: let me know what happens after a hundred years when my father is dying again."

A hundred years passed. It doesn't take long for the years to pass. A hundred years passed and Death once again came and stood at the doorstep.

The emperor said, "All my hopes are still incomplete, no dreams have been fulfilled." By that time his older hundred sons had died but another hundred sons had been born. He said, "Call my sons."

Death said, "Don't you see, nothing could happen in two hundred years either."

The emperor said, "If I just get a little more time, maybe I will be fulfilled."

That "maybe," that "perhaps" is there in the final moments of death too: "Maybe there will be fulfillment." So the hundred sons were called and again one agreed.

Death tried to convince him too, "You are crazy."

But the son said, "It would be better if you could explain to our father that he is crazy. In two hundred years nothing was fulfilled, so what will he be able to do?" The son asked his father before dying, "Hasn't even a little been fulfilled in two hundred years?"

His father replied, "A little? Nothing has been fulfilled at all. I am still standing where I was when I came on this earth."

The son said, "I am going with joy; there is no frustration."

It is said that it went on like this for a thousand years. That old man lived for a thousand years. His sons kept changing, his age kept increasing; in the thousandth year when Death came, Death too was tired – but the old man was not.

Death said, "Enough, not this time. It is enough now. How many times can I keep coming? You have learned nothing at all from your experience."

The old man said, "But still nothing has happened. Everything is still in the same place, empty and unfulfilled. If I get a little time, then maybe something can happen." He had said this to Death ten times.

Don't laugh at this old man. This is not just any story, this is our story. We have said this to Death too, a thousand times, but we don't remember. The old man did not remember either. If he had remembered that the matter had been discussed ten times, then maybe his courage to say it for the tenth time would have broken down. He had also forgotten.

He asked Death, "What experience?"

Death said, "I have come ten times."

The old man replied, "I don't remember anything."

Actually, we want to forget sorrow and we do forget. We forget the sorrows and we carefully hold on to whatever joys were there. We go on making the sorrows smaller and slowly go on making the joys grow in our hearts. That's why an old man can say, "There was so much happiness in my childhood."

No child ever says this. A child says, "How soon can I grow up? Adults seem to be very happy." No child is happy, but all old people say, "My childhood was very happy." But children want to grow up very quickly. All children are troubled because they have thousands of sorrows. In a world of adults, to be a child is very saddening. There are adults everywhere and he is a small child. The adults are having somber conversations and he is not allowed to play. And to that small child, their somber conversations appear to be absolutely stupid; play is important. There is pressure everywhere, there are commandments everywhere – don't do this, don't do that. The child wants to grow up very quickly so that he can say the same to others. But all old people say that their childhood was joyous. They have forgotten all the pains of childhood.

It is a very strange thing. You will say, "No, if a man's death has come ten times, then he cannot forget." You were born. Do you remember your birth? One thing is certain: you have left previous lives behind and you were born this time. But do you have any memory of your birth? Birth is such a painful process that the mind does not create a memory of it. The pain a mother bears at the time of giving birth is nothing compared to what the infant bears. The mother will be free of the pains of childbirth very quickly, but the pain that the child bears is so severe that he erases it from his memory.

Our memory is constantly choosing what has to be saved and what has to be erased. If there was no one to tell you that you were born, you would not even know of it. But at the time of birth you were there, your birth happened to you. You have passed through the birth process, but where's the memory of it? The memory is not there because it was a very painful event. You came from the darkness of your mother's womb, from the utmost state of rest, where even no effort to breathe was needed, where nothing had to be done to live. You were simply alive.

Psychiatrists say that on the basis of thousands of observations, man's vision of ultimate freedom is derived from his memory of the womb. There is so much peace in the womb, so much silence, total silence – and no effort. There is nothing to do; there is just being. From that world of being, all of a sudden he comes into this world where he will have to breath, eat food, cry, scream to remain alive; where life will pass through many difficulties. From such a peaceful and happy existence he enters such a painful experience. The child forgets.

But in deep hypnosis you can be made to remember your birth experience. In a deep hypnotic state or in deep meditation, you can remember the experience in your mother's womb. If your mother fell during pregnancy, the knowledge of the event and of the injury which was sustained would have reached you. It is still a part of your memory, but you have forgotten.

In exactly the same way, we have died many times, just like the emperor whose story I was relating. Death came ten times but he kept on forgetting. He said, "I don't recognize you at all. I think you are coming for the first time. If I can have a little more time I will fulfill my hopes."

But Death said, "No, it is enough now. If you could not learn from the experience of a thousand years, then you will not learn after a million years either."

For someone who wants to learn, one experience is enough. Someone who doesn't want to learn will not even learn from infinite experiences. We have all stopped learning. People like Mahavira, or Krishna, or Buddha learn from their life experience, but we just don't learn. We keep our eyes deliberately shut and do not learn. We go on doing what we were doing, and we go on enjoying what we were enjoying – with the same hopes, the same frustrations, the same repetitions, the same cycle.

There is a Sanskrit word, *samsar*, which means wheel, in which the same spokes return, in which the same axis keeps spinning again and again. You might not have realized that this wheel is used in the

Indian flag – but the politicians don't seem to know why. For them it is a symbol of the emperor Ashoka and they chose it because it was carved on a pillar built by him. But how will a politician understand that this wheel is a religious symbol? No one turns as many times as a politician. He is in a whirlwind; he is clutching the spokes and sitting there, spinning all the time. Other politicians are trying to release him, and even then he does not break free. After releasing him, the others just hold on to his spokes themselves. They never realize that just as they are trying to release *him*, others will try to free them too, once they have managed to clutch the wheel. This is going on all the time.

This world, this samsar, is a wheel, in which we go on doing the same things; we keep on repeating the same things. Only yesterday you were angry, and yesterday you repented too: yesterday you also swore that you wouldn't be angry again. Today you will get angry again, today you will repent again, and today you will swear yet again that you will not get angry. This will happen tomorrow too, and it will happen again the day after. Are we humans or machines? If a machine keeps spinning, it makes sense. If a man goes on spinning, there is doubt whether he is human or a machine.

People say that man is a rational animal, but man does not show any evidence of it. Looking at man, one cannot tell at all that he is intelligent. It is very difficult to find a creature more unintelligent than man; he doesn't learn at all. The most important thing that can be learned in life is that possessiveness is futile. I am not saying that things are useless; I am not saying that a chair in your house is useless. How can a chair be useless? A chair is useful for sitting on, it can be used. I am not saying that your house is useless. A house can be useful for living, it *is* useful, and it *should* be useful. I am not saying that things are useless; they have their own significance. What I am saying is that we can fill our lives with things, but that in itself has no significance. There is no way that things can become the soul.

If we open our eyes even a little toward possessiveness, then we will immediately find ourselves entering a world where its hold on us breaks, is lost and disappears. The day we let go of it, we are simply alone. Neither the wife is there, nor friends, nor brothers, nor our houses.

They are all there in their places, but they are part of a big game. And this game is exactly like playing chess. In chess, one piece is an elephant, or rook, another piece is a horse, or knight, but no one has ever been deluded into riding on the horse. Within the game and the rules of chess, the horse is very significant: it has its own function, it has its own movement, it has its own victory and defeat. But sometimes people get crazy about chess too…

There was a king in Egypt who was crazy about chess. Eventually he became so crazy that he released the real horses in his stables and had the chess horses tied up instead. He began to live day and night among the chess horses and elephants, and when there was the likelihood of an attack he said, "Send out all the chess horses."

Then the people of his court said, "Now his mind is completely mad. This is a major problem; how can we correct it, how can he be cured?"

So all the country's thinkers and wise men were called and they were asked, "How can he be cured? The game of chess has become life itself for him."

An old man who had come with the wise men stood up to leave. He said, "The king will not be cured because there is not much difference between him and the people who have come to cure him. He has assumed the game of chess to be life itself, and these people have made life a game of chess. Both are the same. There is not much difference between them."

The king grabbed the old man, "You are saying something intelligent, that we are both mad. What should I do?"

The old man said, "Don't do anything, just play chess. Play it with gusto."

So great chess players were called and the king was engrossed in playing chess with them. Within a year, the king was cured and the other players went mad. It was bound to be so. He was cured because for a whole year he went on playing day and night. As he played, he began to realize that neither was the horse really a horse, nor the elephant an elephant; it was all a game.

We have played a lot, we have all played; we are all playing. But a chess horse still does not appear to be a chess horse to us; it still appears to be a real horse. All relationships in life are like a game of chess. There are rules and you have to obey them. If you see life as a game, you will find it very easy to obey the rules; there is no problem. Then all the seriousness goes out of it, there is no substance to it. If life is a game you cannot be serious about it.

But some people turn the game into real life; then they become serious even while playing it. Then even in a game, swords are pulled. Among chess players, swords have been pulled many times. If the chess horses and elephants were able to understand anything at all, they would laugh at the players: "What are they doing? They are pulling out swords to threaten wooden horses and elephants!"

In our approach to life, the whole arrangement is appropriate in its place: things are things, having is having, wealth is wealth, position is position – but none of this belongs to the soul at all. So remember that freedom from possessiveness is not about forsaking possessions and running away. That is why the traditional sannyasins of India are upside-down possessors; they are possessive, but doing a headstand. They are merely standing upside down, they are just like you. They are the same as you. In fact, in some respects, they are even more serious than you.

I cannot even imagine it – a sannyasin and serious? It should be impossible. If a sannyasin is serious, it means he is just a worldly person standing on his head. Seriousness means seeing the material world as very significant, seeing the whole web of life's stupidities as very important. We can attach importance to it in two ways – either by entering it, drowning in it, clutching it to our chest, or by being afraid and running away from it.

One last thing…

There were three sannyasins in China. I am ready to call those three sannyasins because rarely can there have been more nonserious men than those three. People didn't even know their names – names and such are all playthings, so those sannyasins never revealed their names.

When someone would ask, "What is your name?" they would look at each other and laugh. They would chuckle so loudly that even the questioner would start laughing after a while. Slowly their laughter would spread through the entire village.

So people only knew them as the three laughing saints. Their names did not survive. Whenever someone would ask them a question they would laugh. They answered by laughing. Whenever someone asked them, "Why are you laughing at our questions?" they would say, "You ask with such seriousness that any answer we give you will be dangerous because you will hold on to it just as seriously!"

Possessiveness is stupid and renouncing it is also stupid. To hold on to things is madness; and to forsake things and run away is no less madness. To be attracted to things is madness; to be repulsed by things is equally mad. Either way it is madness, standing back to back. And both madmen are wondering, "Could it be that the other is right?"

I meet sannyasins who tell me that such doubts often arise in their hearts: "Could it be that we made a mistake?" Doubts will arise. It is natural for such a thought to arise in the heart of a sannyasin: "Could it be that I made a mistake in forsaking everything and running away? Could it be that the people who are running after things are happy?" But the people who run after things are very troubled; they go on touching the feet of sannyasins, saying, "We are in such misery." And they go on thinking that sannyasins must be very happy.

So the illusion continues and our faces, our masks, keep the deception alive. In his aloneness the sannyasin becomes full of doubts, but he is self-assured in the crowd. When people touch his feet, he is convinced that they cannot be happy; otherwise they would not come to touch his feet. In aloneness, when the crowd is gone, his doubts arise. So the crowd is needed to sustain his phony sannyas; otherwise it would be very difficult. In aloneness, the sannyasin becomes doubtful: "You never know, maybe the people of the town are having fun."

So, all sannyasins come into town eventually. There are double benefits there. First, there are people around. Secondly, the people touch their feet and give them respect, so the sannyasins are assured: "No, if they were happy they would not come near us. They are coming to a renouncer."

But the sannyasins do not know that these are *their* moments of doubt. They are also filled with doubts: "You never know; it could be that the sannyasins are having fun." In fact, this idea that other people are having fun is always in our minds – because we only know the facade of other people, while we know our own reality to the very core. We are familiar with our own misery, but we are only familiar with the mask of the other.

No, things are neither worth holding on to, nor are they worth giving up. Therefore, to be non-possessive does not mean to be indifferent to the world. It does not mean to be dispassionate; it is not non-attachment, it is not renunciation.

Take this last point that I have said about non-possessiveness to heart. It should not make you a renouncer. It should not be that you leave the material world and start running away. It should not be that you give up your house and set off for the forest. No, a man who understands possessiveness will not talk of renouncing even by mistake, because only that which has been possessed can be given up. A man who understands possessiveness will find that nothing can be possessed, so there is nothing to renounce. How can one renounce? There is no way to do it. The other is the other, things are things, a house is a house; they cannot be renounced.

Non-possessiveness means that you can be inside the house or outside it, but without any sense of ownership. You have stopped seeking ownership in the outer world. That does not mean that you have to give up the external world and run away. Where will you run? Wherever you go is the outer world. And if you leave home and sit under a tree, and tomorrow another sannyasin comes and says, "Move from here, we want to chant under this tree," you will say, "Stop your nonsense. This tree is mine! I have taken possession of it. I was here first. Don't you see the flag on top of the tree? This temple is mine; this ashram is mine!"

A man who escapes from possessiveness will only recreate it – because if he escapes from possessiveness, he has not understood what it is. He will create it again. Yes, people will stop him; his followers will stop him. They will make every attempt to prevent it. They will say, "Don't build a house, don't build a temple, don't build an ashram." They will say, "Don't build this, don't build that." They will try to stop it in every way. But the sannyasin will find very subtle ways.

When it becomes difficult to possess money, he will seek subtle ways. He will start collecting followers. He will get the same pleasure from counting followers that others get from standing in front of the safe and counting money. He will go on counting – seven hundred, one thousand, ten thousand, one million, two million. How many followers are there? How many disciples are there? He will start whispering into people's ears, distributing mantras and collecting numbers. There is pleasure in numbers; money or followers makes no difference.

Life cannot be understood by escaping. Whoever runs away does so out of stupidity. Life has to be understood just how it is. And when it is understood, you will suddenly find that possessions disappear instantly – but they do not have to be renounced. Suddenly you will find that husband and wife are still there but the attachment is gone; the ownership has disappeared. Now the husband is not a husband; just a friend remains. Now the wife is not a wife, not a slave; just a friend remains. The relationship between them is suddenly gone.

To be non-possessive means to transform the relationship between us and others, between us and objects. Ownership drops. Non-possessiveness has blossomed if the feeling of ownership between ourselves and another has been dropped. So it is more difficult than renunciation. Renunciation is a very simple matter because it is the opposite extreme, and the pendulum of the mind can move to the other extreme very quickly. For someone who overeats, it is always easy to fast. For the man who is crazy for women, it is very easy to take a vow of celibacy. If you are very ill-tempered, it is very easy to discipline yourself not to get angry.

Understand that an ill-tempered man can vow not to get angry, and he can readily keep his promise. If he were less ill-tempered, he might think a little before taking a vow. If he were even less ill-tempered, he might not keep it at all because in order to keep the promise one has to feel it.

Now, by keeping the oath, the bad-tempered one will become angry with himself, whereas beforehand he was angry with others. There is no difference. Before, he was squeezing other people's throats. Now he will squeeze his own throat to avoid getting angry: "Where is the bad temper now?" Now he will clutch at his own neck. From one extreme to the other is always easy. Only those who stop in the middle attain religiousness.

Confucius went to a village. The people of the village told him, "In our village there is a very intelligent man. You have to meet him."

Confucius said, "Why do you call him intelligent?"

They said, "He is very thoughtful."

Confucius said, "I hope he is not too thoughtful."

They said, "He is really very, very thoughtful. He thinks three times before he does anything."

So Confucius said, "Save me from this man. I will not go there."

But they said, "How can you say that? Isn't that intelligent?"

Confucius said, "He has become a little too intelligent, a little too unbalanced. The man who thinks once is at one extreme; the one who thinks three times has gone to the other extreme. Twice is enough."

Confucius means that it is enough to stop in the middle – the golden mean, stopping in the middle – neither renunciation, nor excess. Non-possessiveness blossoms where there is neither possession nor renunciation. It happens in the middle.

With the things that I have said, don't start worrying about non-possessiveness: be concerned with understanding possessiveness. Don't worry a bit about renouncing your possessions, worry about understanding why you are possessive. What is possessiveness, what need does it fulfill?

Three things have to become clear. First, it is impossible for the possession of things to bring fulfillment to your soul – to fill the emptiness, the void in your soul. Second, you become bound by whatever you are clinging to; you become a slave to it. And third, that your entire past experience tells you that even if you acquire everything, nothing is gained. You remain just as empty. If this remembrance becomes total, you will suddenly find that rays of non-possessiveness begin to descend into your life.

Tomorrow we will talk about non-theft. It is an even subtler journey into non-possessiveness.

I am grateful that you listened to me with such love and silence. Now to end, I bow down to the godliness that dwells in you all. Please accept my *pranam*, my offering of respect.

3

Non-Theft

My beloved ones.

One of the dimensions of violence is possessiveness. Without being violent, it is impossible to be possessive. And when possessiveness goes crazy, insane, theft is born. Theft is possessiveness gone mad. If the possessiveness is healthy, then non-possessiveness can slowly arise. If the possessiveness has become unhealthy, then slowly, slowly theft is born. Healthy possessiveness is slowly, slowly transformed into charity; unhealthy possessiveness is slowly, slowly transformed into theft.

By unhealthy possessiveness, I mean that now you consider another person's possessions to be yours, even though you do not see him as part of you. Unhealthy possessiveness means that you see another as the other, but dare to consider his possessions your own. However, if you feel he is part of you, charity is born. When only the other's possessions are felt as part of you and the other remains the other, then theft is born.

There is a great similarity between theft and charity. They are two polarities of the same phenomenon. In theft, the attempt is to make another's possessions your own. In charity, the effort is to feel the other as part of you. In theft, we snatch another's possessions and make them ours; in charity, we make our own possessions become those of others. In a sense, charity is the apology for theft. The donor is often a former thief, and a thief often becomes a donor later. If theft were only in relation to things, then it would not be such an issue. The theft of objects is related to the law, justice, the state, and society, but there is another deeper kind of theft that is related to religion.

Perhaps the day will come when there is excess wealth and affluence and the theft of objects will stop, but the importance of non-theft will still remain. The theft that your normal so-called religious people talk about stopping can soon come to an end. But none of these great disciplines of religion can ever come to an end because there is another deeper meaning of non-theft, which will always be significant, which will always be relevant. If society becomes completely affluent someday, theft will stop. The theft of things is always largely born out of poverty, but there are other thefts; those deeper thefts are connected with the great practices of religion.

So first let us understand this deeper theft a little, in which we are all involved – even those who may never have stolen another person's possessions.

What do I mean? The deeper spiritual meaning of theft is when I declare what is not mine as belonging to me. There is much that I have claimed as mine that is not my own, even though I have never committed any theft.

This body is not mine, but I call it *my* body. From the spiritual point of view, a theft has occurred. The body is not mine: I have found it; it is with me. When I say that I am the body, a theft has occurred. In spiritual terms, I have wrongly claimed ownership of something, I have gone mad. But we all consider the body to be our own. In fact we go on thinking that we *are* the body, not just the owner of it.

You had a body of sorts in your mother's womb. If it were placed in front of you today, you would not even be able to see it with naked eyes. You would need a large microscope and you would never be ready to agree that this was you at some point. Then, when you were a child you had a body that was changing every day. Every day the body is flowing. If we put pictures of a man's whole life in front of him, he will be astonished that he was in so many bodies! And the strange thing is that while traveling in all those bodies, he accepts each body as if "This is me."

The lives of traditional sannyasins are often hollow, there is nothing in them. The so-called good men often have no life at all. So it is very difficult to write a story about such a "good man." He has no life, he is walking on flat, empty ground; there are no ups and downs. Someone we would call "bad" has a life, with all its ups and downs; there are deep experiences of life itself. If he were to use them, he could become a saint. A good man is never able to become a saint. A good man just remains a good man – decent, but mediocre. If he has never even mustered the courage to be bad, he cannot acquire the strength to be saintly either.

I was reading about the life of this American actor…

His life was one of great ups and downs – of darkness and light, sins and virtues – but I was still amazed at his last words. I wish that his final statement, which was about what made him the most restless his whole life, could make you restless too. He said, "My biggest problem is that I have played so many different characters. I have done so much acting in my life, I have become so many people, that now I can't decide who I am."

Sometimes he was a character in a Shakespeare play; sometimes he was another character in another play. Sometimes he was a saint in some story or other, and sometimes he was a sinner in another story. He played so many characters in his life that finally he said, "Now I can't understand who I really am. I had to play so many characters, I had to assume so many faces, that it is no longer clear to me what my own face is."

The second profound thing he said was, "Whenever I go on stage to play a character, I am at ease. This is because it is not necessary to be myself there. A character has to be played, so I am completely at ease; I play it. To step into a role is easy, but to step out of it is complex. As soon as I come offstage after dropping the character, immediately my dilemma begins – now who am I? Before it was clear who I was; but who am I now?"

After playing a thousand characters, it became difficult for him to know who he was.

One could say that in this actor's life, the moment of non-theft has come close. But we do not realize it in our own lives. In reality, no actor does as much acting as we do. We just don't do it on a stage, so the realization does not arise. From childhood to death is one long story of acting. There is no one who is not an actor. He can be a competent or an incompetent actor, but he is still an actor. And when someone stops being an actor, religiousness is born inside of him.

We steal faces and lives. We believe that the body is ours, but it is not, and the personality that we consider our own is not ours either – they are all borrowed. The faces that we imprint on ourselves – the masks, the personas that we put on and live out – are not our faces either. The greatest of all spiritual theft is the theft of those masks, the theft of those personas.

Benjamin Franklin has written a memoir of his childhood. He wrote: "Ever since my childhood I had only one desire – to be self-fulfilled. So I established twelve rules by which I would become fulfilled. In those twelve rules, the best practices that each and every religion has mentioned are included. Self-restraint, determination, grace, peace, silence, courtesy – in those twelve, all the virtues are included."

He wrote: "How was I to accomplish all this? I began to study each and every behavior. I stopped saying bad things and when they came up, I started to suppress them. I started to keep an account every night of whether I had said or done anything bad during the day. Did I show restraint in something today? Did I behave badly? Did I think about stealing today? Was I lazy? I kept those accounts and observed the disciplines every day so that they became ingrained."

He wrote further: "I practiced my disciplines totally, and then a Christian monk told me, 'You have followed everything, but you have become very arrogant.'" It is natural for someone who has paid attention to everything to become arrogant. He has accomplished everything, he has proven himself – there is bound to be arrogance. So the Christian monk said, "Add a thirteenth rule: humility."

Franklin said, "I will observe that too." So he practiced humility, he also became humble.

But in his memoirs he has written one last statement that is very precious. He wrote: "Finally I felt that my accomplishments were just appearances. Whatever I have practiced has been just a facade; it has not become part of my soul."

Naturally, whatever we observe from outside becomes just a mask. Only what comes from inside is of the soul. We all practice religiousness only on the outside – non-religiousness inside, religiousness on the outside. Theft occurs inside while outside there is non-theft; possessiveness inside, non-possessiveness outside; violence inside, nonviolence outside. Then the masks become ingrained. That's why it is very difficult to find more stolen personas than those of so-called religious men. A stolen persona means that they go on believing themselves – and they go on showing themselves – to be what they are not. In spiritual terms, the meaning of theft is an attempt to show yourself as someone you are not, to claim to be what you are not. We are all doing that from dawn to dusk, we all go on making such claims.

It is not only that American actor who has forgotten his original face; we have forgotten it too. We all keep many masks ready. As the need arises we put on the mask for that moment, and we begin to appear as someone we are not.

Don't be misled by seeing a man's smile; it doesn't necessarily mean that there are no tears in him. A smile is often just an arrangement to hide the tears. Seeing someone joyous, don't assume that there is a spring of joy welling up inside him; it is often just an arrangement to suppress sadness. Seeing someone happy, there is no reason to assume that he *is* happy; often it is his way of forgetting sorrow.

Spiritual theft occurs whenever you do not appear on the outside as you are inside, and whoever commits this theft has not stolen a thing, he has stolen a persona. Stealing a thing is not so bad, but stealing a persona is a very great theft.

So anyone who wants to enter non-theft must understand one thing first: that he should not steal a persona even by mistake. Someone who copies Mahavira will be a thief; someone who imitates Buddha will be a thief; someone who behaves like Jesus will be a thief; someone who takes a persona from Krishna will be a thief. The meaning of *thief* is simply someone who has become something which he is not, something which he never was, in fact.

No other man on earth can be Mahavira, he just cannot be. All the conditions which occurred during the time of Mahavira cannot be repeated. Nor can a father like Mahavira's be found again. Mahavira's age cannot come again, nor can the moon and stars of that time be found again. Nothing can be found at all; each moment that passes in this world is gone forever.

So whenever someone tries to become Mahavira he will become a Mahavira-thief. If someone tries to become Krishna, he will become a Krishna-thief. Whenever anyone tries to become someone else, they will fall into spiritual theft. They will begin to steal personas.

We have been interpreting the meaning of religion as becoming like someone, becoming a follower: adopt, incorporate, follow, imitate, become anyone at all, just don't remain yourself. Become anyone at all. Somebody is a Jaina, somebody is a Hindu, somebody is a Christian, somebody is a Buddhist. Not one of them is religious – in the name of religion they have fallen into deep theft.

A follower will be a thief in spiritual terms; he has stolen another's persona and begun to clothe himself in something which he is not. The result is hypocrisy.

Hence a so-called spiritual society is a hypocritical society, because no one is what he actually is. Nobody is what they really are. Understand this, that no one is in their right place, everyone is standing in someone else's shoes. Nobody is looking through his own eyes; everybody is looking through someone else's eyes. Nobody is laughing with his own mouth; everyone is laughing with someone else's mouth. Nobody is living as himself; everyone is living as someone else. But this is impossible. I can neither live in someone's place nor can I die in someone's place, nor can I laugh through someone else's mouth, nor can I feel through another's heart.

My experience must of necessity be personal. And when it becomes personal, on that very day I will attain non-theft; it cannot happen before then. The day I remain just myself, without any imposed personality, on that day I will attain non-theft. Otherwise I will remain a thief.

We lock up those who steal objects in jails, but what do we do with those who steal identities? What should we do with people who have stolen personalities? We respect them; we honor them in temples, mosques, and churches. Those who steal objects have not committed a big theft, but those who steal personalities have committed a very great theft. And the theft of things will stop very soon because everything will increase in abundance. But the theft of personalities will continue. We will continue to steal; we will continue to clothe ourselves in others' personalities.

So consider a little whether you can gather the courage to be yourself or not. If not, then the foundation of your personality will certainly be theft. Haven't you tried to be like someone else? Is there an urge somewhere in your conscious or unconscious to become like someone else? If there is, then it is necessary to understand that urge and become free of it. Otherwise, the state of non-theft cannot come into being.

And this theft is such that no one can stop you from committing it – because stealing personalities is invisible theft. If you steal wealth, you can get caught; if you steal a personality, who will catch you? How will they catch you? Where will they catch you? The theft of a personality is such that you do not take anything from anyone, and yet you become a thief. The theft of a personality is easy and straightforward. From the time you get up in the morning, it is important to watch how many times you become someone else. We cannot be individuals because of these personalities.

Because of the personality, the individual cannot emerge. This word, *personality*, is a good word – it comes from Greek dramas. In those dramas, each actor would wear a mask, a face; they had to wear a mask. They used to call the face a *persona*, and the identity created by that mask was called the *personality*. It meant something they were not. *Personality* means that which you are not.

So the greater the personality, the greater is the theft; much will be stolen. There was a monk who assumed Mahavira's personality. He stood naked just like Mahavira. He would walk, get up, and sit down exactly like Mahavira. He ate and drank exactly like Mahavira. He spoke Mahavira's words exactly. He became Mahavira completely. But this can only be from the outside; this is a personality. Inside he can only be what he is.

That is why thieves often have their own individualities. Monks do not have their own at all. If you go to a jail and look into the eyes of thieves, you will feel that they are who they are. Go to temples and look into the eyes of monks, and you will feel that they are not their real selves.

A sinful man is often himself because after all, no one pretends to be bad. A good man is often *not* what he is because everyone likes to be seen as good. It is very difficult to *be* good; it is very easy to appear to be good. To be good is a spiritual discipline; to be good is arduous. But to pretend to be good is a game; it is easy, it is very convenient.

The world is not good, so there are great difficulties in being good. So someone who is good gets into trouble with the world. To be moral in an immoral society, to be virtuous in a corrupt society is a great dilemma. In a corrupt society, to be virtuous is to invite great difficulty. But it is the only truly ascetic discipline for a monk.

A monk's ascetic practice should not be to stand naked, or to remain hungry. These are very cheap and easy things that any simpleton can do. Actually, if the monk has any understanding, it will be difficult to practice these things. If he lacks understanding, they are easy to practice. A monk's discipline is to be moral in an immoral world. He will be tormented from all directions.

So it is convenient to wear the clothes of personality, to put on the cloak of morality, but to remain immoral. If you put on the cloak of morality in the marketplaces, in public places, you can remain immoral and there will be no trouble from the world.

That's why we have two faces, a private face and a public face. And the rule is: don't ever wear the individual face, the personal face in a public place. Nobody does it. Sometimes if you drink alcohol, you might make a mistake, otherwise never. If you drink, you forget that it is a private face in a public place – then there is difficulty.

Hence decent men are very afraid of drinking alcohol. Evil men are not so afraid because that face of theirs… They do not have a bigger or worse face than what is known. If all the decent men could be gathered up and made to drink alcohol, then you would know their private faces.

There was a mystic in Eastern Europe called Gurdjieff. Whenever somebody came to him, he would ask, "Are you a good man or an evil one?"

Rarely would any man who came ever say, "I am an evil man." It is difficult to find such a good man who can say, "I am an evil man." Usually people would say, "How can you ask such things? I am good. I have come to offer my devotion. Why would I come to do that if I were not good?" In fact the situation is the reverse – why would a good man go to offer devotion?

Gurdjieff would say, "The first practice will be that you must drink alcohol for fifteen days." Often those good men would run away. They could not even imagine that a mystic would talk about drinking alcohol. But that idea of Gurdjieff's was meaningful. He would say, "For at least fifteen days I will make you get drunk so that I can see your private face. Otherwise I don't know who I am talking to, who I am relating with, who I am transforming. It will be a futile effort if I transform what you appear to be; it will only be your mask, which has no relation to your true face. Such a change is useless. I can paint your mask, but it has no relation to your real face. Your mask is a completely different thing, you can remove it and put it aside at any time; you can change it. Don't make me work hard for nothing. First let me see your original face."

Respectable people would often run away upon hearing the mention of alcohol. Running away only revealed that there was something hidden inside them which they were afraid to expose. If someone remained, there would be a big surprise. For fifteen days, Gurdjieff would make him drink alcohol. He would make him drink as much as he could, and he would look for his original face.

It is unfortunate that one has to make someone unconscious to find his original face. The theft is so deep and so ancient that there are many layers of false masks. For an infinite number of lives, this face has hidden itself far, far, far beneath. Remove one mask and there is another beneath it. Man has become like an onion – peel one layer, and another layer, and another and another.

You cannot hold on to the illusion that you will find the onion. Go on peeling the layers, go on peeling and peeling, and eventually nothing will remain. The final layer is peeled, and you will ask yourself, "Where is the onion?" You will discover that the onion was only the layers, it had no identity of its own.

We have stolen so many personalities in an almost infinite number of lifetimes; we have donned so many masks that we have no face of our own left. If those layers fall away, then ultimately a void will be left. You will have to begin with that void because only there can there be movement into non-theft. Before that, there can be none. If you come to know that you have no face at all, it is a very great achievement.

I say unto you: do not think that any attempt to avoid theft is non-theft. Someone who commits a theft is a thief who steals, and someone who avoids theft is a thief who avoids stealing. They are both thieves: theft is inside them, there is no difference. One person's theft has progressed into behavior; the other's theft has remained limited to the mind.

But the real, deep spiritual meaning of non-theft is this: Do you have your own face? You will not be able to find it. You can stand in front of the mirror and a face will be visible. You will discover that it is someone else's face, even though you have considered it your own until now.

And it is not only that we have just one face, with which we make do twenty-four hours a day. In twenty-four hours we have to change so many faces, according to their function. In front of her husband a wife has one face… The husband is someone else in front of his wife: he is one person in front of his own wife, he is someone else in front of the neighbor's wife – instantly, his face changes.

I have one face in front of my boss, another one in front of my servant. If my boss is seated on one side and on the other side my servant is seated, my servant will see something on half of my face, and my boss will see something else on the other half – two faces will be there together. On one side I will be suppressing my servant, on the other side I will go on wagging my tail in front of the boss. I will have to do both tasks at the same time.

So sometimes when you are among a lot of people you become a chameleon – one thing with this person, something else with that person, still something else with a third person. A great difficulty arises.

I have heard…

Nasruddin had two lovers. He must have been a humble person, otherwise who stops at two lovers? He would meet each of them separately. It is very difficult to meet two lovers at the same time. To each one he showed a certain face, and promised that he had only shown it to them. He said to each one, "I love only you."

But lovers are very clever; they find out immediately. They look out for their lover's other lovers more than the lover himself. They both found out, and one day they caught Nasruddin and told him, "Answer both of us at the same time today."

Nasruddin said, "Don't trap a poor man like this. When you are not together it is very easy. I can change faces in between."

But they had caught him and said, "Give us an answer: which one of us is the most beautiful?"

Nasruddin said, "You are each more beautiful than the other."

I do not know if those lovers understood or not. Maybe they understood: love has little relationship with intelligence. I do not know if you understand either! Nasruddin says, "You are each more beautiful than the other." What words! Nasruddin is making a very deep joke on mankind. If he wants to balance both faces at the same time, what can the poor man do? – he becomes a chameleon. He says, "Each one of you is better than the other."

In twenty-four hours, we change faces twenty-four times. Not just twenty-four times; we change much more often, and this changing of masks causes tension. The tension *is* the changing of our masks. Someone who has one face does not feel tension; there is no reason for it. The tension always occurs when faces are constantly changed. You have to change so many times that a great difficulty arises. When you drop one face and bring in another, in the gap that happens in between, you have no face and much anxiety is created. That American actor is right when he says, "To step into a role is easy but to step out is arduous." To come out of any role is difficult, but we have to do it continually twenty-four hours a day. We have to change faces, constantly change faces. But people are very clever.

Cars used to have a conventional gearbox; the gears had to be changed. Now there is an automatic gearbox; the gears do not have to be changed. Very skillful people have an automatic gearbox; they do not change faces, their faces just change. We have discovered automatic gears to change the face; now we do not have to change them. Our servant comes and our face changes. Our boss comes and our face changes. Our wife comes and our face becomes something else. Our beloved comes and our face becomes something else. A friend comes and our face becomes something else. Now our face keeps on changing.

It was easier for people in earlier times to become religious; they had conventional gears. They themselves had to change faces, so they were aware that they were doing it. Modern civilization has removed the conventional gears that had to be changed; now they are automatic. I only make this much distinction between civilized and uncivilized man: conventional or automatic gears. I don't make any other distinction.

An uncivilized man has to change faces. Because of the need to change, he comes to know what he is doing each time: "What am I doing?" He is troubled. For civilized man, for civilization, there is training that saves man the trouble of changing faces. Our faces start changing on their own.

It becomes difficult for a civilized man to be religious because he does not recognize this kind of theft at all. He does not see the gap, the moment that passes between two faces; that empty space is missed. He doesn't come to know of it. Civilized man's tension keeps increasing because it is created by his changing face, but the realization that the face should not change does not occur because the gear is automatic. It happens on its own, so the more civilized a man is, the further he seems to be going away from religiousness.

Jesus, Buddha, and Mahavira were born in an uncivilized world. In a civilized world, we are unable to create men of their stature. There are reasons for this: our anxiety is much greater than before. Uncivilized man was not so anxious. Now there is great anxiety, but no one knows why. Our understanding of why it exists has diminished.

So I would like to tell you that to understand non-theft, you will have to become aware of your changing faces. There is a knack to becoming alert, and it has a result, a consequence: the more alert you become toward something, the less it moves.

Have you ever watched a film? What happens if the machine is damaged? If it starts moving slowly, if the projector starts moving slowly, then the movement of the film on the screen becomes slower. So, if a man would have appeared to raise his hand abruptly on the screen, instead, ten men appear to raise their hands slowly, and in between each picture a gap happens. When I raise my hand it does not rise with jerks because your eyes cannot capture the speed, but my hand has to take twenty positions to move so far. If you look closely and *your* machine slows down, then, by looking closely the activity becomes slower.

If you look at anything very closely, then the process becomes slower for two reasons. First, to look closely you have to stand still, you have to stop. If you look closely when you change faces, then the process will slow down and you will be able to catch it when it happens. Then you will be able to laugh at yourself, that your face has changed.

Look at your changing faces in regard to the great virtue of non-theft. Someone is going from his shop toward the temple. He should keep track of when he changes his face, at what step, on which step of the temple his face changes. His face when he is in the temple is not the same as earlier in his shop; the change has certainly happened somewhere. Somewhere he has changed masks.

Men do not keep vanity cases and such things with them; women do. Before getting off the bus, women change their face; they even keep the preparations with them. A similar, very interior arrangement, in which we remove faces and change them, is in us all. When you are going from your house to the temple, then with a little alertness, watch at which point your face changes. At what point does the shopkeeper disappear and the devotee appear? At which place does the one sitting in the shop disappear and the one entering the temple appear?

Does the change happen where you take off your shoes outside the temple? It may not happen there. Actually that's why the shoes are taken off there: "Now please change your face; now you have come to the place where your old behavior will not work – remove your shoes." Where it is written: "Shoes here, please," there should also be a sign below: "Masks here, please." Many people push their way inside with their masks on. If you go inside the temple with your shoes on, there won't be that much impurity. There will be more impurity if you go inside with your mask, but no one realizes it.

I want to tell you to remain a little aware when you change faces. And it will be great fun. So far you have laughed at others; now you will begin to laugh at yourself. And when you change masks knowingly, then it will become difficult to do. Slowly you will start to ask, "What is this madness? What kind of act am I doing?" Changing your mask will slowly become difficult and the gaps in between will grow. Sometimes you will be left without a mask. Then your original face will be born. Inside you, your original face will begin to appear.

So, first remain aware of your masks changing twenty-four hours a day, and second, do not try to take on someone else's face as your own – Mahavira's, Buddha's, Krishna's, or Christ's. Do not do it even by mistake. Do not become a follower at all; otherwise you will have to just be a thief.

A follower commits two thefts. A very sincere follower – or I should say a very sincere thief, who steals with great honesty – steals faces. Someone who steals dishonestly only steals ideas; he does not steal faces. He does not take on Mahavira's face, he only takes on Mahavira's ideas. A scholar only carries stolen ideas; a so-called monk carries stolen faces inside him.

So be aware: some thieves are weak. They say, "It is difficult to take on Mahavira's face – but nonviolence is the supreme religiousness. At least we can just copy this, we can certainly read Mahavira's scriptures. It is a little difficult to take on Krishna's face, but we can certainly recite the Gita."

So there are two kinds of theft – of ideas, or of faces. Men who steal faces are known as very sincere; they are honest thieves. "That poor man acts according to his principles." Beware, someone who acts according to his principles will be taking on some face or other – and religiousness is not about deciding on a principle and then practicing it. Otherwise the Benjamin Franklin effect will occur and hypocrisy will come into play.

We often say that we act as we think. This is a "thief-creating" maxim, and sincere and honest thieves are created by it. We tell you to practice what you think, but you should at least first find out if your thought arrived through theft. Otherwise, such a practice will take you even deeper into theft. If we say to someone that a person's thoughts and behavior are exactly the same, then we should ask whether his thoughts have come through his behavior or his behavior from his thoughts. If his thoughts have come through his behavior, then he is a religious man. If his behavior has come from his thoughts, then he is a thief. But the distinction is not immediately apparent.

When a thought comes through behavior it feels different because behavior comes from the being. When behavior comes from a thought, then the thought comes from the scriptures, and a thought that comes from the scriptures is, by its very nature, a theft. To mold one's life according to the scriptures is an even bigger theft. And those who fall into this kind of theft lose their souls. They find it difficult to know who they are.

No, I do not say to behave yourself according to your thoughts. I say, think according to your behavior. But you will fall into great difficulty – from where to get your behavior? If your behavior is according to your thoughts, then thoughts can be found – but from where to get the behavior? There is no shop for it, it is not sold anywhere. So where will you get it? If you get it from Mahavira, then it has come from thought; if you get it from Buddha, then it has come from thought; if you get it from Krishna, then it has come from thought. From where will you get it? If you get it from someone else, then the thought comes first. If it comes from yourself, it is a different matter. Then the thought will not come first; the experience will come first.

If your behavior is based on theft, then please think like a thief. That will be sincere. If your behavior is thief-like, then just think like a thief. Further, I say to you that if your actions are thief-like and your thoughts are also thief-like, then you will go beyond theft! If your behavior is thief-like and your thoughts are of non-theft, then you will never go beyond theft – because you will say that your behavior is external, that the real issue is your thoughts.

It's as if I am saying, "I am not really a thief, I only become a thief because of my desires. So slowly I will watch; I will change my behavior too. When my thoughts change, then my behavior will also change – I will take a vow, I will make a promise." Then you will keep on postponing your whole life because you will experience from the inside that your thoughts are of non-theft: you are a good man on the inside. "External circumstances make me a thief, but I am not really a thief."

Notice that your behavior is very distant from you, but your thoughts are very close. So if we point out a fault in a man's thoughts, he will not be ready to accept it. If we say to somebody, "There is a boil on your foot," he does not argue; he says, "Give me the cure!" But if we say to somebody, "There is a disease in your mind," then he gets ready to fight. He says, "There is something wrong with your observation!"

A man will accept a boil in the body; it is far away. He will not accept a boil in the mind; it is very close. An attack on a boil in his mind is an attack on himself. So we have created a device, a technical device: we create good thoughts and we continue to behave badly. This is convenient because we can go on believing inside ourselves that we are good people. If I swear at you, then I will not say that I am a man who swears. I will say, "I don't ever swear, but that man swore, so I had to. It is him who is responsible for my swearing."

When you fight with someone, you do not say that fighting is inside you. You say, "This man created a hostile situation; I had to fight. I am not a fighting man." And you will also believe it yourself because inside you have never thought of fighting. The thought is always of nonviolence, non-theft, non-possessiveness. You read the scriptures about nonviolence, non-theft, non-possessiveness, and celibacy, so your thoughts are very good. But behavior? Someone else is responsible for your behavior. You are saved.

Then there is one more convenience: when your thoughts are good, by gathering courage, by creating determination, by making the situation right – if not today, then tomorrow – you can change your behavior too. So you can postpone.

Beware; if you want to bring transformation in your life, avoid postponement. This is a very cunning device. Someone says, "I am still violent but I believe in nonviolence. I will slowly become nonviolent." He says, "I will become nonviolent tomorrow, or the day after, in this lifetime, in the next lifetime." He goes on postponing it and he remains violent. But he is saved from the pain of being violent because the hope of becoming nonviolent lessens his pain. It becomes a consolation.

So I am saying: if you steal, think in the same way. Burn all the scriptures that exist about non-stealing. Write on the walls of your house that stealing is the supreme religion. And know in your heart that stealing is your supreme duty, that he who does not steal is making a mistake.

If you think about theft like this and also have the behavior of a thief, you will not be able to live with yourself – because no one can live with a thief inside him. You will become a real thief, a perfect thief. It will become difficult to live with that. Your entire personality – your behavior, your thoughts, your whole identity –

will become that of a thief. And it will become difficult for your being to live with that thief, even for one moment.

But there is a trick with which one can live: "I will make it all right tomorrow. At least my thoughts are good. My behavior is bad, but it is bad because of others." This kind of thought finds support too. For example, if a man retreats to the forest he does not get angry. He says, "Look, other people were making me angry. Now that I have come to the forest, where is my anger?"

Hence the so-called holy man runs to the forest; he finds consolation there: "I am really a good man. I was a good man before too, but I was surrounded by bad people; hence all the confusion that was happening." A husband leaves his wife and runs away and thinks: "See, now I am beyond attachment and desire. The attachment and desire was created because of that woman."

So men write in the scriptures that the woman is the door to hell! Those who have run away from a woman, who have escaped, are now saying that the woman is the door to hell: "She was the one who created the mess. As far as I'm concerned, I was always free." Thus they create rationalizations.

If we drop a bucket in a well that has no water in it, the bucket cannot draw any water out. The bucket can only draw out water that is already in the well. The bucket only does the work of drawing it out. When I swear at you, then my curse cannot create anger in you. The word just does not have the power of creating anger. But the word becomes like a bucket; it brings out your anger, the well of anger that is swelling inside you. The curse doesn't create, it only brings out what is inside. It does not create anything, it only makes something emerge.

But if the bucket is not dropped in the well, then the well might think there is no water in it because no water comes out: "It was the bucket's fault. It came inside and created the illusion of water. I am completely empty; there is no water at all. Look, no bucket – now where is the water?"

We all have this misconception; when we are alone we just don't see it. Actually, we only discover our personality through others. Only when we are with others do we discover what is within us. Others become an opportunity for us to reveal ourselves.

So please do not hold others responsible. No one who has held others responsible can be religious. Religiousness means that the total responsibility is mine. The non-religious man puts the responsibility on someone else: "I am a good man; other people are making me bad." No one is doing any wrong to you.

The second trick is: you go on thinking good thoughts inside, so at least you know that you are good inside. When you come into contact with others, you become bad on the outside. So this being bad on the outside seems to be because of others.

Avoid good thoughts if you want good behavior to happen. If your behavior is bad, then please have bad thoughts; become completely bad. It is difficult to live with a completely bad person. Arrangements can be made to live with someone half-good, but a half-good man is even worse than a bad man. Half-truths are worse than complete lies because you can become free of complete lies. You will never be free of half-truths; a half-truth will create bondage.

So I say unto you: do not act according to your thoughts; think according to your actions. Then matters will be clear – and if matters are clear, then no one in this world will be able to live with a completely bad man. You will not even be able to live with your own bad man. And when you know that you are living with a bad layer inside, it will be as easy to strip it off and throw it away as it is to remove a thorn from your foot. It will be as easy to remove – to strip off and throw away this layer of the onion, this bad layer, this personality, these layers of personality – as it is to remove dirt from the body.

But when someone considers his dirt to be gold, a problem arises. If he values his dirt, considers it a decoration, then a great difficulty arises. If a girl's nose is pierced, she will feel pain, but to acquire a gold ornament any girl is ready to get her nose pierced.

Now to pierce the body is insanity, but in the desire for gold we are ready to commit this insanity. Piercing the body is ugly, but with the dream of beauty, with the misconception of beauty, we are ready to do it. We are ready to do ugly acts because behind them we have set up concepts that act as golden ornaments.

Do not act according to your thoughts; think according to your actions and then your personality will get a direct and sincere cleansing. You will be just what you are, there will be no deception. There will be no fear of another's betrayal; no means of deceiving yourself will remain. You will be able to recognize your masks. And the day those masks become familiar from all sides, when their ugliness, their filth, their stench, and their scourge are visible from all sides, inside and out, then you will not be able to live with them. It is just as when your clothes catch fire – throwing the clothes away, you are naked. Transformation happens exactly like that. Revolution happens just like that. When your entire personality appears sick and on fire, you throw it away. You do not think even for a moment that you will throw it away tomorrow. It is not like that.

A man came to Buddha and asked, "Master, give me some instruction."

So Buddha said, "Will you do it now or tomorrow?"

He said, "It is very difficult right now."

So Buddha said, "Then come tomorrow. Come only on the day you want to do it."

The man said, "At least give me the instruction. It will be useful sometime, and you may or may not be available. I will certainly start using it sometime."

Buddha said, "I was passing through a village and a house had caught fire. I said to the people in that house, 'Don't run now, run tomorrow.' They said, 'Have you gone mad? Our house is on fire, how can we wait till tomorrow?'"

Buddha said, "As far as I understand it, you believe that you are content with what you are right now, so you can let it wait till tomorrow. Why do you trouble me now, when you are okay? Why should I say things to you needlessly? The day you find out that you are not okay..."

"No," said the man, "I know that I am not okay. I am not a good man, I do bad things but at least my soul is clean and pure. The soul is always pure. So I will change my behavior, all of it. Just give me the instruction."

We are all very eager and anxious to receive instruction. We think that then we will act accordingly, but our actions will be just like those of an actor on stage. First he gets the script, the outline of the play, and then he recites it. Then he has rehearsals. Then he comes on stage and acts it.

The meaning of acting is behaving according to a prescribed script. But the meaning of being is something else – thinking according to your behavior. If your behavior is bad, then think bad thoughts also. Then you will break down. Your personality will not be able to survive, it will fall apart. And the day your old personality falls apart completely, in that empty space your original face will arise.

In Japan, if anyone goes to the Zen mystics, they ask many questions. One question is this: "Please show your original face, reveal it. What is your original face?" Now, a new man has come and a mystic says to him, "Show your original face." He says, "This is my only face." Then the mystic says, "If this is your only face, there is no need to come here. Go and seek. Bring your original face."

Sometimes courageous people come with their real face. But those mystics are unique, they keep on saying, "We agree that this one is more genuine than the previous one, deeper than the previous one, but it is still not authentic. Go and bring your original one. Bring that face which was with you before your birth and will be with you after your death. Whichever face you had before birth, bring that one. Or bring the face that you will have again after death. Please do not bring these in-between faces." And when a man comes and sits down faceless, without any mask, then the mystic says, "This is correct. You have come to the true place."

Facelessness is a great attainment – but we become very afraid if our face is lost. We find it extremely difficult, so we quickly become engrossed in creating a mask.

You have to lose your mask if you want to drop theft. And the moment must come when you are not sure of who you are. If you want to know who you are, remove your stolen faces, whether you have taken them from Mahavira, or from Buddha, or from Krishna, or from a Mohammedan, or a Jaina, or a Hindu. Remove those masks and seek that which is yours. And the day all your masks drop, suddenly the form which is yours is revealed in front of you. As soon as it is revealed, you attain non-theft.

A man who has stopped stealing personalities and faces, who has stopped stealing behavior, cannot steal objects. It is impossible; there is no way for it to happen anymore. One who has renounced such deep thefts will not go in for such petty thefts. But we remain engrossed in renouncing the petty thefts.

A friend came to me and said, "I do not take bribes." He is a senior officer.

I said, "If someone offers you five rupees?"

He said, "You say such ridiculous things. I do not take bribes at all."

I said, "If someone offers five hundred rupees?"

Forcefully, he said, "No, what a ridiculous thing to say! No, no, I do not take them at all!"

I asked, "If someone comes with five thousand rupees?" He looked at me closely. Doubt entered his mind. I asked, "If someone comes with five hundred thousand?"

He said, "Then I would have to think."

So there can be degrees to our thieving. You may be stealing only two cents, but don't believe that you are not a thief. What difference does it make whether you stole two cents or two hundred thousand? How can there be any degree to theft? Can theft be less or more – the theft of two cents be less and the theft of two hundred thousand be more? Two cents might be less, two hundred thousand might be more, but it is still theft. How can thefts be different, more or less? The act of theft is total. If I steal two cents, then I am just as much a thief as when I steal two hundred thousand.

But it can happen that one theft has a different outcome than another. Someone steals two rupees; someone else steals two hundred thousand rupees. The ones who steal two hundred thousand rupees can put those who steal two rupees in jail. They can do that because the two-rupee thieves cannot build a jail but those who steal two hundred thousand can.

The thieves of two hundred thousand cannot be caught because they can give anyone two hundred thousand rupees in bribes. So how can the magistrate, who punishes the two-rupee thief, punish the thief of two hundred thousand rupees? By then the magistrate himself will also have become a thief. By receiving two hundred thousand rupees, he will also have become a thief. So, big thieves go on trapping smaller thieves. The big thieves are outside the jail walls, the smaller thieves are inside; the clever thieves are outside, the foolish thieves are inside. But the whole of society is based on theft.

This theft is not going to go away as long as we continue to think of it only in relation to objects. It can happen that I renounce everything, escaping and saying that I do not steal. But a thief may bring my food, a thief may bring my clothes, a thief may build the ashram in which I live. What difference does it make? It is just that I am a much smarter thief. I do not commit theft myself; I get others to do it for me. Otherwise it is the same. But I cannot escape the responsibility. Theft exists, society is criminal, and society will remain criminal as long as we understand theft to be the theft of objects only.

Society is based on theft, and we have given everyone an in-depth training to be a thief.

We tell a child to become like Vivekananda. Now, what mistake has this child committed that that he has to become like Vivekananda? Vivekananda was very good, but what mistake has this poor child done that he has to become like Vivekananda? And if he succeeds, he becomes a thief. We say, "Become like Mahavira." Have you committed a mistake by being born as yourself? If only Mahavira had the right to be born on earth, then there would be no need for the world to continue. He was born; the matter was over. What is the need of *your* existence?

What is the need of repeating carbon copies of Mahavira? When the original already existed before, why should we make useless efforts? One Mahavira is enough!

No, no one needs to be a carbon copy. Avoid stealing personalities, avoid stealing behavior, then one day your own inner being will reveal itself and you will attain non-theft. Thereafter there will be no question of stealing objects at all; it would just not be there.

Do not get absorbed in the few things I have said, otherwise they will become thoughts borrowed from me, and then theft will begin. There are very subtle ways of theft. You may say, "What you are saying is absolutely correct, let's do it." Now theft has begun. Please don't just do what I am saying. Understand what I am saying and leave it at that. Let the understanding stay with you, not the thought. Let the perfume remain, not the flower. Understand the things I have said; then leave them here. The understanding will go with you; it has no connection with the words. If this understanding changes your life, then let it change it; if it does not, then let it not change. Please do not try to impose it from above; otherwise theft will continue and non-theft will never be attained.

Tomorrow we will talk about the fourth virtue: non-desire. I said that one of the forms violence takes is possessiveness, and when possessiveness becomes mad or demented, one of its forms is theft. Tomorrow we will talk of non-desire. Non-desire is the basis of all three. Desire, lust, and longing are the basis of violence. Desire is also the basis of possessiveness and theft. Desire is sitting beneath all these three and has slid in at the root of them all. Tomorrow we will understand desire, and the day after, awareness.

I am grateful that you listened to me with such love and silence. Now to end, I bow down to the godliness that dwells in you all. Please accept my *pranam*, my offering of respect.

4

Non-Desire

My beloved ones.

Nonviolence, non-possessiveness, non-theft – we have discussed these three great virtues. Today we will discuss the fourth: non-desire. Desire is the name of man's most important energy; the energy of desire is at work at the foundations of the first three.

If desire is fulfilled, it becomes possessiveness. If desire is unfulfilled through its own defects, it becomes theft. If desire is unfulfilled because of someone else, it becomes violence. On the path of desire, on the path of lust, on the path of wanting, if someone is a hindrance, then desire turns violent. If there is no hindrance from outside, but rather from one's own internal capacity, desire becomes theft. And if there is no hindrance from inside or out, desire is fulfilled and it becomes possessiveness. It is necessary to understand desire in depth.

Man is energy. There is nothing other than energy in this world; the whole of life is energy. The days are gone when people said it is all matter. Those days are finished.

At the beginning of this century Nietzsche said: "God is dead." But before this century is finished, it is matter which will have died, not God. Matter is dead. It is not even correct to say it is dead, it never was matter. This was a misconception because matter is visible. Scientists say that matter is just energy which has become concentrated, it is condensed energy. There is nothing like matter in this world. A stone which is there, so hard, so clear, so substantial, is not there. It too is a condensed form of electrical charges.

Today, in the eyes of science the whole world is a collection of energies. In the eyes of religion it was always like that. Religion calls this energy godliness. Science is now calling this force energy, just mere energy. When science advances a little further, it will dispel another error. Fifty years ago, science used to say that matter is the only truth. Today, science says that energy is the only truth. Tomorrow, science will have to say that consciousness is the only truth. Just as science found out that matter is a condensed form of energy, so it will discover, if not today then tomorrow, that energy is a condensed form of consciousness.

Each individual is a spark of this very same energy, a very small structure of this life energy – you, me, everyone. If this energy flows outward, it becomes desire, it becomes lust. And if it flows inward, it becomes non-desire, it becomes the soul. The difference is only one of direction. When desire returns back toward itself, returns toward home, then it becomes non-desire; it becomes the soul. When the energy of desire continues to flow outward in life, a person slowly begins to weaken; his energy becomes less, without spirit. He may achieve many things in the world through his desires, but he remains unsuccessful in fulfilling himself. Energy can only move in the direction of whatever we want to achieve. If we want to acquire external objects, then energy will have to move outward, and if we want to attain the soul inside, then energy will have to move inside.

Be aware: by desire I mean outward flowing energy. By non-desire I mean inward flowing energy. These are the two characteristics of energy – outward flow or inward flow. When it flows outward, then an individual can achieve everything on the outside but he loses himself. And if the self is lost, there is no value in achieving anything else either. Even if we attain the whole world it has no value, if in attaining it we only get lost.

But if energy flows inward, then it becomes non-desire.

The meaning of desire is longing, wishing. Whenever we desire something, we have to flow outward because our wishing becomes a hope of fulfillment somewhere outside. If there is something to attain outside we have to flow outward. We are all outward flowing people, we are all desires; we *are* desire. Twenty-four hours a day we are flowing outward. Someone wants to attain wealth, someone wants to attain prestige, someone wants to find love. And the big surprise is that even if someone wants to attain godliness, even then he goes on flowing outward. He thinks that God is sitting somewhere in the sky. Someone wants to attain liberation and thinks liberation is somewhere up there, and he wants to attain it.

Religiousness has no relationship with the outside. So those whose gods are outside should understand fully that they have no relationship with religiousness. Those whose liberation is outside should understand fully that they are not religious. Those who wish to attain any object outside should understand that they desire. Liberation from desire is only possible in a state of flowing inward. And outside, any object at all, anything that can be attained, takes our energy outward.

Slowly we become empty, finished. Yet another birth, again we are born with energy, again we flow outward, again we are finished. Again a third birth, again we are born with energy, again we flow outward and are finished.

At birth, we arrive with energy. In death, we lose energy and return. When someone dies with energy, it is no longer necessary for him to come back. At birth, everyone comes with energy. At the time of death, a great part of that energy is lost, spiritless. We are like an empty, spent cartridge whose shell has remained but the bullet is gone. We return, taking that empty shell along.

Someone who saves all his energy and carries it at the moment of death does not need to come back – someone who can say, like Kabir, "At the moment of death, the cloak is returned spotless." Nothing was spent, nothing was lost, nothing ran out. Take care of the cloak and return it exactly as it was given. For one who returns exactly as he came at the moment of birth, without losing anything, it is no longer necessary to be reborn. Non-desire means liberation from birth and death. Desire means to return again and again through birth. There are reasons for this...

No desire is ever fulfilled in the right way, it cannot be. If someone has become used to running after desires, as soon as a desire is close to being fulfilled, a new desire is found. Otherwise how will he keep running after desires? Running after desires has become his only life. Another desire arises even before a wish is fulfilled. In fact, when one wish is fulfilled, he creates several more, and then he begins to run again. We are outward running energies, outgoing energies, so we die like empty cartridges.

That is why death cannot be a beautiful experience. It becomes impotent, a sorrow, a spiritless pain. We get broken up in every way and are finished. That's why there is so much pain in death. That pain is not of death, it is the pain of a spiritless, empty person who like everyone else has become a void, and in whom there is nothing left anymore – only an empty shell remains. That's why death brings sadness.

But to one who is not empty, who is fulfilled, even death brings bliss. The virtue of non-desire is to make us understand how we can remain fulfilled. However, before understanding non-desire, we have to understand the whole journey of desire, how desire makes us move, how we flow outward. This has to be understood. If we understand this, then it is a very simple thing to flow inward, very easy.

We know that for thousands of millions of years, matter has been made of atoms but we were not able to split the atom. Early this century we split the atom. As soon as the atom was split, a miraculous phenomenon occurred. In a small atom which is not visible to the eye, in a small hydrogen atom – or in an atom of anything – so much energy was hidden that when it was split a terrible force was born. With the explosion of a small atom, hundreds of thousands of people in Hiroshima died instantly. There is so much energy hidden in one small atom that when it was split, such an explosion occurred.

By splitting the atom, science revealed a very important thing, that there is infinite energy hidden inside everything. If it is split, then an explosion happens and all the energy flows outward. If it remains unbroken...

But we never knew that there is so much energy hidden inside an unexploded atom. A long time ago religion did the exact opposite of the work that science has done. Science split the atom, religion synthesized it. That is why *yoga* is one word for religion. The meaning of the word *yoga* is union.

Man's consciousness is also an atom, and if we allow that atom to be split, then everything flows out of it, infinite energy flows out. If that atom becomes joined, becomes closed – no division, no split – synthesis happens, integration happens. It becomes closed, it becomes a full stop; the outward loss in all directions stops and infinite energy becomes available inside. The experience of this infinite energy is the experience of godliness, of infinite bliss; it is the experience of infinite courage. After the experience of this infinite energy, nothing remains to be experienced; everything has been experienced.

But understand that man is a split atom; he is a split atom of consciousness. There is a hole in him, as if someone is using a bucket with a hole in it. When the bucket is immersed in water it seems to be full, but as soon as the bucket comes out of the water, it begins to empty. By the time it comes up there is only the noise of the water falling out of the hole in all directions; the bucket comes back empty.

At the moment of birth, we all are full of energy. At the time of our birth, we are full buckets. From the moment of birth, the bucket starts rising from the well and the emptying begins. If understood correctly, dying begins with birth; something of us begins to empty, to pour out. We begin to empty, like a bucket with a hole.

The first moment of birth is the beginning of dying. The emptying has begun.

So from the first moment of birth everyone becomes capable of death – he can die at any time. When this capability will be realized is another matter. Throughout our whole lives we continue to empty, and to become emptier and emptier. Perhaps only in the morning when we get up after a night's sleep do we have a slight feeling of being full of energy. Our energy is able to accumulate a little through the night because the doors to our senses are closed. Our eyes are closed, our hands fall idle, our ears don't listen, our lips don't speak, our noses do not smell. Everything shuts down. The doors shut down. That is why we feel fresh in the morning. We feel fresh because our energy becomes more still during the night.

We have no idea of the freshness experienced by a person who has gathered his whole life energy together. We have no idea of that. Even if we put all the freshness of all the mornings of our life together, still we will not be able to know that magnificent freshness. If someone loses even one night's sleep it will become difficult to have a normal day because the little energy he collects at night is lost. If he doesn't sleep for fifteen days, a man will go mad. If he has no food for fifteen days he can be okay, but if he doesn't sleep for fifteen days there will be trouble.

If someone is ill and cannot sleep, the doctor worries about the illness later – first let him sleep because the energy required for the body to heal needs to be collected, gathered, it needs to accumulate.

We are just losing energy, and desire is the means of losing it. Desire has many forms; the most condensed is sex. That's why *desire* and *sex* have slowly become synonyms. Energy comes from food; in sleep, energy is saved and with exercise, energy is awakened. Then we spend the energy. A large part of this energy is spent just in the organization of life itself.

A lot of this energy is spent creating energy for tomorrow. Much is spent so that energy can move inside and be awakened. When you have a meal, a great miracle happens inside. You take ordinary dead matter inside and your life energy makes it come alive. It makes the inorganic, organic. A lot of energy is used in that. Food gives energy, but a lot of energy is used in eating and converting it into blood. When you walk, energy is spent; when you sit, energy is spent. In sleep, energy is spent – and it accumulates too.

After all the activities of life, what little energy remains with you, you make no other use of besides sex. You use that energy only for sex. It is good to understand what use we make of the energy that is left after our everyday activities. If it is only being used for sex, then be aware that sex is just a relief. Sex is just freedom from the burden of the energy.

Now this is very strange: you spend twenty-four hours collecting energy, and then to save it, you sleep eight hours. You work hard all your life to earn food. Then when the energy comes, you become heavy with the weight of it and you try to throw it out. It is just as if somebody earns money all day, is crazy to earn money all day, and in the evening he throws it in the river because he finds that his wealth has made his bag heavy. Now the burden seems too much, so to get free of it, he throws it in the river.

We collect the energy first. If there is no energy, we strive for it. When the energy is there it becomes burdensome, it becomes heavy on our consciousness; then it has to be thrown out. We use sex to throw energy out. It is just relief, and afterward we become empty again.

How very absurd man's life is! Tomorrow morning he will once more become absorbed in collecting energy, by tomorrow evening he will once more have collected energy, and then he will throw it out and find relief again. Such a strange madness – collect, throw out, collect, throw out! What is the meaning of such a life? What is the purpose of this kind of life? What will you attain in this kind of life?

But it is not visible to us. If we don't get food, we are concerned; if we get food, we are concerned. If we have no energy, we are weak; if we gather energy, we are impatient to throw it out. Man is such an absurdity as he is. As man is, he is utterly irrational. As man is, it seems he has no relation to intelligence. It is as if a spring is just about to become a lake and then the banks break and everything flows out. Then, after the banks break they are built up again, again the spring fills the lake, and again the banks break. Our whole lives we go on collecting and losing energy in this way.

This cannot be life; something somewhere is going wrong. It is right to accumulate energy, but to collect it just to lose it is utterly meaningless. If anyone says he is born in order to die, we will say he is mad. If someone says he collects in order to lose, we will say he is mad. If someone says he builds a house so that he can demolish it, we will say he is not in his right mind. But what is our own condition? What do we do in life? What are we doing? Whatever we collect, we collect in order to lose.

Perhaps we have never thought about this: whatever energy we collect, we collect in order to lose! Hence your so-called holy men start to work in the opposite way. They start to accumulate less energy so they have nothing to lose. But there is no difference. A man earns two cents and in the evening throws it in the river. Another man does not earn at all, out of fear that he will throw it in the river in the evening. But in the evening they are each as poor. The one who throws it away does not have the two cents, and the one who didn't earn it doesn't have the two cents either. They are both poor.

Somehow you accumulate energy and then you simply spend it on sex. Because of the fear of this, your so-called holy man starts accumulating less energy. He starts fasting, starts eating less; he creates only enough energy in his body for his day-to-day needs. No excess energy remains. If there is excess energy he will get into trouble. Then he will have to do the same thing as you. But there is no difference. You accumulate and lose. He does not accumulate at all, so that he does not have to lose. But no energy is saved in this way.

Recently, they were conducting an experiment at a science school in America. It should be fully understood by all the holy men in India. Thirty students were kept hungry for a month in an attempt to understand the relationship between hunger and sex. What is the relationship between sex and hunger?

There were very strange results. For the first seven days while they were kept hungry, their sexuality became acute. But after seven days their sexuality became weaker and weaker. On the fifteenth day, pictures of naked women were put in front of them but they still did not get excited. No matter how they were provoked they took no interest. By the time the thirty days were over, no lust of any kind remained in those thirty young men, no kind of sexuality remained. They became completely cold, frozen. There was no way left to shake them up; it was as if sex had disappeared.

Then they were given food. After seven days, their sexuality started to come back. After fifteen days, they were back to the state in which they had been before. After thirty days, they were ordinary people again. The same juice, the same lust captured them again.

What happened? Sex was not destroyed; it was just that the extra energy that sex required was not available. The serpent remained alive, but the energy to move was not there. The serpent fell unconscious, waiting for the strength to move. When it had the strength again, it started moving; it stood up.

This thirty-day experiment showed that holy men have been deceiving themselves for a long time. Yes, if these young men could be continuously kept on less food, just enough food to provide the energy used in walking, getting up, sitting down, and talking, then they would be able to live without sex. But this, this is not non-desire, this is just dead desire, this is dead sex. This dead desire, this dead sex is not non-desire.

So people who have understood that energy accumulates – and for relief, to be free of it, they have to go into sex – have stopped accumulating energy. But they are under the same misconception as the rest of mankind.

The householder and the renouncer are at the opposite ends of this misconception. But this is not the meaning of non-desire. The meaning of non-desire is that energy is certainly created, but it does not get dissipated by sex; it accumulates. And when energy accumulates on a very large scale and does not get dissipated by sex, then that energy begins to ascend within you.

It is like when we build a dam and stop the flow of a river. The depth of the river – say it is ten feet – will become a hundred feet after building the dam. And to the same extent that the river rises, the height of the wall will have to be increased, and the depth of the dam will continue to deepen – it may even reach a thousand feet. It will start rising upward. Whenever any energy is confined it rises up because it accumulates. When excess energy accumulates inside you, a reserve of energy is formed and it begins to rise upward.

At this moment, your energy never rises above the level of sex. As soon as your energy rises even a little above the level of sex, you use it and return to the same place you were. If that energy would accumulate, it would rise above the level of sex. And understand that sex is man's lowest center, the lowest of the lower doorways. There are higher doorways above it. If this energy rises, it begins to open these other doorways.

Understand that inside man there are six more doorways above sex, and as energy arrives at each doorway, the intensity of bliss increases. It will surprise you. Rising above sex, when energy arrives at the second center, you will be surprised: "I was such a fool. Where was I losing energy? If I use it here I feel a great bliss, a lot more than I was feeling at the first center."

Suppose a man is digging a mine; he gathers stones and pebbles. He comes back home with only those colored stones and pebbles. Then someone tells him that they are just colored stones and pebbles, and to dig a little more. He digs a little more and finds copper; he comes back home and gets some money in the market for the copper. But someone says to him, "You fool, dig a little more." He keeps on digging and he finds silver, he finds gold, he finds diamonds, and he keeps on digging.

We are living at the first layer of our individuality – at the layer of sex – where we find nothing but stones and pebbles. If energy accumulates there and moves upward a little, the second center begins to open, where the level of happiness changes. Remember that at the level of sex, the presence of another is necessary to be happy. At the second center, another's presence is not necessary; we become sufficient alone. The individual begins to be liberated.

When the energy reaches the seventh center, the crown chakra in the head, so much energy has accumulated that it has started flowing from the sex center to the *sahasrar*, the crown chakra. You can call this energy *kundalini* or any other name, it makes no difference. The day your energy has accumulated so much that it activates this center in your head, for the first time you have become self-realized, you have become enlightened. On that day, you know that you have arrived.

But we get lost at the first center. That hole in our buckets wastes everything else in our lives. What does this mean? Am I saying that you should suppress sex, stop it? If you suppress it or try to stop it, you will never succeed because energy has a law: suppressed energy will become rebellious. However strongly energy is suppressed, it will rebel and react just as strongly. Energy cannot be suppressed at all, it can only be directed. There are two ways: either you give energy a new direction and it begins to flow in that direction, or you block the old path and then the energy begins to hammer back forcefully on the same old path.

So everyone who fights with sex will remain in desire their whole lives; they can never go beyond it. No one has ever reached to the higher centers, to the peaks of life through fighting with sex. Yes, by activating life's higher centers, people have certainly become free of sex.

Celibacy is not a fight against sex. Celibacy is the activation of centers higher than sex. So do not take it in a negative way. In this country we have been taking it negatively for thousands of years. Very early, thousands of years ago, it was our understanding that if this energy were blocked, it would open the door to great bliss. But how can you block this energy? You have to block it forcefully. And the more you block it, that same energy pushes back so you have to hold your attention there. And the center at which your attention lies will remain active.

So people who block their energy at the point of desire, at the sex center, become extremely active concerning sex. In truth their whole personality becomes genital. They do not remain outside it; their whole consciousness gets stuck right there, gets entangled there. The more damage that entangled consciousness causes, the more active that center becomes. And when that center becomes intensely active, only one option remains: they reduce their food intake, reduce their exercise, and start living like corpses so that the energy does not arise.

This doesn't change anything. An ordinary householder is better off; at least he creates energy. If energy is created, then one day the upward journey can also happen. The renouncer is in a worse condition. He creates no energy at all. Neither does his energy go out, nor does he have any energy that can rise upward. One certainly needs energy, and what goes outward can go inward too. But what is unfit to move outward is also not fit to move inward. Whoever has become unfit to make the outward journey will never be able to make the inward journey.

So remember: we need excess energy. There has to be a complete system to create energy, but there should also be a system to give this energy a new direction. I will tell you of two or three requirements so that this energy can find a new direction.

First, if we can just live in the present, then energy accumulates and starts moving upward. This is the first requirement: living in the present. If someone thinks a lot about tomorrow and the day after and about the future, and tries to live in the future, his energy flows away because the future is distant. It is not here, it has to come. And our relationship with the future can only be one of desire, no other relationship is possible.

Jesus was passing through a village and he said to his disciples, "Do you see those lilies blooming?"

His disciples said, "We can see them."

Jesus said, "See their beauty, see their blossoming, see their bliss." Then he said, "King Solomon at the peak of his glory, with the wealth of the whole earth, was not as beautiful as these wild lilies."

Someone asked, "But why is it so?"

So Jesus said, "Solomon was always living in the future; these flowers are living now. Their energy does not have the chance to become desire; their energy is becoming life."

Be aware, whenever we turn energy into desire, it is because of the future. Desire means future-orientation. Desire means the wish to live in the future – and life is always here and now. Someone who has a strong wish to live in the future will keep flowing outward, and his energy will go on being lost. The future absorbs our energy in the wrong way, but in the present, energy accumulates. So someone who wants to use his energy and power to attain to non-desire, to celibacy, who wants to move his energy toward his inner self, toward truth and godliness, should slowly reduce his wishes and desires for the future. He should live here and now.

When you are eating your food, then just eat. Do not work while you are eating. And when you sit in your workplace, just sit there and don't eat. When you go to the cinema, go to the cinema; don't let the temple enter at that time. And when you go to the temple, be in the temple; don't let the cinema come to the temple.

Every moment, wherever you are, try to be there totally. It will be difficult but it will become easier. It will be difficult because your habit has always been not to be present where you are, and always to be where you are not. You are never where you are, your mind is somewhere else, filled with desire. When you are in Kolkata your mind is in Mumbai. When you are in Mumbai your mind is in Kolkata.

Your mind is not where you are in this moment, so you have to stretch your desiring mind in order to connect with where you are not. That connection is a way of losing energy. But if you slowly, slowly, slowly prepare yourself to live here and now, it is easy. It is easy: if you experiment, you will be greatly surprised. Eating was never as blissful as in the moment when you are fully present while eating, when you are simply eating.

An emperor went to meet a Zen mystic. The mystic was digging a hole in his garden and the emperor said, "I have come to learn some wisdom from you."

The mystic said, "Sit and watch and learn." The emperor sat down and the mystic continued to dig his hole.

The emperor said, "Would you say something too? You just go on digging that hole."

The mystic said, "Watch carefully. I am not there at all, only the digging of this hole is happening. I do not exist at all. I am so completely engrossed in digging this hole that there is no need to separate me from the digging. It is incorrect to say that I am digging a hole. It is only correct to say that I have become the action of digging the hole.

"Become the action of watching. Don't think about what I will say when I speak, or what you will understand when you understand. Please just become the watching."

The emperor said, "It is very difficult just to watch. I have to go back."

The mystic said, "Go back, but then become the going back."

However, the emperor said, "I have to ask you something too."

So the mystic said, "Then ask, but become the question."

Whatever you are doing, don't be halfhearted. When you are angry, if you can, become the anger completely, and you might never be able to get angry again. But inside, in your anger, you are asking for forgiveness. While being angry, you are apologizing inside. In your anger, you are thinking that you are doing something very bad. Then you cannot even be completely angry.

You cannot be completely in love either. When you find the lover who you waited for years to meet, and he sits next to you, you forget him and start thinking about something else. When you get the wealth which you worked hard for years to achieve, after locking it in the safe, you sit outside and think about something else. You go on missing all the time. You go on wasting your energy by imagining the future.

If you want to accumulate energy – and without accumulating energy, no inner journey is possible at all – then you will have to learn to live in the present. There is great magic in the present. The present is self-contained. A river is not self-contained, it is constantly flowing; it goes on flowing toward the ocean all the time. A lake cannot flow, it is a self-contained phenomenon, it remains contained within itself; its whole journey is within itself. The moment you are in the present, you become like the lake. Energy starts to move inside you because there is no opportunity for it to flow outward.

Opportunity is in the future: What will I do tomorrow? Immediately an opportunity becomes available. What will happen tomorrow? Immediately an opportunity becomes available. But you are *now*, you are *here*.

You are listening to me here. If you are just listening to me, you will not lose even a little energy. You will become a self-contained personality, non-dimensional; you will have no linear dimension. If you are just listening, you cannot flow outward, but if you are thinking as well as listening you will become exhausted, your energy will weaken. If I am just speaking, I do not get tired; if I need to think as well as talk, then I will get tired. If any action is total, energy does not get lost, it accumulates. If love is total, it brings energy. If anger is total, energy is not lost. Whatever becomes total does not get lost. And it is very strange that if anger is total, you become free of anger because it seems so futile. If you are total in love, then you become filled with love because it seems to be so significant.

Any action that can be carried out with totality I call a virtue. And any action that just cannot be carried out totally, I call a sin. There are no other criteria for a virtue and a sin in the universe.

If you can be totally angry, and then you get angry again, that anger is not a sin. But it has never happened. You become *partially* angry, so you can do it again. If you become totally angry once, then all hell will break loose around you, the hell that you have read about in the scriptures will surround you. And you will not want to enter that hell again. Then you will not ask for forgiveness from anyone, but you will go beyond anger. The fire will burn so fiercely that there will be no other choice but to get out of it.

But we live in a lukewarm fire. We go on doing things little by little so they continue for life; our debts don't get paid off and they keep on going. If hell is totally manifest, there can be no delay in going to heaven. But we create hell so slowly that it can never be total; we cannot get free of it.

So I say unto you: the first requirement for the journey into non-desire and for the upward movement of sex energy is living in the moment. The meaning of renunciation is not to leave home and run away. A renouncer is one who lives in the moment, who does not go beyond the moment, who lives now, who lives here and nowhere else. The one who arrives at such a state of consciousness is a renouncer. The meaning of renunciation is to be in the present, to be in the living moment – and if we are available in that living moment, our energy will start moving upward.

It is a very strange thing that if this living moment surrounds us in all directions... If we can be total in anger, we will become free of anger, and if we can be total in sex, then we will become free of sex too. Whoever is totally present in the moment of sex will not want to repeat it. The matter is finished; it has become futile. It becomes so pointless that there is no need to make the effort again. But even in sex, we are not totally there.

Man is eager for sex. He races toward it twenty-four hours a day. He races his whole life. He earns wealth, builds a house – but deep down a race for sexual fulfillment is happening. If all this has been achieved, then he thinks he can fulfill his sexual desire easily. But then, when the moment for sex comes, he is not total in it. He starts thinking of a thousand other things – that celibacy is good, that celibacy is the ultimate way of life. This is what he thinks about when the moment for sex comes. And when he takes a vow of celibacy, he thinks about sex. This is madness, this is insanity. This madness never allows his life energy to move upward.

Therefore, I say to you that the first requirement is to live every moment. Then non-desire will arise inside you; your desire will begin to weaken because the future is necessary for desire, tomorrow is necessary. The truth is that tomorrow does not exist; it is only in your desire. It is just a creation, a by-product of desire; it does not exist, it is nowhere. What exists is always in the present.

We always say that time has three parts – the past, present, and future. That is wrong. Time has just one form, the present; it does not have three forms. Time is always now. How are the past and future created? The past is created from our memories and the future is created from our desires.

The first requirement to free yourself from desire is the effort to be in the present moment. I do not tell you to go to the forest; just be total wherever you are. When you eat, do it totally and when you sleep, sleep totally; when you take a bath, do it totally. Start with very small things.

The second requirement: be creative, because the energy of an uncreative person will want to flow through sex continuously. He becomes heavy because he has energy, but there will be no outlet for it. We are not very creative at all, there is nothing like creativity in our lives, nothing that we can say is creative. What do I mean? "No," you will say, "we are creative. We make chairs, we make furniture, we build houses, we make clothes. We are creative." No, this is not creativity.

Understand the difference between creativity and production. Production means making something useful, utilitarian. One can sit on a chair – it has a use, it has a price in the market, so making a chair is not creativity. Production is manufacture. But when someone sings a song, it has no market value. When someone makes a painting, it has no market value. Someone dances without any aim, without any purpose. As long as there is utility, there is no creativity. Creation begins where utility ends, when you do something in life which has no utility, but doing it makes you happy, regardless of the final result.

Van Gogh created paintings, but no one was ready to buy them. Not one painting was sold in his lifetime. His younger brother thought, "Poor thing, how sad he must be, not a single painting sold." So he gave a man some money and said, "Go on my behalf and buy a painting. At the very least, he will feel a little fulfilled that something was sold."

The man went to buy a painting and Van Gogh started to show him his works. But he was not a buyer, he was not a man who loved paintings. He was just someone's agent. The money was also someone else's money. He just had to buy any painting. He picked up a painting and said, "Take this money."

The tears started to flow from Van Gogh's eyes; he returned the money and said, "It seems that my brother has sent you. Please go back."

His brother came to ask for forgiveness, and asked him, "When you don't even want to sell the paintings, then why do you make them?"

Van Gogh replied, "I get what I want during the painting itself. In the moment of creation itself, I get what I want. When I paint a painting, I get everything, and then I don't want anything else."

When someone sings a song, he attains everything during the singing itself. Yes, if the singer is also hungry for praise then he is cheap, he is not being creative. Also, if a painter makes a painting to sell in the marketplace, it is construction, it is production. It is not creativity.

We say that God made the world, he created it. Whether he made it or not does not matter, but we say God created the world. That has only one meaning. We do not say God produced, we say he created – because it is not for a purpose. God was not getting anything out of it, he was not attaining anything at all by it. If anything was attained, it was in the act of creation itself; outwardly there was nothing to gain.

When a few such moments of living in bliss and creativity happen in life, you slowly reach non-desire. Because the second condition of desire is to want the final result. The effort, the chase, the energy is just for one aim: what will I get out of it? We are always asking…

People come to me and say, "We meditate, but what will we get out of it?" They do not even know that meditation means an action from which one attains nothing except meditation itself. And the attainment of meditation has its own meaning.

When you buy shoes, the shopkeeper cannot say, "You can simply pay with bliss." You will not get anything. No, a shoe is a utility. But if you go to the temple in the same way that you go to a shoe shop and ask, "What will I get from prayer?" you have come to the wrong place. No, whatever is significant in life is not about getting results. Only *being* is significant in itself – but in your life there are no moments that are significant just in themselves.

Whoever wants to enter the world of religiousness and move energy upward will have to find activities that are not work, and work that is simply a play, a game. That's why we do not call Krishna's life a biography, we call it a play. But Rama's life is a biography. Rama's life is a very serious affair. Rama takes everything very seriously; nothing is a play for him. For him, life is work. For Krishna, life is a play, a game. He dances, he does not gain anything out of it. He plays the flute, he does not gain anything out of it.

In whatever Rama does, at the very least, you will find character and discipline; you will find the prestige of family and tradition, and all this has to be achieved. Rama is very utilitarian, his brain is very goal-oriented. So he could throw his wife out just on the word of a washerwoman. There are constant problems with the utilitarian – there's always trouble when there is a purpose. Rama's disciplined life would be threatened; there would be a stain on his character. What would happen to the traditions of his great Raghu clan? Prestige and family are all utilitarian.

If Krishna had been in Rama's place, he could not have discarded his wife, Sita. It could have been that he himself, playing the flute, would have run away. This could have happened, but he could not have discarded Sita. If Krishna was in Rama's place, he would not have given Sita the fire test – it would have seemed a very ugly matter, very utilitarian. Can there ever be a trial of love? If there is a trial of love, then nothing can be trial-free in this life. Sita's trial was to pass through fire, to determine whether her love was pure or not. But love is pure in itself; it cannot have any degrees of purity.

Sita did not say to Rama, "You go through the fire too, you come along too; you were also alone. How can one be certain?" And a woman can be trusted to some extent, it's a little more difficult for a man. But Sita did not say that. For Sita, life is not seriousness, it is love, so she agreed; she went through the fire. Love does not ask for a test; love can take any test. But Krishna does not talk like that; the question does not arise at all. That is why we do not call Krishna's life one of character; we call Krishna's life a play. This is Krishna's play, meaning that the whole of life is creative. It is not purposive, it is not utilitarian. Life is a play.

A religious man's life is not serious. A serious man will become heavy, and a heavy person will have to find relief through sex. Hence as life becomes more serious, sexuality increases to the same extent; the more serious you become, the more you are filled with stress. And the more you are filled with stress, the more relief becomes necessary. So the more stress there is in a country, the more sexuality will increase because there is apparently no other way. When consciousness becomes heavy, energy must be thrown out to lighten it; it is the only way.

So the second requirement I give you is: do not take life seriously. Seriousness is a disease, a very basic disease. But usually our holy men, the renouncers, are very serious. In truth, your face needs to be sad and serious to qualify as a holy man. People who weep often become holy men. Don't imagine that they weep because they are holy men; they become holy men because they weep. Even their weeping begins to command respect and prestige. Normally if you are weeping then someone may ask what the matter is, but in renunciation the weeping becomes prestigious.

No, life is not serious. And whoever is serious in life will be unable to become free of desire. If life becomes a play, man will become free of desire. I am not saying to make your entire life a play; that may not be possible, but let there be something playful in your life. Children are so light, and they are also non-desirous. The whole reason for that is that their lives are not serious, it is a game; their life is a play. A child is playing; he is not serious. As he becomes serious, sex begins to enter his world.

Did you know that the age of sexual maturity is falling every day? In America, it fell from fourteen years old to twelve, to eleven. Some girls have begun to mature at eleven and it is possible that by the time this century comes to an end, the age of maturity may fall to seven years old. Seven years old – what is going on? Girls always used to mature at thirteen years, so how is it they have begun to mature at seven? Actually, girls are now as serious at seven as they used to be at fourteen. Life has become quite heavy even at seven. Education, organization, discipline, civility, and culture are becoming heavier by the day. The heavier little children become, the more quickly they have to find their way into sex to throw their energy outward.

The opposite can also happen. If we can keep children light for longer, keep them very light, then maybe up to twenty years, twenty-five years…

We hear stories, but we don't know what's happening, and those running the schools don't know what the matter is either. The people running the schools are usually serious. But in earlier times, we were able to keep young people in schools free of desire, free of sex until twenty-five. What was the reason? The reason was that we were able to save them from becoming serious before twenty-five.

The more seriousness increases, the more the burden increases, and the more the burden increases, the more stress there is. The more stress, the more relief is needed. We were able to save them from being serious for twenty-five years. Up to twenty-five years old, we were able to make their lives a play. Neither was there the seriousness of examinations, nor the seriousness of fighting with life, nor the seriousness of accountability and responsibility.

Life was just playing in the jungle. Within that play, everything was moving very slowly. Boys were cutting wood, running in the jungle, making saplings, and farming. Sometimes they studied for half an hour, an hour, but studying was not serious work – it was a discussion conducted in moments of leisure. They would talk for a while, sitting near a master. If they then remained free of desire for twenty-five years, it was not a surprise. And it is no surprise if today your children are fully adult at just fourteen or fifteen and are asking for adult sexuality – because you have arranged things to make them completely serious.

Whoever wants to attain non-desire should take the seriousness out of life. Otherwise there will be heaviness, and that heaviness will take you into desire.

How can this come about? Everyone can find at least two or three activities where he is nonserious. Do you ever play with your children at home? You will say, "What kind of madness are you talking about? Playing with the children?" Whenever a father meets his son, the meeting is serious. Either he does not meet him at all, or sometimes if some serious occasion occurs, then they meet. Whenever a son meets his father it is serious. And the son also keeps avoiding his father. When the father wants to give some advice, he meets with his son. When the son wants some money, he meets his father. In this way both keep on hiding and moving.

No, play with the children at home sometimes; try it and see. A family which doesn't gather together and play for an hour is not a family. And you will be surprised – play for an hour and see; within one month you will find a difference. Something different will happen in your sexuality. At least you will have found one nonserious activity.

What do you do, sitting at home? After sitting in the office or shop for six hours, what do you do at home? Do you paint – or do you ever paint the walls of your house? What foolishness that even to paint the walls of our home we have to hire others; we can't even paint our own walls! Do you ever paint a picture on the wall? It doesn't need to be like that of some great painter. What is necessary is that it comes from you.

It is strange: if there is some other painting on my wall, do I even have the right to call it my wall? It is borrowed, stale. On my wall, there should be a painting made by my own hand.

Do you ever gather everyone and dance at home? Do the people in your house start dancing? "No," you will say, "What are you talking about?" If one person in the house becomes religious, he makes everyone sit and he creates such a sad and teary atmosphere that it is beyond measure. But if you dance in the home for an hour… There is no need for any ritual or special arrangement, no need to learn classical dances like *kathak* or *bharatnatyam* or *kathakali*. At least you can jump!

If you can jump for an hour in the house, dance with joy, if you can sing, play, or paint – you will find that the sexuality in your life begins to diminish. What will not diminish by taking a thousand vows of celibacy will begin to diminish because creative work has begun.

Everyone in the world is a part-time poet, and everyone is a part-time painter, a part-time musician, and a part-time dancer. And everyone should be all of these. If you do this, you will be very surprised that your desire, the heavy energy on your consciousness has become creativity. Once the energy becomes creative, it starts to flow upward. The opposite of this also happens; if your energy cannot become creative it becomes destructive.

You may be surprised to know that Hitler wanted to become a painter, but his parents would not allow it. Now, someday in a future courtroom it will be difficult to decide whether Hitler or his parents are responsible for that great World War, for the deaths of so many millions. If Hitler had become a painter, in any case the Second World War would not have happened. But he could not. The energy inside him that could have become creative became stuck and became destructive. He would have created something, but it could not happen, so he began to destroy.

Beware: if you do not create, then you will surely destroy, you will wreak destruction. There is no way between these two. And if you want to remain between these two then you will need to be impotent, you will have to be without energy. If you have energy it will do something, it will destroy or create, break or create.

So the second requirement toward non-desire in your life is to be creative. Find moments, find anything and get involved in creativity. You can work in the garden, dance, sing a song. Put seriousness aside for a little while, become nonserious, be light for a little while. Do not remain adult, do not remain old, become a child. And the life of one who becomes a child for an hour, even in old age, begins to change. Just as in childhood, his energy begins to accumulate once more.

And the third and final requirement… One: live in each moment, be free of the future and desire. Two: become creative – utilitarian work is not enough, purposeful work is not enough; *purposeless* work is also necessary. Do not remain engrossed in building character. Allow a little play to enter your life also. And the third and final requirement: whenever you get the chance, close all the senses and consciously look inward.

We look outward twenty-four hours a day. When the chance to look inward arrives we have gone to sleep; then looking inward cannot happen. We either look outward or we do not look at all; these are the two options in our lives. All day we look outward, and in the night we don't look at all. Or if some people do look they see dreams. That is also looking outward, it is not inward.

What is the meaning of looking inward? Close your eyes and try – there is no other meaning. Close your eyes and try to look. Just don't do anything, close your eyes and try to look. We can look with eyes open; we don't need to make an effort, objects become visible. With eyes closed, nothing is visible. If darkness is visible, then look at darkness. Just try to look at whatever is there. It maybe that a painting is visible, try to look at it; a dream is visible, try to look at it. Whatever happens inside, close your senses and try to look at it.

First start with the eyes because sight has become our most significant sense. Then try to listen inwardly, try to listen to whatever can be heard inwardly. Then try to smell inwardly, and next, try to taste inwardly. Whatever you have done with the senses outwardly, try to do it all inwardly. And you will be amazed. The inner world has its own sounds, its own vibrations, its own colors, its own tastes. It has its own smells. And slowly your inner world will be born.

The day you are able to see the color of your inner world, on that day external colors will start to appear totally unreal. Then the desire to go outward will stop. When you hear the inner music, the outer music will become completely meaningless, it will seem like noise. When you experience the fragrance of the inner, all the perfumes made in French marketplaces will appear completely useless. On that day there will be the realization of the beauty of the inner, and no beauty will remain outside.

So the third requirement: whenever you get the chance, try to move inward. Do not remain active in outward things twenty-four hours a day – because energy flows in the direction of what we are doing. If we do something outwardly, then it flows outward. If we do something inwardly, then it flows inward. Energy has to go wherever there is work, it runs in that direction. Do some inward work so that energy begins to run inwardly.

Complete these three requirements and you will be astonished that desire is gone from your life, and non-desire is attained. Energy will accumulate inside, it will rise upward, and the other doors of your inner world will open. The other inner centers will be activated and the nectar of the inner will begin to flow, the immortality of the inner will arise. Non-desire ultimately becomes immortality, and desire ultimately becomes death. Desire is the search for death. Non-desire is the search for immortality.

Tomorrow I will talk on the fifth and last virtue, "non-unawareness" or awareness. Awareness means consciousness. And tomorrow I will talk about the key with which you can attain what I have talked about in the last four days. Tomorrow is the key.

What should we do to learn nonviolence? What should we do to learn non-theft? What should we do to learn non-possessiveness? What should we do to learn non-desire? What is the door? What is the truth?

I am grateful that you listened to me with such love and silence. Now to end, I bow down to the godliness that dwells in you all. Please accept my *pranam*, my offering of respect.

5

Non-Unawareness

My beloved ones.

Man is a seven-story house, but we live and die on just one floor. First, let me clarify the names of those seven stories for you. The name of the floor on which we live is the conscious mind. Directly under that floor is another floor, in the underground basement. That floor is the unconscious. Below that floor, in the direction of the underworld is the third floor, the collective unconscious. And under that there is a fourth floor, still lower, the lowest; it is the cosmic unconscious.

There is also a floor above the floor on which we live, called the superconscious. Above that there is a floor, which we can call the collective conscious. And there is a floor above that too, which we can call the cosmic conscious. From where we are, there are three floors above and three floors below. This is man's seven-story house. But most of us live and die in the conscious mind.

Self-realization means to become familiar with this entire arrangement of seven stories. Nothing should remain unfamiliar, nothing should remain unknown because if anything *is* left unknown, man can never be his own master, never be his own emperor. What is unknown makes him a slave. The unknown, filled with darkness, is human bondage. What is not known has not been conquered; ignorance is the only defeat and self-knowing is the only path to victory.

In this seven-story building, we know only the floor on which we find ourselves, where we are. To continue living on that floor, to remain there is called unawareness. Unawareness means unconsciousness, insensibility, sleep. It means lethargy, hypnosis. We have become hypnotized by that one floor in such a way that we do not look elsewhere at all. We are not even able to realize that there are other dimensions in our personality, in our life, in our being.

Spiritual discipline means to break this unawareness, to break this unconsciousness. But why call this unconsciousness, why call it unawareness? If someone has a seven-story house and lives on just one floor, unaware of the other floors, then what will we call it? Is that person awake? If he is awake, there is no possibility of him remaining unaware of the other floors. But it can happen that someone is only familiar with one floor of his house and is unfamiliar with the other six floors. It can only be possible if he is asleep on one floor, otherwise he would begin to realize. People *are* asleep, living out their lives just where they are without realizing anything else.

Until recently, Western psychiatry accepted that the conscious mind is all there is to man. But as they investigated a little and thought more and more about it... Freud was the first to begin to consider the idea that there is something else underneath. That proved very significant. The conscious is not everything, there is something else underneath: Freud discovered the unconscious. He discovered the unconscious, and then Western psychiatry accepted two things: the conscious mind and the unconscious mind.

But Freud's discovery is inference, not experience. Experience cannot happen without spiritual discipline. While living on our floor, we might sometimes become suspicious; a noise might come from below. We don't know it, but there could be something down there. Smoke might come from below, flames of fire, and we could feel that there certainly must be something down there... But this is all inference – we stay on our floor, we do not go down below; this is not experience.

The unconscious which Freud spoke about in the West is not his experience; it is inference. Therefore, Western psychiatry has still not been able to become like meditation, the crystallization of the individual. Psychiatry will become like meditation when inference becomes experience. And the strange thing is that a seeker like Freud, who said that there is something hidden, something underneath in man which he didn't know, was affected by the unconscious mind in the same way as the people who are influenced by it unknowingly.

Inference cannot make much of a difference. Freud was engulfed by anger and troubled with anxieties just like those who know nothing about the unconscious. The work of the unconscious was unfolding in Freud just as in those who have no idea of the unconscious. It was inference, but even inference can be very significant.

A colleague of Freud's who took the work further inferred something even below the unconscious. Gustav Jung suggested that a collective unconscious seemed to exist underneath, and that it didn't end there either. But that too is just inference, it is not experience.

Meditation is the journey into experience. Meditation is not speculative, it is not just an idea. It is an experience.

We will not discover those three floors opening above and the three floors down below as long as we are asleep on our own floor. First we need to really understand the fact that we are asleep, so that the journey of awakening can start.

Have you ever considered that you are asleep? Maybe you haven't thought about it. Just realize that you are asleep and the awakening begins. Even the realization that you are sleeping is a sign of awakening. In sleep, you do not realize that you are asleep. It can only be realized when you wake up. A madman does not realize that he is mad, only a sane man can see it. While sleeping, you have never known that you were asleep, but upon waking up you realize: "Oh no! I was sleeping." Knowing that you are asleep is an experience of awakening; it is not an experience of sleep.

I don't expect that you have realized that you are asleep. But those who have awakened say that you are asleep. A few things can be said through which you might get the idea.

Someone gets angry, shouts and swears. In the evening he comes to ask for forgiveness and says, "Forgive me. I said what I did not mean to say, in spite of myself. I did not want to, but the words came out. Forgive me." Can you ask such a man, "If you did not want to, then how could you say the words? Were you awake or asleep?"

Have you not had this experience every time you were angry, that you have done something which you did not want to do? If you have had such an experience, then it means that what was done must have been done in your sleep. Otherwise, you would have realized you were doing what you did not want to do.

Swami Anand was staying with me one night, and he remembered an incident. He said that during Gandhi's early life – when he had returned to India – he spoke badly about the English at a meeting and cursed them. Swami Anand wrote letters reporting what Gandhi had said and sent them to the newspapers, but he deleted the words that Gandhi had used. They were harsh, bitter, poisonous words – swear words, bad words – so he deleted them.

The next day Swami Anand took the report to Gandhi and said, "I have deleted many words."

Gandhi patted him on the back and said, "You did very well to delete them because I should not have said what I did." Swami Anand told me that Gandhi patted him on the back and told him he was a good reporter.

I said to Swami Anand, "You satisfied Gandhi's ego and Gandhi satisfied your ego. You patted each other on the back." I asked, "Did you ever try the opposite experiment? Did you add words, and then write in the newspaper that Gandhi was abusive when he hadn't been? If he had patted you on the back then, you would know." Actually, both actions are the same.

The reporting was false, Swami Anand's report was false. If swear words were used, then that should have been reported. But Gandhi said, "You did well to delete those words because I said what I should not have said." If what was said should not have been said, was Gandhi conscious or unconscious in that moment?

We do something in unconsciousness and when a moment of slight consciousness comes, we repent. In the life of someone who lives consciously, there is no repentance because whatever he does, he does with full awareness. There is no need for repentance at all.

Haven't there been such moments in your everyday life when you have repented? Understand that if you repent you are asleep. Are you conscious of all the reasons for your actions? You fall in love with someone… It is a good English phrase, "falling in love." We use the word *falling*, but in love, rising should happen, rising in love. But people fall in love. There is a reason for it. The word is correct. The word is correct because we love in a state of almost sleep, we become unconscious.

That is why lovers often say that they did not fall in love, it just happened. What does "it happened" mean? In sleep, things happen; in an awake state, things are done. Have you loved or did it happen? If it happened, you are unconscious, asleep. Your love is not your love; it has come through some unconscious path.

When you are angry, do you do it or does it happen? If you *do* it, okay, but if it just happens, then again you are not awake, you are asleep.

Are we the doers in whatever we are doing, or is it all just happening to us? We press the fan switch, the fan moves. If the fan is talking to other fans it cannot say, "I am moving"; it can only say, "Moving is happening to me." Are we machines or humans? Are things happening to us, or are we doing them in a conscious way? No, we are not doing anything, it is only unawareness.

Before his enlightenment, Buddha was passing through a village. He was on the road talking to a monk and a fly came and settled on his neck. He went on talking and swatted the fly away, as we would all have done. He went on talking and swatted the fly, then he stopped and closed his eyes. The fly had flown away – but the monk was very surprised: Buddha put his hand in the place where the fly had been and again swatted a fly that was not there.

The monk asked, "What are you doing? The fly is not there now."

Buddha said, "No, but now I am swatting it as I should have done. I swatted the fly unconsciously. I went on talking with you and my hand swatted it mechanically. I was not in full awareness. I misbehaved with the fly. I swatted it and only afterward did I realize that I had done it. When I was swatting it, I was not at all aware that I did it." He said, "Now I am swatting in the way I should have – consciously."

We are all unawakened people. We are asleep in whatever we are doing. Love, hatred, friendship, enmity, anger, forgiveness, repentance – everything is happening in sleep. If we added up everything in our lives, it would seem like a dream, it would not seem like life at all. If you looked back at your life, it would not seem like you lived it, but rather that you were lived by it. You have been lived; something has been continuously happening to you, like a movie.

The name of this state is unawareness. I am not talking about the sleep during the night, I am talking about the sleep during the day. Even awake, we are asleep; we are asleep twenty-four hours a day. Sometimes, in a moment of danger there is a little wakefulness, otherwise not.

If I suddenly hold a knife to your chest, for a moment at least, you will wake up. In that moment you will not be asleep because it will be a moment of emergency. To stay asleep at such a time is dangerous. If someone suddenly holds a knife to your chest, for a moment, something which was asleep inside you will suddenly wake up. Then you will not be there, the person holding the knife will also not be there, only the consciousness of the knife being held will remain. But it will not last long, it will be very momentary. Fear will instantly overwhelm you and you will start running. Then everything will be lost and you will go to sleep again.

So sometimes in a moment of danger we awaken for a moment or so. If we add up the moments of awakening in an ordinary person's life, then in eighty years it will be difficult to find even eight moments when he was awake. Hence a desire for danger also arises in our hearts; a little fascination for danger grows in us because in danger we wake up. Danger has its own sensitivity.

Say a man makes a bet, betting a hundred thousand rupees. Now for a moment he will wake up, until it is clear whether he has won or lost. In this moment of uncertainty his breath will stop, his mind will stop, and he will be waiting to see what will happen. In such dangerous moments he cannot sleep. Perhaps you do not know that the attraction of gambling comes from the desire to wake up. The attraction to danger comes from the desire to wake up, too. We choose a hundred kinds of danger, a hundred kinds of risks, in which we can wake up for a moment. But these are such momentary events that we have hardly awakened before we fall asleep again, sleep resumes again. No one can ever awaken completely through these accidental methods.

I am explaining this to you so that you come to understand this state of lethargy or sleepiness. If you can, just become aware that you are asleep and you do things that you don't want to do, you live in a way that you don't want to live, and you sit, stand, and move around in a way that you don't want to. You are being the kind of person that you don't want to be.

Mark Twain has written in one of his memoirs: "I was writing a story, and in the story I had decided which character would play which role. But when the story was finished I saw that the characters were not playing those roles at all, they were playing other roles."

Then he wrote: "It seems certain that the characters were born through me, but slowly they became independent and started to do things I did not want. The protagonist didn't do what I wanted him to do, and he started to do something else. Now, what else might the protagonist do to the story?"

He could not understand. Actually, at the time that he made the characters do his wishes, he himself was asleep, so why should his characters obey him? Then another sleeping Mark Twain would do something else, and a third something else.

So whatever story a writer conceives and begins never gets finished that way; the story finishes somewhere else. However a poet begins a poem, the poem never ends that way, it ends somewhere else. Conscious art has not been born, what we can call objective art has not yet been born.

Up to now, sleeping men write poems, so they begin one thing and something else happens. Sleeping people make paintings; they want to create one thing and something else is painted. Sleeping people write stories; they want to write one thing and something else is written. Sleeping politicians govern the world; they want to do one thing and something else happens.

Nothing is certain with a sleeping person. But never mind about stories: even in life, did you become what you wanted? Perhaps just the odd person can be found in the world who says, "I became exactly what I wanted." Almost everyone wants to become something else.

First, it is not even clear what you want to become. How can it be clear in your sleep? You don't realize that there is just a dim, sleepy aspiration of what you want to be – but nowhere is it clear what you want, even though it is clear that you are unable to become what you wanted. And at the end of life only one or two people can say that they are leaving having become exactly what they wanted to be. No, everybody reaches somewhere they never wanted to reach. They become somebody they never wanted to become. Life becomes what they had never wanted it to be.

If you feel like that, understand that you are asleep. If you feel like that when you are dying, not many options remain. If you feel it now, there *is* another possibility. At death everyone feels that life was wasted, that they were not able to become what they wanted to be – though even a dying man cannot clearly say what he wanted to be. But he feels that something was missing somewhere; something was lost.

You must feel this also. Whoever has a little intelligence feels that something is missing, is lost, not happening. That is man's only frustration, his only sorrow, his only worry, his only pain. Man's only worry is that he finds that he cannot get what he wants from love. He finds that he just cannot do what he wants to do in love.

You decide to go to a friend's house to talk about something. When you get there, you find that you are talking about something else. A husband decides, "Today I don't want to fight with my wife," and goes home. He decides everything as he goes home: "I should behave in this way, I should say this, I should show my love in this way." During the day, his wife vows that yesterday evening will not be repeated: "I shouldn't do what I did yesterday." Then when they both come face-to-face, suddenly they find that the evening before has returned. What was vowed is gone and what was to be avoided happens again. Are they asleep or awake? No, this is our sleeping state.

Mahavira called it unawareness: unawareness means being asleep. If you can remember that "I am asleep," then the search can begin. So the first spiritual practice of awareness is to understand this point: "I am asleep" – to be aware of your sleep, to realize this first. And understand that as soon as you realize you are sleeping, the morning is near. This realization can only come when sleep begins to disperse.

The first requirement for dispersing this sleep is to recognize it properly. Understand this first truth well: I tell you that you are asleep. Tending your shop you are asleep, going to the temple you are asleep, making friends you are asleep, making enemies you are asleep. Sleep is our twenty-four hour state.

Another thing: a person only begins to become religious from the point when he realizes that he is unaware, when he experiences his sleepiness. Some unaware people even go on practicing religion in their sleeping state. They go on turning their prayer beads and dozing. They continue to sit in temples and sleep, they keep fasts and sleep. Just as they tend their shop, they also go on fasts. Everything continues while asleep. Their religion also happens while they are asleep.

But religiousness cannot happen in sleep, only non-religiousness can happen. So in the name of religion, only non-religiousness happens; in the name of religion, the unawakened practice of non-religiousness happens. These people cannot practice religiousness at all, it is impossible. Religiousness can have no relationship with the unawakened state. Sleep cannot take you into religiousness; it can only take you into non-religiousness.

So what is to be done when the recognition "I am asleep" happens? The first truth is the realization of being asleep. The second... What is to be done to break this sleep? What is the method?

When someone breaks his sleep on the current floor of his house, he automatically drops down to the floor below. If anyone awakens in the conscious mind, he drops into the unconscious. To drop into the unconscious it is necessary to awaken in the conscious mind. It's just like when we get up from our sleep, we drop into the waking state; our state of consciousness immediately changes.

You shake someone in his sleep; he wakes up, sleep disappears and awakening begins. Another state of consciousness arises. If we wake up in a dream, the dream breaks instantly and we come out of the dream. The state of consciousness in which we are living is our conscious mind. If we awaken in it, we drop into the unconscious mind, we drop into the unconscious.

But before I explain how to awaken, let me also make you understand that the more we descend, the more we rise up too. It is a law of life, like with the trees: the roots go down, the tree grows upward. Meditation goes down, enlightenment goes upward. The deeper the roots descend downward, the higher the tree grows upward to touch the sky. The foundations of the flowers that open to the sky lie in the roots that have descended deep into the earth. If the tree wants to grow upward, then it has to grow underground too. It will seem illogical that one has to grow downward to grow upward. Spiritual practice will always take you downward, into the depths, and enlightenment will always be reached above, in the peaks.

Meditation is the depth, and enlightenment is the peak. Whoever descends within himself also finds himself rising upward from within. There is no direct method to go upward. One has to go downward – from the conscious to the unconscious, from the unconscious to the collective unconscious, from the collective unconscious to the cosmic unconscious.

And each time you go from the conscious to the unconscious, suddenly you will find that a door above has also opened – that of the superconscious. When you go into the collective unconscious, you will find that another door above has opened – the door to the collective conscious. When you enter the cosmic unconscious, suddenly you will find that the door to the cosmic conscious has also opened. The deeper you descend, the more you rise upward. So stop worrying about the heights, worry about the depths. How do we wake up from where we are?

If someone asks how to swim, what do we say? We say, "Start swimming." He might say, "I don't know how to swim at all, how do I begin?" This creates a very big dilemma. If I take you to the riverbank and tell you I will teach you how to swim, and you say, "I cannot enter the water until I learn how to swim," your argument will be correct. All seemingly correct arguments are not necessarily those that take you closer to the truth. Your argument is absolutely correct: "How can I get into the water before I learn to swim? First teach me how to swim and then I will enter the water." This seems absolutely logical. But I say to you, "As long as you don't enter the water, how can you learn to swim?"

Only when you enter the water can you learn to swim. If you are not ready to enter the water, you cannot be taught to swim. My argument is also completely correct. Both are logical statements, but my argument is close to reality; your argument is just an argument for discussion. For discussion purposes, what you are saying is absolutely correct – without learning how to swim, how can you enter the water? But you do not know that you have to enter the water to learn to swim. And the first time someone gets into the water, he does so without knowing how to swim. Getting into the water is the beginning of learning, the beginning of swimming. Yes, it is clear that you don't go into very deep water, only shallow water – deep enough to swim, but not so deep that you might drown. You will have to start from there.

So I do not expect supreme awakening from you. Begin by entering shallow water. From where you are sleeping, begin to wake up with small activities. Walking on the road, you can walk and be awake; you can also walk and be asleep.

Most people sleep while walking. If you stand on one side and watch people walking on the road, many of them will seem to be talking to themselves as they go. Someone is gesticulating, answering someone who is not there; someone's lips are quivering, talking to someone who is not there. They are asleep. If you stand on one side of the road and watch people for an hour, you will be astonished at how many people are sleepwalking. Walking is happening just out of habit. It is not necessary to be awake in order to walk. Sometimes someone honks a horn and the person is startled and moves, wakes up a little, otherwise he keeps on sleepwalking.

Going back to your house, you do not wake up. Your feet turn toward your house just like a machine. You step over your doorstep and open the handle. You don't need to wake up to do all this; it all happens in sleep, it is habitual. The handlebar of your bicycle turns around on its own at the right spot. All this happens mechanically and you go on sleeping inside. So it's easy to go on repeating habits because you don't have to be awake for them. It is more difficult to form new habits because you will have to wake up a little. Then when the habit is formed, you will fall asleep again. So you go on doing the old tasks over and over again. It's all happening in sleep.

Someone puts a cigarette in their mouth, strikes a match and lights it, smokes, throws it away. No one would say that he is asleep because if he was, his hand would burn. No, he *is* asleep. Before his hand can burn, he will wake up a little, throw away the cigarette, and fall asleep again. It is a habit. From habit he knows that when the cigarette comes close to the end, his hand will throw it away. It all happens in sleep.

You have to begin by waking up in these small activities. Start with very innocent activities, where there is not too much conflict, where it is very innocent. Walking on the road, eating food, taking a bath, putting on clothes; start with these very small activities in which there is not much involvement. Yes, this is practicing in shallow waters. Awakening to anger will be entering into greater depths. You are wearing clothes; be awake while you wear them – you will be greatly surprised. Be awake while you wear your shoes; you will be greatly surprised. It will seem odd: "What kind of feeling is this? I wear shoes every day but this never happens."

Now you are listening to me; you can listen in sleep, or you can listen while awake. When you are listening to me, don't just listen; watch yourself listen too. If you just listen to me and forget the one who listens, you are asleep. Your arrow of consciousness should be double-arrowed – one directed toward me, what I am saying, and the other toward yourself, the one who listens.

If your consciousness, even in this moment, points in both directions – when you can listen and also know that you are listening – then you will immediately experience that your quality of listening has changed. Even now, here, experience that your quality of listening is changing. Then you will not be able to think, you will just be able to listen. If you think, that second arrow – the arrow directed toward yourself – will be lost. If you just listen, if you just look, the change in your consciousness can begin now. Your sleep will start to disperse and a ray of awakening will begin to appear.

Start being awake during small activities, then wake up during activities for which you have to repent: anger, hatred, rudeness – start to wake up to these. If you experiment with being awake from when you get up in the morning until evening, in just a few days you will become a very different person. Your unawareness will stop during your waking hours. And what will be the proof of this? The proof will be that awareness will also happen during your sleep. The day your sleep stops during your waking hours, that very day you will be able to enter into sleep consciously.

It is such a strange thing: you sleep every night, you have slept a thousand times, but you don't know what sleep is. When does it come? You sleep every night, you have slept so many times, but do you know when sleep comes, and how it comes, and what it is? No, you don't know anything. You only know how long you were awake: you stayed awake until midnight. Have you ever come to know when sleep came – in which moment did it come, how did it sweep over you, how were you drowned in it? If there is no knowing of "I," you will sleep all your life.

A man who lives for sixty years has slept for twenty of them. Such a big phenomenon, which takes twenty years of our lives, and yet we have no idea what sleep means. What is this sleeping? What is this sleep? What is going on inside?

No, but how can a person who is not even aware during waking hours be aware while sleeping? First you will have to remain alert during your waking hours. And the day you wake up, you will be very surprised. It's as if I am sitting in this room and darkness falls: I can see that darkness is falling, it is deepening, becoming total. Then when the light comes, I can see the light has come; it intensifies, becomes total. But I know both.

You neither know how the darkness of sleep gathers over you when you fall asleep, how you drown in sleep; nor do you know how sleep disperses in the morning, how it ends, how it leaves you. When you are awake during your waking hours, and begin the activities of your waking hours in an awakened state, you will eat consciously, wear clothes consciously, walk on the road consciously.

Someone asked Mahavira, "What should we do?"

Mahavira said, "Don't worry so much about what to do. Whatever you do, do it consciously."

Become angry consciously, and you will see that it is very difficult; it is a matter of depth. You can use a method: pretend to be angry one day – then it is easy to be awake in it. When you go home today, make a decision to act totally angry with someone, for no reason, and you will find it easy to be awake.

There need be no reason from your wife; if there was, you would act unconsciously. Just decide and go crazy without reason, and if you are totally angry you will be able to see your anger. Your anger will play out, and you will be able to *see* that it is playing out. And if you can see the acted anger, then when anger arises again it will become acting. If you can act out the anger once, it will never happen again without acting; it will become just acting. The inner connection will simply break down.

So begin the deeper matters of life with acting. Consciously act out those deeper elements and you will be able to wake up in them. And if waking up arises during your waking hours, it will begin to arise during sleep. The day you wake up during your sleep, that day you will enter into the unconscious. Krishna has spoken about this in the Gita: a yogi remains awake in the night when others sleep.

That is the second step. If you wake up during sleep you will be very surprised. You will be so surprised, it will change your whole life. If you can sleep with awareness at night, it is a miracle. The day you sleep and stay aware is a unique, very amazing occasion. You simultaneously stay awake inside and sleep outside, and in the morning you will get up so refreshed, with a kind of freshness you have never known before. This freshness has no connection with the body, but it has a deep connection to the soul.

On the day you sleep awakened, your dreams will begin to disappear because you will be awake to your dreams. It is not that you will remember later that you dreamed. The moment the dream comes, you will know that a dream has come.

As I told you, become awake to the activities of the conscious mind and you will enter the unconscious mind. Then become awake to the activities of the unconscious mind and you will enter the collective unconscious. The activity of the unconscious mind is dreaming. When you become awake to dreams, you will suddenly find another door opening underneath, which is the door to the collective unconscious. This is not *your* unconscious; it is the unconscious of all of us.

That collective unconscious has its own activities which have been given great importance by religions. There are great experiences, very deep experiences of the unconscious mind. Jung has called them archetypes, religious symbols. The mythologies of the whole world were born in that deep unconscious called the collective unconscious. The birth of creation, the threat of annihilation, the forms, colors, shapes and sounds of God, were all born there. These are its activities.

So whoever awakens in dreams will enter the collective unconscious, which has its own activities. What people call religious experiences are not; they are the psychic experiences of the collective unconscious. The expansion of color, the production of light, extraordinary smells, extraordinary sounds – they all arise there. The birth and death of the world can also be seen there. The moment when the earth was born and the moment when the earth will cease to exist can also be seen. All the creation myths of the whole world arose there.

It is very strange, but this is why all the creation myths of the world are similar. Whether they are Christian, or Mohammedan, or Hindu, the difference is only of words, it is not much. It was in that moment of consciousness, in that state, that many things became known throughout the world.

For instance, throughout the world it is thought that at some time there was a total annihilation. Christians have this idea, Hindus also. All the tribal peoples of the world also have tales that at some time a total annihilation took place. And the strange thing is that there was no communication between them. Communication came recently, but their tales are hundreds and thousands of years old, at a time when they were completely unrelated to each other – and their tales are the same. What is going on? Just one thing: there is one collective unconscious for all of us. So deep down we are all one, and that's why there are no great differences in those things at these deeper levels.

For instance, dance arises from the collective unconscious. So it is not necessary to understand another's language to understand a dance. If an Englishman dances, a Chinese man can understand; he doesn't need to know English. If a Hindu dances, a Mohammedan can understand.

For a painting there is no need to understand any language. Someone who does not understand French can understand Picasso's painting. There is no need to know the language because all these things are created in our collective unconscious. We know it all already: there is no need to be familiar with each other's language, each other's culture, each other's society, or each other's principles.

That is also why the symbols of the religions of the world are all similar. In many aspects, there are such startling similarities that it is difficult to say anything. The sound om is born from the collective unconscious, and it is found in all the religions of the world. There are just a few variations; they are variations in understanding.

Hindus have understood it as om. It is a matter of our understanding, which is of our conscious minds. So we have conceived it as om. The Jews and the Christians have understood it as amen. That is just their version of om, so today after prayer they say "Amen." *Amen* comes from *om*. The English words *omniscient*, *omnipresent* have been formed from *om*. But they have emerged from deep down; they have not come from Sanskrit. Sanskrit scholars think that all the world's languages were born from Sanskrit. It is not so. The similarity that exists between the languages of the world is from the collective unconscious. The languages of the world are not born from any one language.

There is a foundation to our minds that is ours collectively. On top of the ocean the waves are separate but underneath, the ocean is one. Just like the waves we are separate but deep down all is collective. That collectiveness has its own manifestations, which Kabir has called unwounded sounds. We know one kind of sound, a sound born of a wound. If I clap, a sound will arise when two hands collide. If I strike a blow on a table, a sound will echo but only when I strike a blow. We can call it a wounded sound, born of a wound, wounded, a sound born of a wound. There are sounds in the collective unconscious where there is no wound. That is why they are called unwounded sounds – sounds created without making a wound, like the sound of one hand clapping.

A Zen master in Japan will ask his disciple, "How will it sound if a clap is made with one hand? Go and find out." A great difficulty arises. Can a clap be made with one hand? How can a clap made with one hand make a sound? Sometimes he claps on the table, sometimes he claps against the wall. But the master will say, "The wall has become the second hand, it won't do. How can a clap be made with one hand? Go and find out and then come back." He cannot find out until he descends to the unwounded sound. The master is telling the disciple to descend to seek the sound of one hand clapping.

If we awaken to the activities of the collective unconscious, we descend into the cosmic unconscious, which has been called *prakriti* in this country. It will be appropriate to understand the word *prakriti*. *Prakriti* means what was there even before everything was created, what was there even before creation – pre-creation. The English word is *pre-creation*: that which was there even before creation, from which all was created. Whatever was there even before being born, we call that pre-creation. The cosmic unconscious is pre-creation. Everything arose from it.

Understand it like this: the conscious mind is mine, the unconscious mind is also mine, but the collective unconscious is ours, it is not mine. It is not yours; it is ours. The cosmic unconscious is not even ours, it is of everything. Even the rocks are included. The birds are included. The rivers are included. The mountains are included. It is pre-creation. For one who descends there, no further descent remains. It is a bottomless abyss and there is no way to descend beyond it. The process of descending into it is called awareness.

Start waking up just where you are. When you wake up, you will find the key to the doors below. Then begin to awaken there, and you will find the key to what is still further below. And an upward process will follow alongside. As long as you are in the consciousness, you cannot rise upward into superconsciousness. Your roots will have to descend into the unconscious. When your roots have descended into the unconscious, your branches will spread into the superconscious. They will rise upward.

Freud and Jung could not reach the superconscious because they were making inferences. That's why they talked about the unconscious and the collective unconscious, about the lower levels, but they had no awareness of the upper states.

But the world is always in balance. There are as many ways of going up as there are of going down. Actually, without the higher the lower cannot exist; they can only exist together. If the left is not there, then the right cannot be either. Or can it? If the right is there, the left must also exist, whether one knows it or not. Can the lower exist without the higher? If so, then how will you call it the lower? The lower cannot exist without the higher. Can sorrow exist without happiness? Then how can you call it sorrow? Sorrow cannot exist without happiness.

Life is always dual. There is as much above as below. Whatever is below, the same is above too. There is only this much difference: below is underground, in darkness; above is the open sky, in sunlight. The further you descend, the more the darkness will go on growing. At the cosmic unconscious, at the level of pre-creation, there is total darkness, supreme darkness; it is darkness and darkness alone.

The higher you rise, the more the light will go on increasing. And at the cosmic conscious, there is total light. It is light and light alone. But the upward road passes through the underworld. The peak is to be reached via the abyss. This is the only great difficulty in spiritual practice. This is the most difficult thing to understand, that to rise up, one will have to go down.

We think that we should go up directly, but we cannot do that. If we go directly up, only speculation will arise. Then we will create only a vision of the higher levels: the superconscious, collective conscious, cosmic conscious – we can create principles out of them. But those principles will be just principles, imaginary. Those who ascend directly will be entering the realms of philosophy and worship. They will not be able to go into religiousness. To enter the experience of religiousness one will have to go downward first.

This is a strange thing: to be a saint you have to become a sinner in a very deep way. So whoever avoids going deeply into sin cannot become a saint either. This seems a very odd thing, but it is exactly so, this is the essence of it. There is no way around it. That's why it often happens that great sinners suddenly become great saints, and lesser sinners continue being lesser sinners. Whatever transformations happen in the world, they always come from the depths. Descent is necessary to rise upward.

Let me tell you one of Nietzsche's statements. Nietzsche has said that the tree that wants to touch the sky will have to muster the courage to make its roots reach deep inside the earth. It is a very frightening thing to descend because there is darkness there. When you descend from the conscious into the unconscious, you will be descending into great darkness. But the more you gather the courage to enter the darkness, the more light you become eligible for and entitled to. Eligibility for light comes from descending into darkness. Courage comes from descending into darkness. Worthiness comes from descending into darkness.

So stop worrying about the higher; worry about the lower and go on breaking down your unawareness at each and every step. From where will you start? You always have to start from where you are, from the level you are at, and the name of that level is the conscious. Start by doing activities at the conscious level with awareness.

Buddha's disciple Ananda stayed with Buddha for years. One day he said to Buddha, "I have a great difficulty. Sometimes I can't sleep at night so I watch you. You sleep only on one side. You continue sleeping on that side; you do not even move your hand, you do not even switch legs. All night you keep your head in the same posture, the same position in which you placed it in the evening. I am puzzled: I have to change sides a lot. I have to move my hands and legs a lot."

Buddha said, "Are you aware that you are moving your hands and legs, changing sides?"

Ananda said, "I am not aware of anything. I only know in the morning that I have not slept in the position I went to sleep in. My head has moved. How can I know while I'm asleep?"

Buddha said, "I sleep knowingly and I go on sleeping knowingly. Where my hand was placed, my hand remains; I do not move it. If my hand moves on its own, then my mastery is gone, then I am no longer the master."

So Ananda said, "Do you even sleep awakened?"

Buddha said, "Definitely. Because I remain awakened during the day, I have become worthy of sleeping awakened at night."

As long as you remain asleep during the day, there is no possibility of your sleeping with awareness. If you remain asleep during waking hours, you will remain unaware while sleeping also. You will have to begin with awareness during waking hours, break down your unawareness from there first.

Mahavira used to tell his monks continuously, "Arise with *vivek* – awareness – walk with awareness, sit with awareness." What does that mean, to arise with awareness, to sit with awareness? It seems that his many monks understood that walking with awareness meant: do not put your feet on a bed someone has made, or do not walk on a carpet that has been laid down. Walk on dry land, not on wet land. Similarly, for thousands of years Mahavira's monks have understood eating with awareness to mean: eat this, do not eat that. But this is not Mahavira's intention. People have understood *vivek* to mean discrimination, but this is not Mahavira's meaning of the word. By *vivek*, Mahavira means awareness, not discrimination. Because where there is awareness, discrimination comes on its own like a shadow. For discrimination, awareness does not need to come, it is not needed.

Mahavira says: "Walk with awareness," meaning walk knowingly, walk with the consciousness that you are walking. Then with this consciousness everything else will come. Nothing wrong can happen because no one has ever consciously done anything wrong, they cannot. Whatever is done consciously is always right, one can only be virtuous. Sin cannot be committed consciously.

So when Mahavira says eat consciously, he doesn't mean "Eat this, don't eat that." He means to eat with awareness. The act of eating should happen with awareness, then what to eat or not to eat will come naturally. There is no need to make separate rules about what to accept or reject. Someone who makes separate rules is saying that their awareness has yet to awaken.

If I go to the temple and vow to leave by the door rather than through the wall, people will say, "Are you blind? Such a promise can only be made by the blind." But however much a blind man promises, sooner or later he will crash into the wall. It is beyond his capacity to fulfill the promise. A sighted person never promises to leave by the door and not through the wall. A sighted person will always leave by the door and not go into the wall because his eyes will tell him that the wall will break his head, and that there is a way through the door. There is no way through the wall.

One who lives with awareness does no wrong, but never promises to do no wrong either. If someone promises not to do any wrong, then know that he has discovered nothing about awareness so far; he is blind. Only blind people keep vows, people with eyes do not need to. The way people with eyes live their lives is a spiritual practice in itself. No vows are kept.

But we all take vows in temples. We make promises: "For a year I will do this: I will not eat like that; I will not drink." This means that our consciousness wants to drink, so to stop it we make a vow to do the opposite.

You make a vow in the temple, where there is fear of God. You make a promise in front of people who keep checking on you: you have said you will not smoke a cigarette – and now you are smoking. You make a vow in front of a monk, then the fear remains that you promised a monk, so you must fulfill it. One thing is certain: the desire to smoke a cigarette is present inside you. You take a vow because you are not conscious.

Against whom is a vow taken? Against yourself! And vows taken against yourself are very difficult to keep. Even if they are fulfilled, there is no benefit from them. There is only a deadening, a weakening in the sensitivity of your personality; nothing else happens.

No, when Mahavira says walk with *vivek*, he means that the act of walking is to be conscious, with awareness. It should not be in unawareness, in unconsciousness. If your foot lifts, then know that it is lifting. If it falls on the ground, then know that it is falling. If your head turns, then know that it is turning. If you sit down, then know that you are sitting down. No action should happen in unconsciousness.

Hence, when someone asked Mahavira whom he would call holy, he didn't say he would call a monk holy who ties a cloth over his mouth. If Mahavira had said that, he would have been a very ordinary man, with as much worth as the cloth covering the mouth. Mahavira didn't say that someone who lives naked is holy. If he had said that he would have proved to be very ignorant; the sages would have laughed at him for eternity. No, the answer that Mahavira gave was quite unique.

Mahavira said, "I call one who is awakened, holy, an awakened saint. One who is not asleep, I call him holy." Mahavira gave a unique definition: one who is not asleep.

The questioner asked, "Whom do you call unholy?"

Mahavira could have said, "One who drinks alcohol." But it seems that Mahavira had no association with bars. Those who know about bars are constantly explaining that one who does not drink alcohol, or who doesn't eat meat, is religious. It appears that Mahavira also had no association with a slaughterhouse. Those who do are constantly declaring that someone who doesn't eat meat is holy, one who doesn't smoke cigarettes is religious – who does this, who doesn't do that.

Mahavira said, "One who lives asleep is unholy." This is a very brave, very deep idea, of great understanding. Everything becomes dependent on just one small condition. Either you live awake or you live asleep. If you live awake, religiousness will descend into your life. If you live asleep, there can be nothing but non-religiousness in your life. You can become holy while asleep too, but it will be a fake holiness. Fake religious men are in worse shape than unholy men because they have the misconception that they are holy. And when an unholy man has the misconception that he is holy, it will take him lifetimes to drop this delusion.

Awareness is the basis of spiritual practice. Awareness *is* meditation.

I have shared these things with you over the last four days. Violence is a state of unawareness, nonviolence is an outcome of spiritual practice. Possessiveness is a state, non-possessiveness is an outcome. Theft is a state, non-theft is a result. Desire, lust, longing, is a state, non-desire is a result. Awareness, remembrance is the key to changing a state into a result.

Each activity should be carried out with remembrance and with awareness; not even one activity is to be carried out unconsciously. And that's it: your religious journey has begun. You will begin to descend and the key will be the same. When you reach the second level below, then again bring awareness into your activities. When you awaken totally to your activities, then bring awareness further down. And the deeper you go, the higher you will reach. When you touch the last layer of this abyss, on that very day you will attain the ultimate, the immortal layer of your soul.

Go into the abyss so that you can reach to that ultimate freedom. Descend deep down so that you can touch the peaks. Touch hell to reach heaven. Go deeper and deeper into the darkness so that you become eligible to reach the light. But go with awareness – this is not possible by any means except awareness. Whatever has been said by anyone in this world – whether by Buddha, by Mahavira, or by Krishna – it all comes down to one small word: *awareness*.

Krishna says: "Be awake, even in your sleep." Jesus says: "Stay awake because you don't know when it will come. It should not happen that you are asleep when God comes, that he finds you asleep and goes away. Be alert and waiting." All of Jesus' words revolve around this key: be aware and waiting. And the message of Mahavira's whole life repeats just one thing over and over again: live consciously; live with awareness, not in unconsciousness.

Two or three more points and then I will finish. Understand the first key well: you are asleep. Don't try to make yourself believe that you are not asleep. Do not rationalize with yourself that you are not asleep. The heart will say, "Me, asleep? I read the scriptures, how can I read them while asleep? I know that the soul is there, God is there. How can I know that while sleeping? No, I am not asleep. Others are sleeping." A sleeping man always accuses the other of sleeping and believes himself awakened. This is a way of protecting his sleep.

This is sleep's safety measure; it has its own ways of protecting itself.

Be aware – your sleep wants to protect itself from being broken. It makes all kinds of arrangements not to be broken. If you go to sleep hungry at night, sleep gives you food in your dreams to protect itself. If you don't get food in your dreams, your sleep will break. So sleep arranges food – unreal, because sleep produces only fakes, it cannot produce anything real. An invitation is delivered to the hungry man in his dream: "There is a feast at the emperor's palace today and you are invited." And sleep puts food in front of him that he has never eaten in his life. Sleep is protecting itself.

You need to urinate in your sleep, so sleep will say, "Go to the bathroom. Go in your sleep; there is no need to..." If you get up, your sleep will be broken. You set the alarm to get up at four o'clock and the alarm rings. Sleep says, "It's not the alarm, the temple bell is ringing. Sleep peacefully."

Sleep has its safety measures in place, its arrangements so that it is not broken. And there is an arrangement in your waking hours too. Sleep will say to you, "You are awake and everybody else is asleep. It is fine if you try to awaken them, you are already awakened." If your heart tells you that you are already awakened, be careful. This is sleep's safety measure. Don't fall into this trap.

The day you discover that you are asleep, realization happens. And there is no need to wait for tomorrow: the realization that you are asleep can happen right now, here. Begin this technique for awakening: in small acts and in deeper matters, act them out and try to be awake in them.

If you are determined and try to remain awake, while being careful of sleep's tricks, then what was possible for Mahavira and for Buddha can be possible for you too. You have the same potential as anybody else. At any time you can become whatever anyone in the world has become.

So try to awaken, and do not stop as your effort goes deeper, otherwise sleep will catch you at the second step. You will stay at the second level. Try to awaken there too. The journey is long, but not impossible – difficult, but not impossible – and only the one who tries can do it. Go on descending, don't worry about the heights. The fruits of the higher levels will come on their own.

The further you descend, the more flowers will blossom above. Their fragrance, their light, and their bliss will begin to shower on you. The more you descend, the more you will rise upward. And the day you touch the deepest depth, the ultimate depth, that very same day, you will touch the ultimate peak also. And the day you touch both, that day the depths and the peaks will become one. They do not remain two. On that day all becomes one.

When this seven-story house is known completely, it becomes one. Then the seven stories are no longer there. All the curtains in between drop away, the walls fall away, and one house remains. That experience of oneness is the only experience of godliness. That experience of oneness is the only experience of ultimate liberation. That experience of oneness is the only experience of nonduality. That experience of oneness is the only experience of enlightenment.

The past five days, I have not said these things to you because I get pleasure in saying them, nor because you are entertained by listening, but so that maybe somewhere a chord is struck. Perhaps some harp string is vibrating in you – and the journey begins.

To end, I pray to existence that you do not give up until you know yourself, that your journey of knowing, that your quest to become completely familiar with yourself may begin. But by itself there can be no meaning in a prayer to existence: I pray to you too to give existence a little support so that your journey can be completed.

I am grateful that you listened to me with such love and silence. Now to end, I bow down to the godliness that dwells in you all. Please accept my *pranam*, my offering of respect.

6

Transcending the Animal Heritage

Question 1

Osho,

In one of your talks you said that violence is a disease, and to recognize it in all its aspects is the first condition toward becoming nonviolent. Please shed some light on its biochemical and psychic structure, so that we can understand violence in greater depth.

Violence is a disease of human beings, but it is not so for animals. For animals, it is their nature. There is no possibility of nonviolence at the animal level; hence they have no idea of violence. Violence is a natural thing for animals – nonviolence is impossible. Violence is a disease that man has inherited from animals, and it is obstructing the evolution of his consciousness. As soon as his consciousness starts to evolve, his past becomes a bondage for him. Someone who is evolving is also every day tied to his past.

So, a person who wants to evolve must each moment break from his past and move forward. It can be said that someone who does not want to wipe out his past is denying his evolution.

If I continue to be what I was yesterday, it means my today is wasted. If I want to make progress, there is no other way but to go beyond my yesterday. The past must be transcended. In fact, only the transcendence of the past is evolution. Man's past is his animal heritage, and his future leads him to godliness. Whoever does not transcend his animal heritage cannot enter the temple of godliness. And whoever desires to attain this future – to attain godliness – has to die every day to the past. One who does not die to the past is diseased.

This disease is like a child who refuses to throw away his old clothes, even when he grows up. Changing clothes along with the growth of the body is absolutely essential. A child's clothes are fine for a child, but they would be ill-suited for a young man and they would be painful; they would be like a prison. Those clothes may protect the child, but the youth must protect himself from those same clothes!

The animal heritage is man's past; we have all passed through that stage. This fact is confirmed by science as well as religion. Some years ago, Darwin declared that man is descended from the animals. But thousands of years before Darwin, here in India, Mahavira, Buddha, and Krishna declared to the world that man's soul evolved from the animals. The last link in man's past was an animal. And before stepping onto the next link, he will have to disconnect from the previous one. Being human is a state of transition, a bridge over which the animal passes to be transformed into godhood.

But we experience the past as something heavy because it is the known. It is not so easy to be free of it, to get rid of it. We start feeling that we *are* our past. Millions of years ago, when humans were cavemen living in caves in the mountains with no fire and no way to light lamps, a fear of darkness entered man's mind. The fear from those times pursues people even today. Now there is no darkness outside – there are no caves surrounded by darkness – but in spite of this, the fear of darkness remains even today. This fear, which entered man's mind millions of years ago, pursues him still; it is still part of him.

I have used fear as an illustration. In exactly the same way, violence is an imprint carried by man from his past as an animal. Animals cannot survive without violence and we cannot live *with* violence. Man is not born violent, but we see that for many thousands of years he has done nothing but fight. He does not live, he just fights. It would be no exaggeration to say that man lives simply to fight.

Thousands of wars have been fought in the last three thousand years. Those many thousands of wars were on a grand scale – but we quarrel and fight with one another twenty-four hours a day. It is difficult to find even a few moments in twenty-four hours when we are not involved in some kind of fight. Sometimes we fight with enemies, sometimes with friends, sometimes for wealth, sometimes for fame. We fight for status, and then our fight takes on a political dimension. We fight for wealth, and our greed becomes exploitation.

Sometimes we fight for no reason; the habit of fighting just makes us fight. When a man goes hunting, he fights without a cause; he fights and calls it sport. Man has sought and developed sports to satisfy his fighting instinct. All our sports are small forms, miniatures, of fights. Sports are our fights – futile fights, without reason. And when we have no reason to fight, even then we want to fight without a cause. If we cannot enter actual warfare, we can fight to win in a game of chess. Even in chess it is not a surprise if swords are drawn! Deep down, there is a strong desire to defeat others, so even in a game of chess the urge to fight with others is there.

All our sports are different forms of warfare. Either we can say that our sports are different forms of warfare or we can even say that warfare is our most terrible sport. But man *is* fighting. What we call relationship is also a fight. If a traveler from planet Mars comes and watches a husband and wife for twenty-four hours, he will not believe that these two people had agreed to live together. His understanding will be that these two people have agreed to keep fighting twenty-four hours a day! Perhaps what we call family is an organization of people who have decided, "We will fight and never leave!"

Life is full of violence on all sides; it is a disease of mankind. It may be inevitable for animals but not for humans. It should be remembered that with each new step in evolution, new responsibilities and new burdens are also assumed. Every step in evolution is a step toward greater responsibility. Nonviolence has become a responsibility since the day we left our animal heritage and evolved into man, because the flower of being human can never blossom in the midst of violence. Man can only fully blossom in an atmosphere of love. That is why I say nonviolence is health, violence is a disease. A more dangerous disease than violence perhaps does not exist.

It is difficult to find a human being who is not mentally ill. What we call normal, healthy, does not mean health; it only means normal madness. It only means that all the other people are insane in the same amount: it is average madness. What we *call* mad is in fact "abnormal" – someone has gone beyond the average. He has made a jump. Perhaps we are all mad people boiling at ninety degrees, and so those whom we call mad, those evaporating at a hundred degrees, have "become mad." There is no qualitative difference between us; it is only a matter of quantity.

Between the inside and the outside of a madhouse is only a matter of a few steps. No matter how high we build the walls around a madhouse, it makes no difference. It is only a matter of a few steps between us and the mad people. And this distance between the two is not such that we are standing with our backs toward it, rather we are facing that direction. And it is not that we are standing in one place: every moment we keep moving toward it and so decreasing the distance.

Those who are able to see the human mind say that mankind is very slowly becoming a madhouse. And even what we call the diseases of the body, more than ninety percent of them are created as diseases of the mind which then spread toward the body. And the basic sickness of the mind is violence.

What does violence mean? I will talk about this, so that you will be able to understand the disease.

To be violent means to have a mind which is always restless unless it is quarreling, a mind which cannot be content without hurting someone or making someone miserable. Naturally, a mind which is eager to hurt others, or whose only intention is to make others miserable can never be happy. Deep inside, such a mind will be miserable.

It is a profound law that we can only give to others what we have within ourselves; we cannot give anything else. When I am eager to give misery to others, it only means that I am filled with misery and I want to push it onto someone else. Just as the clouds shower rain on the earth when they are filled with water, when we are filled with misery, we start throwing misery on others.

The thorns with which we want to pierce others have to first be born in our beings – where else will we bring those thorns from? The pain that we inflict upon others, we have to endure its birth pangs within ourselves first. The darkness that we want to spread to other people's houses is not possible without extinguishing our own lamp.

If my lamp is lit and I come to spread darkness in your house, the opposite will happen – together with me, your house will be lit: darkness will not happen.

Someone who is interested in violence toward others has become violent to himself too; he has been violent to himself. Hence I will like to give you a maxim, and that is: violence is the evolution of violence toward oneself. When we are violent to ourselves inside, that violence overflows, spreads over like a flood, breaks the banks, and so reaches others. So, a violent person can never be healthy; he will be unhealthy within. Inside him there cannot be harmony, balance, and concord. He will be filled with discordance, conflict, and struggle. Someone who wants to be violent with others must first be violent with himself. That is a prerequisite.

Hence, to me, violence is inner conflict. It spreads onto others and becomes their misery, and when its seeds sprout and grow within, it becomes conflict, inner struggle, and inner pain for that person. Violence is a condition of inner conflict, inner disharmony, inner strife, inner discordance. Violence fights with the other later; first it fights with oneself and so moves forward. Each violent person is fighting with himself.

One who is fighting with himself cannot be sane: sanity itself means harmony. A sane person is one who has achieved harmony, synchronicity, and rhythm within himself. The imprint of harmony and music on the faces of Mahavira or Buddha is not even seen on the faces of master musicians sitting with a harp in their hands. It is seen in Mahavira, though his hand is devoid of a harp. That kind of music cannot come from a harp. It is a symphony of the soul within, which spreads and flows out in all directions.

The symphony in Buddha's walk, the rhythm in his movements and the lightness in his eyes are not to be found in any composed song, nor in the music produced on instruments. That rhythm is created from the depth of the soul when all inner conflicts have been dispersed. Nonviolence is music from within. When a person's vital energy within is bathed in this music, life becomes completely harmonious. When life is filled with disharmony, it becomes full of disease.

This English word *disease* is very meaningful, it is made up of *dis-ease* – when ease within is lost, when all balance within is disturbed, all rhythm is destroyed. All the lines of the poem are scattered all over the place. That condition which is happening inside is really a dis-ease, like that created by breaking the strings of a sitar. The body cannot be kept in a healthy condition for long when the mind within becomes diseased. The body always follows the vital energy as a shadow.

Hence I say violence is a disease. Nonviolence is freedom from disease. Nonviolence is a perfect state of health.

Just as the English word *disease* is meaningful, so is the Hindi word *swasthya*. The meaning of *swasthya* is not only health, just as *disease* doesn't only mean illness. *Swasthya* refers to someone who stands within himself, rooted within himself; one who is absorbed or immersed within himself, who has become himself – a state in which there is no "other," so there is no scope for any conflict. There are no differing tunes; all tunes have merged into one. Such a condition is called *swasthya*. In this sense, nonviolence is *swasthya*, and violence is disease.

Someone has asked what I would like to say about violence from the point of biochemistry. Biochemically, violence is sickness. As soon as the mind is filled with violence, the body becomes filled with a poisonous substance. As soon as the mind is filled with violence, a poisonous substance starts flowing in the body. There are glands in the body that collect poison so that it is available when needed in critical times for its defense.

When you are filled with anger, you don't have the same blood that you had before the anger. Your blood becomes poisoned. Those glands release their poison into your blood and it gives you the insanity to fight and die. So, in times of anger you can lift such a big stone, which you could never have lifted in times of non-anger. In a state of rage you can even throw a man who is stronger than you, which you could never have imagined in a peaceful state. Chemical changes have taken place in your body. Your body is not the same. The body has released the accumulated poison into the blood; now you are not in your senses.

Anger is a temporary madness. And so, when he is mad, a man can do things that in his normal state he would never do. Hence in anger, people have murdered and later they have cried and repented their whole lives. For the whole of their lives they will be asking, "How did I do this? It happened in spite of me – I have not done it! How did this happen?"

In anger we have all done things that we did not want to do. Then who did it? Certainly we have done it, but we have done it in the same way as someone does when they are drunk. But this alcohol comes from our blood, from our inner sources, so we know nothing about it. When we drink alcohol from outer bottles, only then do we know about it: this alcohol comes from inner sources so we know nothing about it.

In its journey over millions of years, the human body has acquired glands of poison, which were necessary for emergencies.

They were necessary when man was an animal. If a lion attacks someone, he needs an instant superhuman capacity to run. It is not that he will learn how to run, practice running, and only then be able to run. This is an emergency: the body should immediately have enough madness to enable it to escape, abandoning any consciousness. It might be difficult for the body to save itself if it were conscious; so, in its journey over millions of years, the body developed poisonous substances that are automatically released into the blood when an emergency arises, so that in panic or madness one can run. In fear, a man trembles: this trembling is a chemical process.

In the same way, many chemical changes take place in the body of someone possessed by the sex urge. If you see animals madly excited by sex, you will realize that something of this remains in human beings. As soon as they are in this condition a peculiar kind of unpleasant odor is released by their bodies. Actually, animals only know when their females are ready for sexual intercourse because that particular smell is released by their bodies. At the moment of sexual intercourse, that same smell is released by men and women's bodies. Their bodies are passing through a sort of chemical change.

Whatever happens in a man's mind, immediately the chemistry follows it. When you eat, your body releases substances needed for digesting the food. And when you are filled with violence, the body releases the substances which are helpful in committing violence.

Hence, violence is not just a mental fact, but is a biochemical fact too. It is *also* a chemical fact – when I say this, I am not saying that it is only a chemical fact. There are some chemists who say there is no need to educate man about nonviolence: "We will just cut a few glands off, then people will become incapable of being violent!" What they are saying is correct up to a certain point, but the suggestion they are giving is more dangerous than violence.

It is possible to cut off some of those glands: you have seen a bullock and a bull. The only difference between them is the removal of one gland. But what a difference between the meekness of the bullock and the pride of the bull! The soul or spirit of the bullock does not develop, and his body becomes meek and pitiable.

If not today, then tomorrow, the scientists will give the suggestion to remove those glands in man – are giving, have already given – and it will not be surprising if the Communist governments of China and Russia follow it very soon.

If those glands were cut out of the human body, man would not be able to commit violence, but he would also not be nonviolent. These two are quite separate matters. Then man would be a meek, pitiable human being. He would be like an old person suffering with sexual desire but unable to enter the world of sex. Such a person cannot evolve. Such a person, if created, would not rebel or rise in up revolt. Slavery would be his soul. He would not be a rebel. The governments would like that a man could be made nonviolent chemically. It can be done, but that man will fall below the animals, and can never go beyond human nature.

So, I say to you that very soon man will have to raise his voice against this – and state that these suggestions from the chemists are very much against the human soul and put it in danger. No greater slavery has ever come before, nor can come in the future, than there would be by following these suggestions.

A great chemical revolution is nearing. Work on its first phase has begun. It is certain that some substances exist in the body for violence, but by removing those elements, man's soul does not become nonviolent. There would still be violence, but in an impotent form. It would accumulate and go on circulating, and there would be disease in the soul – the soul would be devoid of harmony. But the body would be incapable of sharing that disharmony with others.

We can break a light bulb, but breaking the bulb will not cut off the electric current, although the current will not be seen. Electricity is shining through the medium of the bulb but the bulb itself is not electricity. Violence is produced through the secretions of glands but they are not the violence itself.

One more thing: when violence leaves a man's mind, the same accumulated poisons and stimulating substances that were creating disharmony in him begin to create a new chemical revolution in his life.

It is said about Mahavira that his perspiration did not emit an unpleasant odor. This may look like a made-up story, but it is not wholly unscientific. It is possible; it does not matter much whether a sweet or an unpleasant odor came from Mahavira's body, but it is sometimes possible for a pleasant smell to come out of the human body. A sweet odor can come from the same source as a bad one. All sweet smells are nothing but the transformation of bad smells, just as manure is thrown on gardens and sweet-smelling flowers are produced. If you visit factories where various kinds of scents are prepared for sale in the markets, you will know that sweet smells come about through the transformation of bad smells.

If the body can release an unpleasant odor in certain circumstances, there is no reason why it cannot release a sweet-smelling odor in other circumstances. Hence I say to you that the story of Mahavira is not just a story. The body has released pleasant odors many times, even today it can do so. If the mind transforms completely and you stop using the poisons in the body – they are produced but you stop using them – then a very interesting thing happens: a quantative change turns into a qualitative change. As soon as there is a quantitative change, the qualitative change begins. There is no difference between ninety-nine degrees and one hundred degrees, only a difference of quantity. But up to ninety-nine degrees, water remains water, at one hundred degrees it becomes vapor. The difference is of quantity, but eventually it becomes a qualitative difference.

All qualitative changes are basically a change in quantity. If the poisonous substances in the body that have been spreading unpleasant odors accumulate beyond a certain level, they transform and a pleasant odor starts releasing from the body.

Nonviolence has its own sweet smell and violence has its own unpleasant smell. Love has its own sweet smell, lust or passion has its own bad smell. Similarly truth has its own sweet smell, while untruth or falsehood has its own bad smell.

This is why I am not in favor of making man nonviolent by transforming him biochemically. If someone becomes nonviolent in the spiritual sense, his biology, his body chemistry will be transformed and a sweet fragrance will start flowing from where there was previously a bad odor.

Another question has been asked about this:

Question 2

Osho,
Is violence a disintegration of the mind into many parts from the point of view of psychic anatomy?

Nonviolence is integration of the mind – becoming whole. We have a mind, but it is perhaps incorrect to speak of it as singular. We should say we have minds, not one mind; we are polypsychic, not monopsychic. We have not one mind but many minds. Ordinarily we think that we have only one mind but that is wrong. Everybody has many minds. Now Jung and other psychologists say man is polypsychic. But you will be surprised to know that Mahavira first experimented with the polypsychic condition of the human mind twenty-five centuries ago. Mahavira declared that man is polypsychic.

There is not just one mind inside us, there are many minds. So, this evening you decide not to be angry tomorrow, and the next day you are angry. You think to yourself, "What kind of person am I? Only yesterday I decided not to be angry and I am angry again today. Then I repent, and again I try to understand, and again I become angry."

People don't commit new mistakes every day, they repeat the same mistakes for which they have already repented thousands of times, again and again. Why is this? In fact, they have two different minds, one that acts and the other that decides. The minds have no information about each other; there is no communication between them. When you resolve not to be angry any more, it is decided by just one part of your mind.

To illustrate this, let us say that mind *A* decides not to be angry. Then the next day you become angry with your wife, and then it is mind *B* who is angry. As soon as *B* disappears, *A* returns and repents that in spite of your resolution not to be angry, you became angry. Again it happens: somebody's foot injures you slightly, and *B* at once appears before you and shows his temper immediately, as *A* recedes into the background. Just as the spokes on a wheel go on revolving round and round, changes are taking place every moment in your mind. There are many minds inside you.

Gurdjieff often used to say that he had heard about a palace whose owner had gone on a long journey. The building was very large and there were many servants. Years passed but there was no news of the owner. He had not returned, nor had he sent a message. Gradually the servants forgot there was once an owner of the house. They were happy to forget about him, so they forgot very quickly. And if a traveler passed by the palace and asked any servant about its owner, the servant would reply, "I am the owner."

But the neighbors were very confused because they met different people at the door each time. There were many servants in the house and each one claimed to be the owner. All the people in the neighborhood were puzzled about how many owners of the house there were. Then the people of the town gathered together and found out the truth. All the servants were brought together, and it was discovered that there were many owners.

A difficulty arose: all the servants began to quarrel. They each declared, "I am the owner." When the quarrel became serious one old servant said, "Please pardon me, we are quarreling uselessly. The owner of the house has gone away, and we are all his servants.

The owner has not yet returned; a long time has passed and so we have forgotten him. Now there is no need to remember him; perhaps he may never return."

When one day the owner came back, those twenty-five owner-servants disappeared at once, and they immediately became servants again. Gurdjieff used to say that this is the story of the human mind.

As long as the being does not awaken, each and every part of the mind says – each and every servant says – "I am the master." When the part that gets angry comes in front, it says, "I am the master," then it becomes the master for few moments and the whole body follows it. The body does not know anything. It follows the master. Then the one who repents comes and says, "I am the master" and the body cries. The same body that had lifted the sword cries. It does not know anything, it just follows any master. Whoever says loudly, "I am the master," the body immediately follows. The mind says, "Celibacy," the body says, "It is a very pure thing, I am ready." Another part says, "Indulgence," then the body says, "I am totally ready. I follow the master."

Man is polypsychic. The psychic structure, the structure of his mind, is in many parts. The mind is split into many parts, and it will remain split until the unfragmented being awakens. Violence is the fight among these different parts, as all these servants each have their own claim of "I am the master." When they encounter each other face-to-face, the mind is split. It fights twenty-four hours a day over who is really the master. And the duality, pain, and misery that arise through the fighting of the conflicting parts of our mind, we then solve by fighting with others.

It is interesting that we generally project our conflicts onto the outside. There is a thief within you, and you are quarreling and fighting with that thief, trying to suppress him so that he will not commit theft. If a theft is committed in your neighbor's house and the thief is caught, you will be the one who beats this thief the hardest – because there is already a repressed thief within you. You have wanted to punish your inner thief many times but you have not been able to. Now you have a thief on the outside, so you project your inner thief on the outer one, and you make certain to punish him. A thief needs to be present for the punishment to take place.

A religious person cannot beat a thief because there is no source for projection. So all the time thieves are condemning thieves, scoundrels are insulting scoundrels, and those full of lust are censuring sex. We project on the outside what is within us. Bertrand Russell has said somewhere that when someone cries aloud, "There goes a thief, catch him, a theft has been committed! This is terrible!" and so on, then our first duty should be to apprehend the person who is shouting because he will commit a theft, if not today, then in the future.

We usually project our illnesses and our mental diseases onto others. So, if a person is saying bad things about someone else, he is not saying so much about the other person but he is saying a lot about himself. The act of speaking badly about others tells us what he is projecting. A conflict is going on within him, which he is projecting onto another. When there is no conflict within, the projecting stops immediately – there is no longer any way of projecting outside.

The human mind is fragmented, and frustration is born in that fragmented mind. When the mind becomes nonviolent, it will become whole, unfragmented – it will be one. And when the mind becomes one whole, there are no different or opposing tunes. Then a dance of joy begins. A joyful flute begins to play in one's life. People traveling on that joyful route reach godliness: they cannot reach and have never reached godliness by any other route.

There is another small question on the same subject:

Question 3

Osho,

What changes take place in our life force under the conditions of violence and nonviolence?

Water from the mountains flows downward, seeking deep holes, ditches, or lakes. Water runs downward but when heated, that same water is transformed into vapor and rises up to the sky, reaches the heights, rides on the clouds, travels toward the sun. It is the same water, the same energy, but it is transformed – there is a revolution.

A violent mind is in search of ditches and deep holes. It flows downward. It is heading for a fall. A nonviolent mind becomes finer; it is transformed into vapor and reaches the mountain peaks. It is a journey toward the sky; an upward journey begins toward the sun. It is a flight to the highest peak. It is eager to move in the direction of liberation and godliness.

A violent mind is always in search of another; the other is the abyss. A nonviolent mind is in search of the self. When we are in search of the other we feel as if we are on a downward journey. Why is it so? Because the other is the abyss, the other is our downfall, the other is hell. Why does the road to the other lead to our downfall? Why? One thing is clear – we have no joy or tranquility within ourselves. We are in search of the other because there is no joy within ourselves.

Even with our enemies, we are not as miserable as we are with ourselves. Even with the greatest of bores, we are not as bored as we are with ourselves. What does this mean, what is the cause? It is significant to see that no one wants himself as a companion. And we become unhappy when someone else does not want us as his companion, even though we had already rejected ourselves. We had already declared that we could not be our own friend.

You are unwilling to sit alone with yourself even for one hour. If you are required to sit alone for a whole day you become anxious, or perhaps you may think of committing suicide, or get confused about what to do. If you had to live alone for one year, would you be able to do so? It is very difficult to live with yourself because only a person who has reached the highest inner joy can live with himself. A person who is full of misery within is always anxious to live with someone else.

I have told you that violence means unhappiness, uneasiness within. So a violent mind is always in search of another. Sometimes the mind is in search of a friend and sometimes in search of an enemy – and it doesn't take much time to go from one frame of mind to the other. Very quickly a friend can become an enemy, or an enemy can become a friend. In reality, if you want to make someone an enemy, first you have to make him a friend. Without making a friend it is very difficult to make an enemy – other than family members. Because relatives are enemies right from the beginning! Anyone else, if you want him to be an enemy you have to first make him your friend.

Man is always in search of another as he strives to save himself from himself. So I tell you: the other is an abyss. Whoever desires to be saved from himself can never begin a higher journey. How is it possible for someone who is not willing to reach his own self to gather the courage to reach godliness? Can someone who is not willing to touch his own peaks touch the highest peaks of existence? That's why we are in search of another, and as long as we remain in search of the other there will certainly be violence within us.

There is also another kind of companionship: when a person lives with himself. He can then live with others too, but the other is not a necessity. Others can be around him, can participate in his bliss, but he is not dependent on the other. Even when the other is not there, he will be in the same bliss. Even if no one goes to Buddha, Buddha's bliss will be the same. And if thousands of people go to Buddha, then too it will not make any difference. But for us, if one day someone turns his face away and does not come to us, then immediately we enter hell.

And anyone who is so dependent on others will create chains for them, to prevent the other from going away, from turning his face away. He will enslave the other. He will bind their feet: sometimes by making them into a wife, sometimes by making them into a husband, sometimes by making them into a son, sometimes by making them into a father; he will enslave the other in thousands of ways. And whenever he binds someone in chains, violence begins. Because nonviolence makes one free, bondage makes one violent. Violence enslaves others.

There are many kinds of slavery, and the sweet kinds of slavery are worse than the bitter ones, because in the bitter ones there is some honesty, some sincerity. The sweet kinds of slavery are very dangerous because they are sugarcoated. They have poison within and sugar on the outside.

We have made all our relationships sugarcoated but they contain poison inside. The poison comes out as soon as a little of the covering is removed. Then we somehow repair the covering and carry on with our relationships. But the fact that we go in search of others is solid proof that we cannot find joy in being with ourselves. So violence begins again and we go in search of the other because we cannot live without him. We will certainly enslave him if we cannot live without him; we will possess him, be his master, claim ownership of him. And we will destroy and kill those whose masters we become.

That mastership can be of any kind because all types of ownership kill and destroy. Ownership is a very subtle form of violence; it is subtle murder, it kills slowly. Alexander the Great can make someone a slave and kill him; Hitler too makes someone a slave and kills him. A religious teacher can also enslave someone and kill him. There are many types of slavery. Whenever we chain somebody, grip him tightly by the neck, become dependent on him, then we hang like a stone, like a weight around his neck. And this weighing him down is a downward journey. There is no end to this journey, it goes on and on. Whoever is doing this is not satisfied with one, they want a second one, third one, and then want thousands. A politician wants hundreds of thousands, then millions. Until he becomes the president of the country and hangs around the whole country's neck, until then he is not satisfied. He wants to hang around the neck of the whole country; he wants to become a heavy stone for everyone.

Our minds are continually in search of the other, and such minds journey downward. Their violence goes on increasing. Such minds will assume many forms, will have thousands of faces, will have thousands of ways to suppress others, to harass them and to torture them. There can be very subtle and cunning ways of torturing others.

A father can torture his son, the son can torture his father; a mother can torture her son and the son can torture his mother. Psychologists say that humanity has been doing this for a long time. We have been torturing one another, but we have not been aware of it at all. This situation will continue as long as people are discontented with themselves, as long as they are not ready to live with themselves – until the journey toward the self begins. As soon as a person is ready to live with himself, his journey will shift away from the other, from the outer. Because the other is always the outer, the other is always the without, his journey will continue outside.

People must leave the outer world and enter within because the other is always the outer, the other is always outside. As long as the search for the other continues, they will certainly be outside. The other will always be outside, even when that other may be a wife, or a beloved, or a lover, or even God.

Even seeing God as the other means that violence will continue, and there can be no freedom from violence. Hence Mahavira rejected an outside God because he thought if God is the other, there would still be violence. Very few people understood why Mahavira rejected God. The ignorant thought Mahavira was an atheist; they thought Mahavira said it because perhaps God did not exist.

Mahavira said: "There is no God except you." The only reason for this statement is that if God is the other, the violent mind will make even God a means for going outward and downward.

Mahavira said: "There is no God outside, we have to journey within. The soul within is God himself." And as soon as one enters within, the journey toward the highest peak begins. There are great heights within and there are very deep valleys outside. There are peaks as high as Mount Everest within and there are depths as deep as the Pacific Ocean in the outer world. Anyone who goes deeper and deeper into the outer world will fall into a bottomless pit where there will be darkness, misery, torture, death, and hell.

For anyone who climbs within toward the self, there will be great heights, there will be the peaks of Mount Kailash, there will be peaks of gold, there will be liberation, moksha, there will be heaven. This is the inner journey.

When the life force becomes violent it degenerates, and when it becomes nonviolent it transformed. In both cases the life energy, or the life force, is one and the same. When it flows in the outside world it brings misery, pain, and unhappiness; when it travels within, it brings happiness.

If you have experienced joy at any time, you must have known that you are absolutely alone. If thrills of joy have spread in you at any time, you must also have experienced that you are within yourself. If a single drop of joy has showered within you at any time, you must have realized that you are alone, no one else was there. In association with others, you have always been in misery, and you have always known happiness only within yourself.

Yes, there is a happiness that seems to be coming from others but it never really materializes. There is a happiness that creates the illusion it is coming from others, but when it comes and we open our eyes, we realize that we were seeking happiness and have actually found misery. There is a happiness that beckons from others, but when we come closer, we find that the call for happiness from others was a deception.

Just as in the story, when Rama went after the golden deer… And everyone knows that there are no deer made of gold. At least Rama should have known that no golden deer exists anywhere. But it is a sweet story, and meaningful too. We all go on chasing golden deer and everyone knows that they don't exist, and still we go on chasing them. So Rama went after the golden deer. Who would be mad enough to believe that a deer made of gold could exist? But

Rama went after it. The Rama within us is also chasing a golden deer, and in the end we find that nothing has been attained. How can anything be found by chasing a deer made of gold?

Happiness is just such a golden deer. Whenever it seems to be coming from another, then understand well that Rama is starting to chase the golden deer, and his wife, Sita, is certain to be stolen. When you go seeking happiness, your inner soul, call it Sita, is stolen: you have fallen. Then there is a long war; then follows the long battle with Ravana, who stole her. Then there is bloodshed and killing. That whole world of trouble and violence began merely because Rama went chasing the golden deer. That troubled journey began with the golden deer, but it continued until the whole range of violence was complete. As I see it, it is a symbolic story, it is a parable.

When we see happiness in the other and run after it, then we too are chasing the golden deer. Then there will be a falling downward of energy. The downward fall happened the very moment we believed that the golden deer exists. Our downfall begins the very moment we believe that the other can give us happiness. It has begun at the very moment when we believe that happiness can be found outside. It is the experience of our whole lives that we get nothing but unhappiness and misery from the outside world. Except unhappiness, what have we got from the other? But the hope persists that happiness will come one day, although it has never happened. We always hope it will come in the future, but looking at our past, can we say it was ever achieved? Has anyone ever received happiness from the other? On the contrary, the fact is that the more happiness we expect from the other, the greater is the misery we receive.

That is why the son whose marriage is arranged by his parents is not as unhappy with his wife as is the son who marries for love. There is a greater possibility of a love marriage failing. Someone whose marriage is arranged after horoscopes and the like were consulted does not entertain high hopes of happiness. So, the possibility of the marriage failing is remote. He will also be unhappy but only in proportion to how the astrologer had predicted his chances of happiness. We get unhappiness in life in proportion to the happiness we hope for. Whoever hopes for great happiness is rewarded with great unhappiness. But there is no way to bring unhappiness to someone who does not hope for happiness.

So the life force becomes violent when it flows toward another. It flows toward misery, it flows toward hell. We are all in search of our own hells. Occasionally a few people turn back and find their heaven, when their life energy travels back, travels inward, and then rises upward. But the energy is the same. There are not two different forces in the world, only the directions differ. The energy is the same; the only difference is of its rising up or going down.

The energies of life are not different, only the directions are different. The energies in the world cannot be different: there is only a difference of upward or downward. It is like climbing or descending the steps of a temple. Or when you and your friend are standing on the same step and you are facing downward and your friend is facing upward. Then both heaven and hell will be there on the same staircase. Your friend who is facing upward will be in heaven, while you with your face downward will be in hell on the same step. So, understand well that there are no such geographical locations as heaven and hell; everything depends on the direction of one's mind. Everything depends on the direction of one's mind. Violence is the downward flow and nonviolence is the upward flow of the life force.

Question 4

Osho,
In a previous talk you said that nonviolence is man's intrinsic nature, and violence is his creation. Will you please explain this one more time? Isn't violence a phenomenon given to us by nature?

Violence is something given to man by nature, but it is not the intrinsic nature of man. For animals it is their intrinsic nature, it is the nature of beasts. Man has passed through that state and that's why he carries with him all the experiences and impressions of that animal life.

Violence is like this: suppose a man walks along a road and gets covered with dust. Then he enters a palace but refuses to remove the dust, saying, "It has come with me, it is part of me." Dust has covered the human soul while it was passing through animal life. It has become stuck there but it is not man's nature. Violence is natural for animals; it is their nature because they have no choice in the matter. Violence is not natural for man because he has a choice. In fact, to be human begins with this choice. To be human begins with this decision, with this resolve. Man is standing at the crossroads; no animal is standing at the crossroad. All animals are on a one-dimensional road. Therefore they have no choice.

Man can become violent or nonviolent as he wishes. This is his freedom. Animals don't have that freedom; they are helpless: whatever they can be, they are. It is good to understand that the animal already is what it can be. Thus there is no difference between animals' nature and their reality. There is no distance between the past and the future for an animal. The animal is only what it can be; there is no difference, no distinction between an animal and its potential. It is already all that it can be.

The case of the human being is a totally different matter. Man can be different from what he is; his reality is not his potential. Tomorrow he can be something different from what he actually is today. We can't say to a dog, "You are something less than a dog," but we can say to a person, "You seem to be less than a human being." To say this to a dog is utterly absurd, it has no meaning. All dogs are complete dogs. There may be weak dogs and strong ones, there can be sick ones and healthy ones, but there is no difference in the degree of their "dog-ness."

But in the human being there are differences of degree. We cannot say there is no difference in humanity between a Krishna and a Hitler. We cannot say there is no difference in humanity between a Buddha and a Ravana.

No, to one person we must say, "There seems to be very little humanity in you," but in someone else the human qualities are so immense that we have to coin a word like *bhagwan*, the blessed one, to describe him.

Whenever we use the word *god* for someone, it means that there is so much humanity in them that it is not enough to call them just a human being. Being human is not everything; much more can happen to us, we have great potential. Our past is linked to the journey through our animal heritage and its violence, but we have the potential for nonviolence.

It is the nature of being human to have this potential become fully evolved, and someone's reality is what he has accumulated on his journey so far. That is why I say that violence is acquired, nonviolence is our nature. So violence can be renounced but nonviolence can only be attained, it cannot be renounced. It is very important to understand this difference. Violence can be renounced; nonviolence can only be attained. And if nonviolence is attained, it is impossible to renounce it. No matter how violent a man is, it is always possible to renounce it because it is not his nature.

Every sinner has a future and every sinner has the opportunity to be a saint in the future. Every sinner has a future: every sinner has the opportunity to be a saint in the future. We can honestly say to every sinner that he is the saint of the future. Every saint has a past and in every saint's past there is the past of a sinner. We can honestly say to every saint that he was a sinner in the past – but a saint has no future. By "saint" is meant someone who has realized his entire nature, who has become all that he *can* become. His flower has fully blossomed.

A bud has a future. If a bud wants to become a flower, it can. But a flower cannot go back and become a bud, even if it wishes to. A flower remains a flower. So if we say to a bud, "It is your nature to become a flower," we are not stating a fact, we are simply talking of potential. When we tell a bud, "It is your nature to be a flower," it means, "You can become a flower if you want." If a bud remains a bud and says, "The fact is I am a bud. Hence I will remain a bud because it is my nature to be a bud, as I am a bud," it will be the same as if someone says he is violent by nature. He is talking like the mistaken bud that thinks it will be a bud forever. Violence is not man's nature; it is an acquired thing and an imprint from his past. Violence is man's conditioning, which was an inevitable part of the process of evolution from his life as a beast. Just as if someone comes out from a room filled with soot, his body is covered with soot, it spreads onto his clothes – it is inevitable. Animals can be forgiven because violence is unavoidable in their lives. Man cannot be forgiven because violence is now his choice: it is not inevitable that he choose violence.

If the bud insists on remaining a bud, then it can do so. This is not its destiny; it is its own misunderstood decision. And so the bud itself will be responsible for it. It cannot go in front of some God and ask, "Why did you keep me a bud?" because God has given the bud full potential to become a flower. It could have become a flower. To be a bud remains our responsibility.

Violence is inevitable for animals; for man it is a responsibility. It is a fact for beasts, for man it is merely a prehistoric memory. It is the present for beasts, the past for man.

We have a choice before us. We can make a decision to be nonviolent, or decide to be violent. When someone decides to be violent, no beast can compete with him. In fact, no beast can be as violent as a man because a beast is violent by nature and man becomes violent by design. Search the whole animal kingdom and you will not find beasts as violent as Genghis Khan, or Tamerlane, or Nadir Shah, or Hitler or Mao or Stalin. If we consult all the beasts of history trying to find a parallel for Stalin or Genghis Khan, and ask if they had similar examples, they would reply, "We are very poor in that respect; we have no memory, no recollection of such degrees of violence." It is interesting to know that no animal besides man becomes so violent toward its own species. No animal will kill a member of its own species, no animal will commit violence against it. This is a distinguishing feature of the violence of mankind as opposed to that of animals.

Man is the only animal who kills his own kind. It is an interesting fact that if an Indian wolf is left near a Pakistani wolf, it will not harm it; but to leave an Indian person near a Pakistani is dangerous. Language experts say this might be due to differences in language, and they seem to be right. They say that neither wolf speaks any language; the Pakistani wolf does not speak Urdu and the Indian wolf does not speak Hindi, so they don't know they are foreigners. But a man from one province becomes a foreigner in another province. Gujaratis are foreigners in Maharashtra. Hindi-speaking people are foreigners to Tamil speakers. If what the linguists say is correct, and I feel there is some truth in it, we shall be compelled to make man silent one day, just to make him a human being. Perhaps it will be difficult to create humanity in the world without becoming silent.

It is such an unfortunate thing that although no animal attacks its own species, man does! And no animal kills without a reason – this too is significant – except man. An animal does not kill without a reason; if sometimes it kills, then that is its need. If it is hungry, it kills. If it wants to defend itself, it kills. Man kills for no reason. Even when there is no need, then too he kills. Sometimes it seems that because he wants to kill, he just creates the reason. He cannot live without killing, hence he creates the reason. Sometimes he creates a reason in Vietnam, sometimes in Korea, and sometimes he creates a reason in Kashmir.

There is no necessity. Neither is it needed in Kashmir, nor in Vietnam, nor in Cambodia. There is no necessity anywhere. But man creates the necessity because if he kills without a reason it will not seem right.

Man is rational only in the sense that he rationalizes his follies, he is not rational in any other sense. Aristotle certainly said that man is a rational animal, but the history of mankind until now does not support him. History has disproved Aristotle. Man seems to be intelligent in one thing only: rationalizing his faults. Even when he kills someone, he rationalizes his action. He says, "I have to kill him because he is a Mohammedan, he is a Hindu. He is not an Indian, he is a Pakistani," and so on. As if being a Pakistani or a Mohammedan is sufficient reason to kill him.

Men will find reasons to kill. A man is rich, he should be killed; a man is a communist, he should be killed. As the old reasons become worthless, new ones are found. New reasons replace the old ones that have become useless, which cannot be used now: "Let's find new ones. Until now we have been killing many Hindus and Muslims, let's make Hindus and Jainas quarrel now. If we don't succeed in making Hindus and Jainas quarrel, let's start dividing them into rich and poor, let's have a class war." So people find convenient reasons whenever they want to commit violence, to kill.

Animals never kill without reason. I am telling you this because if you can understand man's violence, you will see that his violence is without reason. Violence is his choice, so no animal can be as cruel and as violent as man. Violence is natural for animals; it is not out of choice. But among mankind there can be a Nadir Shah and there can be a Mahavira. Nonviolence is not a choice for animals, but for man this choice has to be made.

We have seen the valleys of men such as Nadir Shah, Stalin, and Mao, we have also seen the peaks like Mahavira, Krishna, and Christ. Both are our potential. Those valleys are the memories of our past, and the peaks are the longings for our future.

We will discuss the rest tomorrow.

I am grateful that you listened to me with such love and silence. Now to end, I bow down to the godliness that dwells in you all. Please accept my *pranam*, my offering of respect.

7

We Are Free to Choose

Question 1

Osho,

You have said that ignorance of the self is the source of violence. And yesterday you said that man himself is responsible for his violent instincts. Does this mean that man himself is also responsible for ignorance of the self? Please clarify this for us.

It makes no difference if someone sitting in a cave on a dark, moonless night keeps his eyes closed or open – either way there is darkness. But there is a difference if that same person continues to sit with closed eyes when morning comes, when the sun is rising, and the sunrays are falling on the mouth of the cave, and the birds begin to sing. In the darkness of night, there is no difference if his eyes are closed or open. The person in the cave is not responsible for the darkness of the night; the darkness is there, that is the reality of the situation. But if he continues to sit with closed eyes and sees darkness when the sun rises, it will be his responsibility. If he wants, he can open his eyes and be free from the darkness.

An animal's life is like that dark, moonless night. There is no possibility of self-knowing in that situation. Animals do not know of their own existence; there is no alternative for them, no freedom, no possibility to know themselves. So it cannot be said that animals are responsible for their self-ignorance. They are in a dark night and are not responsible for their darkness. So they cannot be at fault if they do not go in search of self-knowing. But man has journeyed through that animal world and entered the world of consciousness where there is bright sunlight. If someone remains in darkness, he alone is responsible for it.

If we do not know ourselves, it is because our eyes are closed. It is not our natural state, it is our choice. There is light on all sides. Man is standing at a point on his evolutionary journey where he can know himself. If he does not know himself, who else is responsible? This does not mean that self-ignorance is created by man. No, self-ignorance exists, but if someone does not try to eliminate it, the responsibility is his. He did not create his self-ignorance, but he can eliminate it – and the responsibility lies on his own head if he does not try. If someone prefers to remain self-ignorant, it will be his decision; he has kept his eyes closed although there is no scarcity of light.

I just remembered a rare and very famous statement of Sartre. He wrote: "Man is condemned to be free." Man has all manner of freedom except one, which is that he cannot choose *not* to choose. He can make all other choices except this one: he cannot choose not to choose because that will also be a choice. He has to make choices every moment because to be human is a constant journey of choosing. But being an animal is not, an animal is what it is. And if anyone can be held responsible for what an animal is, it is existence itself. Man is beyond the responsibility of existence, whereas the responsibility for the animals lies with existence. An animal is as it is, the trees are as they are; we cannot hold them responsible for being what they are, nor can we praise them. But man has moved out of this state, he is free to choose.

So if someone is unenlightened, the responsibility is his, and if he is an enlightened being, that responsibility is his own too. If he is sad, the responsibility is his and if he is happy, that responsibility is his own too. To keep his eyes open or closed is everyone's choice. The light is present all around, now it is up to us to live in light or in darkness.

That's why I said man is responsible for his unenlightened state; now he cannot throw his responsibility on others. Now he will go on becoming more and more responsible each moment. This responsibility is his dignity, his grandeur, his very humanity. This is where he goes beyond his animal heritage. Therefore, I would also like to say to you that whenever someone starts doing something without making a choice, he is equal to an animal.

It is interesting to note that generally it is not that we choose violence; we go on committing it out of old habit. Nonviolence is a choice. So nonviolence is a responsibility, whereas violence is our animal heritage. Nonviolence is a destination on our journey, violence is just an old habit. I have certainly said that violence is the result of unenlightenment. And there is no contradiction in the two statements. To be unenlightened is of our own choosing, to be violent is also of our own choosing. If we want to be nonviolent, no one can stop us.

Man can become whatever he wants to become. His very thinking forms his personality; his every choice becomes his destiny. His every desire, his every longing is of his own creation. Therefore, no one should ever think, even by mistake, that he is helpless, that there is nothing he can do about what he is. What can he do if there is anger in him? What can he do if there is violence? What can he do if he doesn't know himself? No one has the right to ask this. The moment someone asks, "What can I do?" he is showing that he *can* do, he is only trying to console himself with such a statement. No animal ever asks, "What can I do?" It is out of the question.

When someone says, "I am helpless. What can I do? I have to be violent," he is making a choice and he is also relinquishing his responsibility for that choice. Not only is he violent, he is putting the responsibility for his violence on others' shoulders – on the shoulders of nature, on the shoulders of existence.

When someone places the responsibility for his humanity on someone else, he is falling back into the animal world. In fact, he is denying his humanity. In refusing to choose, he is denying his humanness. He is saying, "No, I feel better being an animal, where there is no question of making choices, where there is no responsibility, no decision-making, no trouble. Where whatever is, simply is. I am going back to the animal world."

Drinking wine, man returns to the animal world. Committing violence, he returns to the animal world. Being angry, he goes back to the animal world. So if you look at a person filled with anger, you will see a human form, but not a human soul. If you look into angry eyes, you will not see human eyes but a different kind: a beast which was hidden within appears in his eyes. In anger or violence, man acts like a beast – he cuts, he shouts, he beats.

Human nails have now become very short as there was little need of them. Wild beasts have very long claws which can tear out the flesh and bones of their prey. For millions of years, man has not needed to use his nails to tear out flesh and bones, so they have become shorter and shorter. He has manufactured knives, spears and swords, which are substitutes for doing the work of animals, because now his nails have become shorter. His teeth are not for cutting and tearing flesh. So he has made deadly weapons and bullets which can penetrate someone's chest. All the weapons, tools, and missiles man has invented are a substitute for his lost animal past, they are replacements. We don't have what animals have, so we have to create substitutes, and they are undoubtedly better than those of animals.

Has any animal got an atom bomb? Does any beast have the means and wherewithal to throw bombs hundreds of miles away? No, beasts have only the tools given by nature. Using his intelligence, man has produced what could not be produced even by millions of animals. It is of his own making, his own choice.

When anyone sees clearly that he is responsible for what he is, that very day, his transformation and evolution begin. The door to religiousness can never open in the life of someone who thinks, "I am what I am, nothing is under my control, I am helpless." Understanding that you are responsible for your destiny, that you alone can decide your fate will transform your life. I had said that man is responsible for his ignorance of himself. He is responsible in the sense that he can eliminate his ignorance, but does not do so. He can be a free man, but he does not liberate himself.

Question 2

Osho,
Please explain to us how the dissolution and sublimation of the violent instinct occur in the practice of meditation.

The desire for violence is not isolated; it is linked to the suppression of many other desires. The desire for violence is already there, the longing to commit violence is there, but on many occasions there is no opportunity for it. We want to commit violence but are unable to do it because of our civilization, our culture, our way of life – inappropriate situations and circumstances get in the way.

It is difficult to find somebody who has not at some time or other thought of killing someone. It is also difficult to find somebody who has not at some time or other thought of committing suicide. And if such thoughts had not arisen in the daytime, they might have occurred in a dream at night. Not everybody kills others and not everybody commits suicide. They think and think about it, but due to circumstances, murders and suicides do not actually take place. But once the desire for violence arises in the mind and it is not possible to carry it out, that desire persists. The force of the desire is blocked toward the outside, and this force goes on accumulating.

The desire for violence remains inside, and along with it, other unfulfilled desires accumulate, together with any fresh desires to commit violence that arise. These accumulated desires are not of one life but of many lives. We go on living with this collection within us, birth after birth – all these desires and the suppressed flow of longings.

On the one hand every desire creates a new charge, and on the other hand, the collection of old charges continues to increase, until there is a potential for an explosion at any moment. To be free from desire and violence, it is therefore necessary to understand two things. Dissolution of both the desire for violence and the suppressed collection of violence are equally essential. If the desire for violence itself disappears, new violent forces are not created in the future, yet the dissolution, a catharsis, of whatever forces have been suppressed in the past is still needed. Mahavira has used a very good word for this: *nirjara*, purging, which Western psychologists call catharsis.

Nirjara means withering away, like falling leaves. It is a wonderful word. It is the scattering of something which has been collected. It means to separate something by discarding the dust particles collected on it. So many forces of suppressed desires are lying accumulated within us. It is only in meditation that the release of these forces can be accomplished. There is no other way to release them.

How is it done in meditation? Whenever you have a desire to hit someone, try a small experiment and you will be amazed. I am not joking about this experiment. A large human potential growth center in America, the Esalen Institute in California, is practicing it. There is a very significant teacher there at present; his name is Fritz Perls. For anyone who has a strong desire to commit violence, he asks them to put on a blindfold, then puts a pillow in front of them and asks them to beat the pillow while imagining it is an enemy.

He says, "Beat anyone you want to." At first, the man laughs and asks, "How can I beat a pillow?" but Perls just tells them to do it. The hands don't distinguish between beating a person and a pillow. There is no difference in releasing the poison in the blood while beating a person or a pillow. What is the other person anyway, more than a pillow? So Perls asks his violent client to beat the pillow. At first, the client laughs but Perls tells him not to laugh and to start beating. The client might ask him if he, Perls, is making fun of him. Perls will say, "There is a little fun in it, but beat the pillow anyway."

The client starts beating the pillow, and in a short time the people standing around are surprised to see that not only does his intensity of beating increase, but his way of beating it shows such hatred toward the pillow. He tears it to shreds, and bites at it with his mouth.

Those who undergo this experiment say their minds become very light afterward, that their minds have never felt so light before. What does Perls say about this happening? He says that up until now the violence has only been released with a purpose – it has been released onto someone. Let your violence out in the air, don't let it out against a person because there will be a reaction if it is let out against someone. If I hit someone, the violence will not be lost in the air, the air will not absorb it. The person I hit will react; he may react today, or tomorrow, or further in the future. He may wait, but he will certainly react. If I hit someone and he happens to be someone like Buddha or Mahavira, *he* may not react, but as soon as I hit him, there will be a reaction as well as a repentance in *my* mind.

Remember that repentance and anger are equally bad. Repentance is anger upside down. In fact when a person repents, he is doing nothing but preparing to become angry again. When someone repents and says, "It was very wrong that I became angry," he is trying to convince himself: "I am not such a bad person. I acted wrongly once, but that is not very important."

So by repenting he tries to reestablish himself as a good man. From his own point of view, he is reverting to his old mind, and when he reestablishes himself in this way, he will be ready to hit someone again. Again there will be violence and again repentance. In this way, the vicious circle of anger and repentance will go on and on. So when he hits somebody, what follows is not only repentance but also a preparation to attack again because that person is going to react. Thus violence creates a vicious circle, and it is difficult to get out of it.

But when we hit a pillow, this does not happen. In hitting the pillow, catharsis takes place. So Perls is asking us to hit pillows, because the present world in which we live has become very material. Mahavira lived two thousand five hundred years ago. He would say: "Beat the air, who needs a pillow?" But we would object to that

– beat the air? A pillow can be punished. At least it looks like the back or the stomach of a person. When we hit or beat a pillow, we feel we have touched somebody. The pillow will also react, although only a little.

In the two thousand five hundred years since Mahavira, the world has become very material. The meditation which Mahavira talked about does not even require a pillow. No pillow is necessary in the meditation I am talking about either. But in America it would perhaps be difficult to punch without a pillow; there has to be an object – if nobody is there, use a pillow. Mahavira would not even allow us to beat a pillow. He would say to Perls that there is some violence in this act, if only a little. When you beat a pillow, you project your enemy onto the pillow. No enemy is being beaten but you enjoy beating, you take pleasure in it. This pleasure will keep the violence going, more or less.

Complete catharsis cannot take place with this method. So after undergoing the treatment in Perls' center, people would return to him about six months later and say, "Violence has accumulated in our minds again." Now they will have to beat a pillow again.

The process of meditation tells us to forget about the other, and to commit violence in an individual way. This does not mean doing violence to ourselves; it only means allowing the violence to happen, but without an object. Suppressed impulses of violence in the mind will disappear when you shout out loud, scream, hit the air, or jump and dance in your meditation. They will disappear. Experiment for an hour one day, and you will see that your suppressed impulses have disappeared and you feel lighter, as if you have come out of a closed cellar. On that day you will not be able to get angry as easily as the day before. You will not be able to punch anybody as easily as before. The same energy which made your eyes red hot yesterday will turn them as blue as the water of a lake today. And you will laugh at yourself, when you see how this way you can cleanse the vicious circle of violence that used to cause pain for others.

Once Mahavira was standing near a village, and some people came and beat him severely. Somebody pushed nails into his ears. He just stood there and watched.

After some time, somebody asked him, "Why didn't you say anything? You should have said something. You should at least have asked them why they were beating you unnecessarily."

Then Mahavira replied, "They were not beating me unnecessarily, there must have been some reason for them to beat me. The reason may have nothing to do with me but there must be some cause within them. And I thought it is better that they beat me because if they had beaten someone else, they would have got a beating themselves. It would be difficult to find a better person than me to throw their violence on." Mahavira behaved like a pillow with those people.

In meditation, all the impulses that have been suppressed can be released by catharsis – they may be of violence, they may be of anger, they may be of sex, they may be of greed. In meditation, all these suppressed impulses are released. And when these impulses are released, when the suppressed energies are let out, then it is very easy to be free of the instincts. If someone's wealth is thrown out, then before long the safe too can be thrown away. Man keeps a safe because it contains riches. If all the wealth from the safe has been distributed, then it is not difficult to give the safe away too.

In the same way, it is not difficult to become free from the instinct of violence. The first and the real question is of getting rid of the impulse for violence; it has settled in by using the instinct for violence as its safe. When all the suppressed impulses are released, we can see violence in its total nakedness. And when someone is able to see violence in its utter nakedness, he cannot remain violent even for a single moment. Because, being able to see violence in its utter nudity is itself liberating. Violence is such a misery, it is so ugly, it is so dirty that one is not able to live with it even for a single moment. Seeing violence in its utter nudity is just as if someone's house is on fire and when they see the flames, it will be impossible for them to stay in the house even for a single moment. They will jump straight out. In the same way, a man surrounded by the flame of violence will jump out of it.

But we don't see the flames of violence because so many layers of suppressed impulses exist between the violent instinct and ourselves. It is because of these impulses that we are not able to see the violent instinct. We cannot see the naked violence due to them; in fact, because of the impulses, violence is seen as a friend, as if we need it: if tomorrow there is an enemy, if someone attacks, then how will we respond? All those suppressed impulses that are between ourselves and the violence create thick smoky layers, so we don't see the violence in its nakedness.

Meditation liberates one from the impulses and so enables a direct encounter with violence. And one who is able to see violence becomes nonviolent. There is no way for someone who has recognized violence to be violent. It is just as no one wants to enter hell knowingly: even if he enters hell, he enters thinking hell to be heaven. No one knowingly enters the flames of hell, and if he enters, it is because he thinks those flames to be the doors to heaven.

Meditation is cleansing, it is catharsis. Meditation means to let out what is inside, without any reason. That catharsis will not be put on anyone, but onto a void. It will be given to the void.

Try a small experiment when you feel angry. Shut yourself up in a closed room and express your anger. Be as angry as you can in that empty room. You will laugh a lot because the whole thing will look very absurd. You have always felt angry toward others, but when you look at it in isolation, you will find that it becomes difficult to feel angry toward others. At first, you will laugh at yourself in your aloneness, but after that, you will laugh when you feel anger toward others.

Keep a mirror in the room and be as angry as you can, and see how you look in the mirror. You will realize that you cannot then even do this kind of madness alone because it makes you laugh. And then imagine what kind of a picture you create in the minds of others when you are angry. You can break the mirror if you want and standing amid that destruction, see what kind of poison there is inside you. The poison will be eliminated, there will be a catharsis, and after this catharsis you will be able to see your violence. You have to see it to be free of it.

Question 3

Osho,

You have said that there is subtle violence in the sexual act. But isn't sexual intercourse an arrangement to create biological pleasure through the mutual contact of two people? Since both participate in this pleasure, is it not based on love and mutual affection?

From the time of the first Jaina tirthankara, Rishabha, to that of Parshavanth, the twenty-third, religion had four key elements; or you can say that the chariot of religion had four wheels, or you can say that religion had four legs. Religion was a four-wheeled vehicle. Mahavira added one more element, celibacy. None of Mahavira's predecessors made celibacy a religious element. It is a very interesting fact and worth understanding. It seems amazing that the thinkers and wise men from Rishabha to Parshavanth did not include celibacy in the key elements of religion.

Up to Parshavanth, it was thought that one who attained nonviolence would also be celibate naturally, celibacy would enter his life without effort. Sex itself was considered to be a very deep and subtle form of violence. Why was this? It will be useful to understand a few key points about why sex is violent, and it will also be appropriate to reflect on why Mahavira made celibacy a separate element.

Mahavira's name is very intimately connected with nonviolence. No other name is so closely connected with it. But you will be surprised to know that Mahavira had to separate celibacy from nonviolence. The whole reason he did this was that the people he was addressing were unable to understand violence in its deepest sense; they could only understand it at the physical level. As long as one only understands nonviolence at a superficial level, one cannot realize that there is also violence in sex. When one understands the deep and subtle nature of nonviolence, one realizes that sexual desire is also a form of violence. But this point was not raised; it was not discussed up to the time of Parshavanth because nonviolence was understood in its deepest sense by the people. Why was this so?

Two or three points are to be understood in this regard. As I told you, if somebody begins to love someone else, it is proof that he is unhappy. It is like this: if someone expects to get happiness from someone else, it is clear that he is miserable. If he cannot be happy by himself, it will be impossible to get it from someone else. He will find illusion, not happiness; he will find deception, not truth; he will have dreams, but he will weep when he wakes up. The desire for another person is positive proof that someone doesn't yet have the key to happiness. And there can be no sexual enjoyment without the desire for another person.

Sex is violent because the desire for somebody else is hidden in it. It is also violent because semen is full of life. Today, there are three billion people on the earth. From the semen produced by each ordinary man, vast numbers of people can be produced over the whole earth. And a man releases his semen during sexual intercourse throughout his life, with all the sperm cells that are released dying within two hours afterward. If a sperm cell enters a woman's egg, it begins a journey as a new life but the rest die within two hours. Thus millions of sperm cells die in one sexual encounter. Those sperm cells are lives in seed form. Each cell has the potential to become an individual, a person. So there is already a massacre – the killing of millions of people – in one sexual act, and this killing is violence.

It is important to bear a third point in mind. Those who have understood nonviolence in its true and deepest sense say that every individual who is born, or to whom you have given birth, is created by you to die. In reality, birth is the beginning of death. If birth is one end of life, the other end will be death. If a father is responsible for the birth of a child, he is taking only half the responsibility. Who will be responsible for its death? If a mother accepts responsibility for the birth, she is assuming only half the responsibility. Who will be responsible for the death? When the father or the mother assumes responsibility for the birth, it becomes a dishonest transaction. Where is the responsibility for the death?

Therefore, a fully nonviolent mind is unable to assume the responsibility of becoming a father or a mother. The profound reason for this is that such a mind is incapable of becoming the cause, the instrument of anybody's death. To give birth to a child becomes the cause of the death of that child. It makes no difference if the death comes after seventy years. The time element makes no difference.

So the whole thing comes down to this: most sperm cells released in sexual intercourse are certain to die within two hours, and those which survive will also die after seventy or eighty years. Sexual pleasure goes on producing death, although it looks like it is giving birth. This is the sole deception of life – that on the back door of life, *death* is written. When you enter life, you see the gate of birth, but when you die, you exit from the gate of death. This is the deception of life – that *happiness* is written on the front door, and *unhappiness* is written on the back door. You enter life with hopes of happiness, but when you leave, you are frustrated, anxious, mad with misery.

I have heard a funny story...

A man in New York had collected many wonderful objects and kept them in a museum. The pieces were so beautiful and remarkable that the people who went there to see them kept on gazing at them and were unwilling to leave. And as long as they did not leave, other visitors who wanted to buy tickets stood at the gate. There was no other way to enter, and it was very difficult to manage the whole show. Finally the visitors inside were asked to leave because the people outside continuously knocked on the door to enter.

So, the collector invented an ingenious device to solve the problem – perhaps he learned it from nature. There were ten or twelve halls in the museum. To direct visitors from one hall to another, a small board with an arrow was placed in each hall. On the board was an inscription: "More wonderful objects," with an arrow pointing to the next hall. He played a trick and put the largest arrow on the board in the twelfth hall, with the inscription: "Please proceed further to see even more wonderful objects, things you have never seen or heard about."

When a person left this hall, he came directly onto the road. Now it was impossible for him to turn back to the hall. A watchman stood at the door. If he wanted to enter the museum again, he had to buy another ticket and enter through the front door. From the day these boards were placed in the museum, there was no longer any congestion because in their curiosity to see more astonishing items, people went directly out onto the road.

The signboard labeled "Birth" is on the front door, the signboard labeled "Death" is on the back door. Those who have lived nonviolence deeply, those who have known, say that to give birth is also violence.

For these three reasons, the sexual act too is a form of violence. An unhappy person, as I said earlier, wants to find happiness from the other. But have you ever thought that the other person who is engaging in sex with you is also unhappy and wants to find happiness from you? These two beggars are begging from each other.

I have heard, there were two astrologers in a village. Every morning they used to go to the market place to pursue their profession of astrology.

Whenever they would meet on the way, they would ask each other to read their palms about how the business would go that day.

This is how we behave our whole lives. Everybody is unhappy and is begging for happiness from each other. The person I beg for happiness from is approaching me to ask for their happiness from me. Naturally, the final outcome of two unhappy people meeting will only be unhappiness doubled, it cannot be happiness.

The unhappiness will be doubled. Rather, it is not right to call it doubled, because in life there is no addition, there is only multiplication. Here, things don't add up, they multiply. Here, four meeting four do not become eight, they become sixteen. In life, when two unhappy people meet, their unhappinesses do not just add up, their happinesses multiply manyfold.

Becoming a cause for another's unhappiness is violence. And as long as I am unhappy, every relationship that I will develop will only impart unhappiness. Therefore, a nonviolent person will say that as long as there is violence in your mind, unhappiness in your mind, don't create any companionship, don't create any relationships, because all such relationships will only spread unhappiness. Be alone, stay away from relationships. The day you are filled with bliss, you can relate.

But the problem is that those who are unhappy want to relate, and those who are happy no longer think in terms of relationship. Not that they do not relate, but they don't think in terms of relationship; they no longer desire it. Even if people form relationships with them, it is always one-way traffic. Others relate with them, but they remain standing alone, unrelated. Others touch them, but they are unable to touch others in a personal way. Yes, their bliss certainly keeps on showering over whoever comes near the one who is happy. He showers just like the rays of the sun do. He showers just like the flowers on the trees go on showering their fragrance. It is not a showering for somebody in particular, but because they have become so full there is an overflowing. Things are in flood and they go on overflowing.

An unhappy person seeks relationship, and whoever he seeks it with, he can only leave them unhappy. Who has ever found happiness from relationships? Who has ever given anybody happiness through a relationship? Nobody is able to do it. This whole earth is made up of unhappy people. And through millions and millions of people trying to give happiness and receive happiness, the unhappiness all over the world has multiplied millions of times, turning it into a hell.

Sex is a form of violence because it is a discovery of an unhappy mind. Nonviolence is a flow from a happy mind. And violence is an infection of insane diseases spreading from one unhappy mind into others. That is why, up to Parshvanatha, celibacy was not even counted as something separate.

Mahavira had to mention sex separately because the society he was born into was decadent. It was a dying society. The society Mahavira was born into in India was a society at the peak of its progress, and when a society reaches the peak, its downfall starts. All societies at the peak of progress start declining. For example, America today is a decadent society. It has touched a peak; now the decline will begin. Everything will start to disintegrate. Wherever a peak has been touched, disintegration will set in.

At the time Mahavira was born, Bihar particularly was at the golden peak of its prosperity. All around was golden; all around, progress was at its peak. And at the same time, everything was starting to rot and decline. Amid *that* society, a man like Mahavira had to talk of nonviolence, taking the subject to profound depths at a time when the available ears were deaf.

The people Rishabha had encountered were simple and innocent. It was a progressing society, not a decadent one: it was evolving, progressing. People were innocent, simple, and straightforward like children. It was possible to talk of deeply profound things with them and they were able to hear profound things. They had not yet gone deaf. The tumultuous noise of civilization and culture had not yet damaged their ears. There was still the simplicity and freshness of a child in their souls. As yet, the songs could still reach; the voice could still reach. Therefore, they simply did not talk of celibacy because celibacy was automatically contained in nonviolence.

But Mahavira had to bring in a fifth key element. Instead of just four, he had to add one more – because it was difficult to explain to the people of that time that nonviolence can go so deep that even sex is included as violence. And that is the reason the system of thought based on Mahavira could not touch the depths of nonviolence that Rishabha and Parshva had in mind. The system of thought that developed based on Mahavira remained confined to superficial nonviolence such as: don't kill even an ant; drink only strained water; do not be violent, do not hit anybody, do not hurt anybody; do not cause anybody suffering; do not eat meat, and so on.

Mahavira is not responsible for this. The people who were around him, the people he had to talk to, were responsible. This is why his system remained at the level of mediocrity.

Just see what remarkable people Rishabha and Parshva must have been who did not even talk of celibacy. Because, they said, if you become nonviolent, celibacy will follow on its own. There was no need to create a separate system for it.

Confucius once went to Lao Tzu and said, "People need to be taught religion."

Lao Tzu said, "Have you heard about the time when people were so religious that no one talked about religion?"

One needs to talk about religion only in a nonreligious society. If people are religious-minded, where is the need to talk about religion? Lao Tzu said, "There was a time when people were religious – at that time it was pointless to talk about religion. Because when people are religious, there is no need talk about it." No one but a sick person talks about health. A sick person just talks about health twenty-four hours a day. Generally, the sick person himself becomes a kind of doctor because he always talks about health and medicines; he reads magazines and leaflets on health, and books on naturopathy. A sick man talks a lot about health, because his sickness keeps him so self-conscious that he uses his constant discussion about health to divert his attention from his illness.

Similarly, an immoral society talks about morality; an amorous or sensual society talks about celibacy; a fallen society talks about progress; a poor community talks about wealth. We discuss whatever we are lacking.

There was great violence in the times of Mahavira. Nonviolence was not deeply understood, and so he was compelled to discuss celibacy separately. For Rishabha, to talk of nonviolence was sufficient, and in the times before that, it was perhaps not even necessary to discuss nonviolence. When violence gets a tight grip on the mind, discussion about nonviolence begins immediately. Hence I say sex is a kind of violence and the absence of sex is the flowering of nonviolence.

Question 4

Osho,

Until now, our idea was that sympathy is an aspect of nonviolence. We have believed this for a long time. But during these talks on the Panch Mahavrat, the five great virtues, while explaining nonviolence, you told us that there is violence hidden in sympathy because the other is present in it. Then you took it further, giving an example of empathy from Ramakrishna's life. You told us how a farmer was being whipped, and the whip marks appeared on Ramakrishna's back.

Please explain to us if there is some subtle difference between sympathy and empathy in the context of nonviolence. Also please tell us what you mean by empathy – is it a psychological phenomenon, or is it on a spiritual level?

Sympathy has been looked upon as a very valuable attribute, but it is not. It means to be unhappy and show your sorrow when you see someone else's unhappiness. It also means to experience along with the other. But one who experiences unhappiness when the other is unhappy never experiences happiness when the other is happy. You show your feelings of sorrow and unhappiness if someone's house catches fire, but you do not show happiness if someone else builds a big house. It is very important to understand this phenomenon. What does it mean?

It means that sympathy is a kind of deception. Sympathy is genuine only when we experience joy in the happiness of others as well as unhappiness in the miseries of others. But we are only able to experience or share unhappiness in another person's unhappiness; we are unable to experience happiness in another person's joy. So it is not right to say we are able to show sorrow when someone else is sad. If we were able to be happy about the happiness of others, then and only then would it be right to show sorrow for their unhappiness.

On the contrary, we take pleasure in the unhappiness of others; we take pleasure in another person's difficulties. We become completely delighted with other people's miseries. So when you show your sorrow while in sympathy with other people's miseries, try to examine within whether you also derive some pleasure in that moment or not.

In such a situation, you feel that you are the one showing sympathy and the other is in the position of receiving it. When another person is in the position of receiving sympathy, he becomes a beggar, and you effortlessly become the giver. When someone is receiving your sympathy, you move into a superior position, and he becomes inferior and humble. If you look into your heart, you will find a kind of pleasure in sharing your sorrow for his condition. You are sure to find it. If you don't, you are someone who can also be utterly happy in another's joy.

Normally we become jealous of another's happiness, we are resentful. This other side tells us that we are in fact unable to be unhappy in another's unhappiness, but that we have just been calling it sympathy. I have been talking about the feeling that is generally known as sympathy. So I thought it good to also speak of another word, *empathy*.

Sympathy is a false thing, it is a deception. If we understand fully, when our sympathy is genuine, we experience unhappiness in another's unhappiness, and joy in another's happiness. Even then it is still violent; it cannot be nonviolent because as long as the other is there, it cannot fulfill the conditions of nonviolence.

Nonviolence is an experience of nonduality, and violence is the experience that there is an "I" separate from the other. It will certainly be violent if your experience of feeling unhappy when you see someone else unhappy is false. And even if the feeling is genuine, you remain the "I" and the other remains the other. The bridge between the two is not removed, and there is no possibility of nonviolence. To know someone else as "the other" is also violence. Why? Because I am living in ignorance as long as I consider another to be the other. In fact, he is not the other.

Empathy does not mean knowing that the other is unhappy; it means I myself have become miserable. It is not just knowing that the other is happy; it means I myself am happy. It is not that the moon is shining in the sky, but that I am also shining. It is not that the sun is rising, but that I am rising. It is not that flowers have blossomed; it is I who have blossomed. Empathy means nonduality. Empathy means oneness; nonviolence *is* oneness.

So there are three states: one is false sympathy, which is violence pure and simple. Two, genuine sympathy, which is a very subtle form of violence. And three, empathy, which is nonviolence. Sympathy may be violence or a subtle form of violence; it may be genuine sympathy or false sympathy – both of these are at the psychological level. Empathy is a spiritual phenomenon.

We can never be one with someone else on a psychological level. My mind is one entity; your mind is a separate entity. My body is a distinct entity; your body too is a distinct entity. It is not possible to have unity or oneness on a physical or mental level. Unity or oneness is possible only on a spiritual level. It is possible because we *are* already one on the spiritual level. It is just as the water in a pitcher dipped in flowing river water is the same as the water outside the pitcher; there is only the earthen wall of the pitcher between them. If the wall is broken, the two waters become one.

Mind and body have a wall which prevents us from meeting the other, which stops us from becoming one with the other. We all are like earthen pitchers in the ocean of consciousness. The pitchers will be distinct and separate but what is inside is not separate. One who experiences nonviolence knows the self, and also knows that even though the pitchers may be separate, what is within them is one and the same. That experience of oneness is nonviolence. Therefore, it cannot be sympathy because for sympathy, the other is needed. This is empathy because the other is no longer there.

Empathy is that which is beyond the mind. It is not in the mind or below it; it is above and beyond the mind. And a phenomenon which takes place beyond the mind is spiritual. Only a spiritual person can say, "That which you are, I am." Only a spiritual person can say, "The flame burning in the sun, that very flame is burning in this small earthen lamp too." Only someone who knows that what is in an atom is also in the universe, can call it spiritual. Only someone who knows that a drop of water and the ocean are one, can call it spiritual. Empathy means the drop and the ocean are one. A man who has completely known one drop of water has nothing more to know about the ocean. When a drop is known, the whole ocean is known. Whoever has known the drop within himself has known the ocean within all. Then he does not die because there is nothing else left.

That ego, that "I," has disappeared because no "thou" is seen. As long as there is a thou, there is an I. This pair of thou and I is always together. Martin Buber's book, *I and Thou* is very valuable. According to Martin Buber, all the relationships of life are the relationships of I and thou. But there is another world which is beyond I and thou. There is another world of real life which is not of relationships but of life energy, of godliness, where there are no I's and thou's.

There is a small play in Bengali, in which it is said that a man goes to Vrindavan and his luggage gets stolen on the way. But he thinks, "It is good that I go empty-handed to Lord Krishna, it seems appropriate. Because how can even Krishna fill the hands which are already full? If I want to fill my being with Krishna, then it is right that I go empty-handed. Perhaps the Lord Krishna sent the thieves!" He bowed in gratitude and moved onward.

When he reached the temple doors, the doorkeeper stopped him and said, "You cannot go inside. First leave your luggage outside."

The man replied, "I have no luggage now, the thieves of Krishna stole it."

The doorkeeper said, "No, first leave your luggage outside; only then can you go in. Here, only empty hands can go."

The man looked at his hands – they were empty. He showed his empty hands to the doorkeeper, but still he said, "No, hands which are full cannot go in."

The man said, "I am completely empty-handed now."

The doorkeeper said, "As long as *you* are, how can you be empty-handed? As long as you say you are totally empty-handed, how can you be empty-handed? Your hands are filled with 'I.' Drop this 'I' outside."

Without dropping the "I," one cannot enter the temple of godliness. But someone who lives by dropping this "I" attains empathy. For someone in whom the "I" dies, whatever happens to others happens to him too. Or it is not even a question of "him too," it is just happening. No matter where the thorn pierces, its pain reaches him too. A flute of happiness may be playing anywhere, those notes too become his. Now nothing is outside, nothing is unknown, nothing is the other.

Empathy is the highest peak of spirituality. But sympathy is our temporal, worldly training and is generally ninety-nine percent false. We do not just deceive others, but we deceive ourselves as well. And even if it is one percent genuine, I and thou still remain, the pitcher remains. Perhaps we glance from one pitcher into another, but even then we do not have any idea that there is oneness between two pitchers, that oneness is flowing between the two.

I call that state empathy when only one remains, when there is no other. You may call it nonduality, or *brahman*, or God, you can call it what you like. You can also call it existence. Life attains its highest peaks, its peak experiences when there is only one. When I and thou have fallen away, you realize that the relationship of I and thou is clearly one of violence. It will be a little difficult because we do not know any moment without I and thou. Perhaps by experimenting a little, you will have glimpses of it.

Sometimes on the banks of the river, on the sand, stretch out your arms and legs. Cover your chest with sand. Close your eyes, hide even your face in the sand. Forget that you and the sand are separate. Break the boundaries, the distance that is separating you from the sand. Let the coolness of the sand enter you. Let your warmth enter the sand. Experience that you have expanded and become one with the sand.

Sometimes stand under the open sky with open arms. Embrace the sky, the emptiness. Sometimes just be silent with the sky. Drop this idea that at the boundary of the body, you finish. Expand your boundaries; let your boundaries be as vast as the sky.

Sometimes lie down on the ground with the stars in the night. Let the stars reach you and let yourself reach the stars; forget that the stars are there and you are here. Let only the exchange between you and the stars be there. Only the communication remains.

Then very soon, an explosion will happen in your life: soon you will begin to feel that neither is there any "thou" on the other side nor is there an "I" on this side. Perhaps there is only one: the right and the left hand are the two ends of one phenomenon. There was only one gust of the wind; it had come here and has gone there.

The breath you take in comes to me, it becomes mine, and I am barely able to take it in before it moves out and becomes yours. Just now the tree was taking it in and now the earth is taking it; now you took it in, and now I have taken it!

Life is a continuous flow, it is an unbroken stream. It is one, but we are unable to experience that oneness because we have built walls around ourselves. We have built our own walls, we have surrounded ourselves from all sides, we have created boundaries. Those boundaries are actually not there; they are made by us and they are temporary. The boundaries do not exist.

If we ask a scientist he would say this and if we ask a mystic he would say it too. The mystic would say it because he has experienced the expansion of the soul.

The scientist would agree because he has tried to find the boundaries but could not see them anywhere. If you ask a scientist, "Where does your body end?" he would reply, "It is difficult to answer that question. Does it end with the bones? No, it does not end with the bones because there is flesh on the bones. Does it end with the flesh? It does not end there because there is a covering of skin on it. Does it end at the layer of skin? It does not end there because a layer of atmosphere, of air, is necessary outside it. If that is not there, there would be no bones and no flesh. Does it end at the atmospheric layer? No, the atmospheric layer ends two hundred miles above the earth. And if this atmospheric layer did not get the sun's rays, it would no longer be there either. The sun is almost one hundred million miles away from the earth. So does my body end at the skin or one hundred million miles away?" Even our sun would be cold if it did not continuously receive rays of light from greater suns. So the question is, "Where *does* my body end?"

The scientist says, "We have investigated all the so-called boundaries, but we did not find them." The spiritual person says, "When we looked within, we saw the limitless." The scientist talks in negative language; he says there are no boundaries. The spiritual person talks in positive language; he says it is limitless. Both statements mean the same thing. Today, religion and science stand very close to each other, all their pronouncements are very close. The scientist cannot say where this body ends. This body ends there where the universe might end.

This experience I call empathy: when the stars are not far away, rather they begin to move within me; when I am not far from them and I begin to dance with their rays. When the waves of the ocean are not far from me, when they become my waves; when I am not far from them, when I become a part of them. When the flowers of the trees become my flowers and the dried leaves fallen on the ground become my leaves, then I am not separate from all these things. We are not separate. There is no greater delusion than the feeling of separateness. To have the feeling of separateness is the greatest illusion but we go on cultivating it.

On the other hand, to cultivate such a feeling is useful, otherwise it would be difficult. I cannot call your money mine; I cannot take away your clothes and make them my clothes. In worldly terms, your shop is not my shop, your house is not my house. When I am a guest in your house you might say, "Everything is yours," but I don't take it seriously and our purpose is served.

In day-to-day life, this separation seems to work but life is not only practicalities. Life is not only your shop, your house, and your clothes. Life is not only your means of livelihood; it is not only your safes and cupboards. It is a much larger phenomenon. Life is not merely a utility, life is also bliss, life is also a play, life is also a boundless mystery. So anyone who takes utility to be all will be in difficulty. In the world of utility we say many false things, but they serve a purpose, they take care of the practicalities.

The world of utility functions through beliefs. I stay at someone's house and ask for a glass of water. He brings me a glass of water. So far I have never seen anyone bringing a glass made of water. But this serves our purpose, although it's a complete lie. How can you bring a glass of water? It is not possible. But both have understood what is being asked and our purpose is served. He does not bring a glass made of water – the tumbler is made of glass, of copper, of brass and he brings water in it. Neither do I fight with him, saying, "You did not listen to me!" nor does he fight with me saying, "You are speaking a very spiritual language!" This serves our purpose.

But life is not only functional; it is beyond all functionality, it is beyond such temporary arrangements. All our languages are functional; they indicate something and the purpose is served. But someone who thinks that life is only functional and practical remains ignorant of the great mysteries of life. The doors to the great palace of life are not open to him, there is none of the music of life for him, the voice of existence calls but he does not hear it.

In the pursuit of utility, don't miss the life which is nondual, boundless, infinite. Keep searching for it beyond utility. Go on searching for it beyond I and thou. You have to search for it until the day you find it. I have called that meeting with it, empathy. That alone is nonviolence, that alone is love, that alone is nonduality, that alone is liberation.

You can ask one last question.

Question 5

Osho,
What is the relationship between violence and social justice? Sometimes it is said that both nonviolence and violence are means to social justice and that Mao, Stalin, and Hitler were all inevitable historically. What is your viewpoint on this?

Nonviolence is not about social policy or law. If it were about social convention or law, it could never free itself from violence. Nonviolence is not social, it is spiritual. If we make nonviolence a social law, then one day we may also consider violence a necessity. And it would be such a disaster for violence to be considered necessary to protect nonviolence.

Suppose a man commits violence against somebody. The court will also commit violence, will punish him because he committed violence. If a country or a nation commits violence against another country, then the latter will react with violence against the former because it is thought just to respond to violence with violence.

To endure violence is injustice: it is not right to endure injustice. But the kind of nonviolence that I am talking about is spiritual. If we wish to discuss social nonviolence, there will always be a law of nonviolence related to it. It will accommodate both violence and nonviolence. The two will be joined, it will be like a mixed economy.

Violence and nonviolence will stand side by side, only their characteristics will go on changing. Complete or total nonviolence is not possible at the social level. It is extremely difficult to achieve total nonviolence even on an individual level; it is not right to even hope for a time when we will achieve it on a social level, on a mass level.

Similarly, it is not right to even hope that everyone will attain self-knowing because that is a matter of choice. If somebody wants to remain without self-knowing, he cannot be compelled to attain it. There will always be the freedom to attain it or not, there will always be the choice. We can simply hope that more and more people may gradually attain self-knowing. But there is one danger to be concerned about, which I will tell you also. Whoever achieves self-knowing cannot return to this society of ours. He does not come again. There is no new birth for him because for a new birth, wishes, hopes, and desires are needed. Whoever has unfulfilled desires returns for a new birth in which the desires continue.

If people like Mahavira or Buddha returned for one more birth, it would be because at least one desire had remained unfulfilled: to tell others what they had come to know. That is also a desire in its true sense. It is also a desire in its true sense. If I have something which I want to impart to others, I shall come again. That is also a desire, the final desire. But when that desire is left behind, how can one come again?

Those who attain self-knowing disappear into space. They become one with the great cosmos, with the supreme consciousness. Those who do not attain self-knowing return to the earth. At times, society brings forth a flower of self-knowing. Such a flower blossoms, fades away, and its fragrance is lost into the air. And then society carries on as before. Society cannot know enlightenment, it will always remain ignorant of it. But the flowers of self-realized people have been blossoming, go on blossoming, and will go on blossoming in a society ignorant of enlightenment.

Nonviolence can never become a fact at the social level. Therefore those who have promoted nonviolence on the social level have admitted the presence of violence, they had to. Violence will continue, then violence and nonviolence will be two aspects of society, as needed. There will be nonviolence when it is required, and equally violence will be adopted when it is required.

When India was fighting for freedom, the freedom fighter was nonviolent. And when he came into power, he became violent. It was possible to fight for freedom with nonviolence because there was no scope to fight violently. So, he fought for freedom with nonviolence. But on achieving authority, the nonviolent fighter did not even think of ruling nonviolently. Now his authority was running on violence.

The English did not use their guns as much as these nonviolent people have done in this country. Whoever considers nonviolence a matter of policy, or a convenience of society, will become violent if the need arises. It will just be a matter of convenience for him whether to be violent or nonviolent.

But Mahavira cannot be made to be violent under any circumstances. To him, nonviolence is not a social policy or principle, it is a spiritual truth. It is not a matter of convenience for him; that he can be whatever he likes. It is his great destiny – everything can be sacrificed for nonviolence, even the self. That nonviolence cannot be sacrificed for anyone. But it is only possible for an individual to be such a nonviolent person. And if a society ever commits the mistake of becoming completely nonviolent, it will simply become cowardly, it cannot be nonviolent.

If a society thinks that it is following Mahavira's nonviolence, then a nonviolent society will emerge – but a truly nonviolent society is not possible. A society made of Mahavira's nonviolence is not possible. Only individuals can be followers of Mahavira's nonviolence. So the society that tries to be nonviolent with the idea that it is following Mahavira's nonviolence will simply be cowardly. It will proclaim its cowardice as nonviolence: it will go on declaring its lack of courage to commit violence. But if we scratch the surface a little, we will find streams of violence flowing underneath. A coward is also a very violent person – but only mentally.

So remember, a society cannot be nonviolent. I say it is never possible; it is very difficult, it is impossible. Only an individual can be nonviolent. The nonviolence which I am talking about is not a social truth; it is an individual achievement.

The second thing the questioner has asked is whether Hitler, Mussolini, Stalin, or Mao social inevitabilities. If they are social inevitabilities, they are no longer individuals. An individual is one who may rise above social inevitability, above the compulsions of society, who is free, who chooses, who makes decisions. But if they are social inevitabilities, social compulsions, then they are no longer human; and they will be violent in the way the society is violent. If they are not individuals, then they are not human – they fall back to the animal level.

To be at the human level, it is necessary to rise above social inevitability. Only someone who has individuality is a human being. He can say, "Whatever I am is my decision, not imposed by society. Whatever I am doing, I am doing it. The society is not making me do it."

Communism believes that the individual does not exist, only society exists. Communism believes that man does not create history, it is history that creates man. Communism believes that it is not consciousness which determines social conditions, rather it is social conditions that determine consciousness.

So according to communism, the individual does not exist. There is no Mao, no Hitler, no Mussolini, and there is no Mahavira and no Buddha. But the kinds of unscientific things communism goes on saying in the name of science are unbelievable. No social condition can give birth to a Mahavira. And if a social situation gave birth to a Mahavira, then was this social condition applicable to Mahavira alone? There were millions of other people in the state of Bihar at that time. If it was the social condition which produced Mahavira, then why didn't it produce hundreds more Mahaviras? If the conditions in Russia produced a Lenin, how many more Lenins did it produce?

No, social conditions don't produce individuals. And if they do, then they are not individuals, but rather social events. Social events cannot be nonviolent. They are bound to be violent because they go back to the animal level. To be an individual is a choice.

I would agree that Mao or Stalin do not rise much on the human level, they go deep into the depths of the animal level. But you might say, "They are committing violence for humanity's good." Whenever violence has been committed, it has been in the name of good.

In the Middle Ages, Christian priests burned millions of people alive – for the sake of humanity. A Mohammedan kills a Hindu – for the sake of human welfare. A Mohammedan does not kill a Hindu because he has enmity against the Hindu, he kills because the poor Hindu is a *kafir*, a lost soul, and he has to be brought to the right path. If he is not ready to come to the right path, then at least kill him so that his soul has a chance to be on the right path in his next incarnation. Similarly, cows, horses, and other animals were sacrificed in rituals called *yagyas*, so that they would go to heaven. In the same way, people have been sacrificing people of other faiths on the altar of religion – for their own good! Communism kills millions of people – in their own interest. Fascism destroys millions of people – in their own interest.

Violence spreads itself fiercely, wearing a mask of good intentions. It is clever – it is not ordinary violence, it is cunning. Ordinary violence says, "I want to kill you for my sake." Cunning violence says, "I want to kill you for your own good."

Each time, man changes his excuses. Now the Mohammedan, Hindu, Catholic, and Protestant justifications have become outdated. In their place, communism and socialism have become the new justifications. Over time, these too will become outdated. By that time we will have invented yet newer excuses. Man does not commit violence because it is justified, rather he invents justifications because he has to commit violence.

If we were to analyze the minds of Mao and Stalin, we would find insane people within. But those insane people were very cunning, they rationalized their acts. Under the label of social revolution, utopia, the coming golden age, they butchered millions and millions of people.

But those golden ages never arrived and since time immemorial, people have been slaughtered in their name. Golden ages came neither in Russia, nor in China, nor in Germany, nor in Italy. How many revolutions have happened in the world, how much bloodshed – and no golden age has ever arrived! Old revolutions ebb away, new revolutions begin, killing afresh, but those golden ages don't arrive. The experience of thousands of years tells us that man wants to commit violence, so he invents philosophies for it. These are not inevitabilities of history. They show the inevitability of violence within the human being, for which he has given new turns to history and then made history itself the basis for his violence.

To me, accepting the very idea of inevitability is to lose human dignity. Whoever says that there is a destiny which has to be lived is a slave; he has lost his soul. An individual who says that there is no inevitability anywhere, no compulsion to do anything, and whatever he will do will be his own choice, reaches the soul. Such decisiveness gives birth to resolve in man, and to the soul.

We will talk about the rest tomorrow.

8

Experience Leads to Liberation

Question 1

Osho,

You say that material affluence is necessary for spiritual growth. But in your last talk on non-possessiveness you said that the fewer the possessions, the less one becomes a slave to them; the more the possessions, the greater the slavery. Please explain this basic disparity between affluence and non-possessiveness. How do more possessions make one more of a slave and how does the possessor become the possessed?

Material prosperity is the foundation of spiritual life. But no building comes into existence just because the foundation is there. It is possible that the foundation is there and the building is not erected. No building can exist without a foundation, but the foundation can exist without the building. If someone abandons construction after laying down the foundation, there will be no building although the foundation will be there. But a building can never exist without a foundation.

Material prosperity is the foundation for being beyond attachment. Without being materially prosperous, no one can realize the futility of material prosperity. Without acquiring wealth, no one can know that nothing is achieved through wealth. The greatest gift of wealth is the disillusionment as to its value. If you don't get rich, you can never know the worthlessness of wealth.

The poor, the needy have great difficulty in being free from the temptation of riches. How can you be free of something you don't even have? To be free from something, you have to have it. You can only become free from something you have. That is why I always say that only an affluent society can become religious, and only affluence takes an individual beyond riches.

So in my previous discussion on non-possessiveness, when I said that the fewer the possessions the lesser the bondage they create, and the more possessions the greater the bondage, many of you might have felt that there is a contradiction. There is no contradiction.

To be free from a lesser bondage is very difficult; it is only possible to be free when the slavery is great. If the chains are few, one can endure them, but when they are many, one revolts. A poor man has so few chains that the very idea of breaking them doesn't arise. The chains of a rich person become too many, so he wants to break them. There is no contradiction. When things are multiplied, I realize that I have collected a useless load around me. A load which I thought would give me freedom does not free me, rather I am simply weighed down by it. A load which I thought would help me to fly offers no flight; on the contrary I can't even walk anymore. Greater slavery brings one closer to freedom.

Just as darkness increases before early morning, slavery has to increase before freedom becomes possible. An affluent person is in deep bondage; as a result, he realizes it and becomes conscious of what bondage is. We become accustomed to lesser forms of bondage, we swallow them, we endure them. But the greater the bondage, the harder it is to endure. We endure small chains in the hope that they will be reduced in the course of time, or in the near future. So the idea of renouncing possessions does not occur to a poor person because he continues to strive for what he doesn't have.

Now, a rich person who has everything for which he was constantly striving realizes that he has really achieved nothing. On one hand there is nothing left for him to obtain, and on the other hand he has achieved nothing at all. Everything has been accumulated in the outside world, but inside there is a total void. These are the moments when the spiritual life of an affluent person begins; this is his first ray of light. But I do not say that all affluent people reach this transformation, this revolution. The majority of people stop at the foundation; they are unable to create a revolution in their lives. There are reasons for this.

Please understand that it is not that a poor person can never be spiritual. A poor person can also be transformed, and there are reasons for that too.

The first thing to be remembered is that there is no knowing without experience. Only experience leads to knowing. Only the experience of wealth leads to liberation. If an individual, even in his poverty, has become spiritual in this life, then he must have experienced wealth during one of his many previous births. Otherwise, without that experience, it would not be possible to attain such knowing. Nobody can be free from the desire for wealth without having experienced wealth. How can we realize that a particular thing is worthless without knowing it first? How can we come to the conclusion that misery is worth dropping without having first experienced it?

Whatever is unknown we fear, if there is no opportunity to become acquainted with it. If we wish to understand our enemy, we must get to know him first. To know what is wrong, we have to pass through it. People who lose their way and fall into ditches along the road know those ditches very well. There is no other way to attain knowing in life. What we now call life may be short, but the actual journey through eternal life is long.

Look at it like this: an individual may have become so saturated with experiences of wealth in previous lives that even if he is poor in this life, it is possible for him to jump into the spiritual world. There can be no other reason. Likewise it is also possible that a man may accumulate all the wealth possible in this life and yet remain pitiable, poor in spirit. Even after acquiring sufficient wealth, he cannot free himself from it.

So I would like to say that whoever becomes free from the desire for wealth has attained wealth in the true sense of the word. This will be his proof: whoever can renounce his wealth is truly wealthy. And if he is unable to do so, there is a poor, pitiable being somewhere within him. If, after accumulating abundant wealth in this life, someone is unable to arouse a thirst for religiousness in himself, it can only mean that he has lived in abject poverty and wretchedness in his past lives. Even with so much wealth in this life he cannot eliminate that image of wretchedness and poverty; it stays within him. This experience of wealth must be new for him; it cannot be transformed into knowing. Knowing comes after passing through many experiences, it is the substance of experience. Knowing is the fragrance of many flowers of experience. For this man, the experience of wealth is a first. The experience of wealth has not become knowing for him yet. As soon as the experience of wealth becomes knowing, an individual is free from the greed for wealth.

So both my statements mean the same thing, there is no contradiction in them. Similarly, I say that an individual who has not known religious scriptures cannot become free from them. One who comes to know the scriptures becomes free of them. Likewise, I say that a person who has not known anger cannot become free of anger. One who comes to know the full fire and agony of anger becomes free of it. Similarly, I say that a person who has not known desire, who has not known sex, cannot become free from desire and sex. Someone who has known sexual desire can transcend it.

Experience is liberation because experience is knowing. Only the experience of wealth takes one beyond wealth.

Question 2

Osho,

In the same context I have another question about contradiction. You always maintain and you have just said that only by moving into the depths of indulgence is man able to transcend desires and passions and be free of them. But in your earlier talk on non-possessiveness, you said that desires and passions move in a circle, they can never be satisfied. Please explain this contradiction to us.

An individual becomes free from desire only after experiencing it because there is no other way toward freedom. This mortal world itself is the door to liberation; through hell is the door to heaven, the prison opens the door to freedom. The miseries we experience in this mortal world also become the path to lead us beyond this world.

I also said that desires are never satisfied, they move in a circle. You can go on running after them, there is no end. You can run as much as you like, but there is always a road ahead of you. You may run still further but a road is still ahead of you, it is endless. Desires never end, just as for an individual running in a circle, the circle never ends. No desire can ever be satisfied. But on the other hand I say an individual can be free of desire only through a deep experience of it. These statements appear contradictory, but they are not. Man is not satisfied by a deep experience, a deep experience *frees* him. If he were satisfied, there would be no need for him to be free.

His dissatisfaction becomes his path to freedom. He has already run in that circle thousands of times and seen where he is, and yet there is no satisfaction. This experience in itself is the deeper experience of desire. He runs far, he seeks so much, he gets what he wants and yet remains empty-handed. He goes deep into the experience, not once but many times, but his desire is not satisfied. On the contrary, he stops running and stands there saying, "I have run so far on this road, I am running in a circle but I don't reach anywhere. I have reached nowhere." This is the depth of experience.

Even so, if he thinks that by running a little further he may perhaps reach his goal, then the experience is not deep enough to free him from desire. If he says, "If I run one more round, I might get what I want," then know well that his experience is not yet complete. The meaning of total experience is not the fulfillment of desire, but the exhaustion of running. Now there is no more running. We have known many times, run many times, but have not reached anywhere. Now the man stops running. Now, no matter how much you tell him, "One step more and there is a gold mine," he says, "I have walked a thousand steps, and the gold mine is there like a mirage, but it does not exist." No matter how much you tell him, "Go a little further and you will get what you want," he will say, "I have never got what I desired. Now I know that desiring is not the way to attain."

This is the depth of experience. He is saying, "I ran a lot but I did not reach the goal." You may say, "Run faster, then you will reach your goal" and he will say, "I ran very fast and I have seen the outcome; I ran until I was breathless and I have seen the outcome. Now I am sweating, I have been running for many lives and now I know one thing, that I didn't reach the goal by running. Now I will make a different attempt to attain the goal by not doing anything, by just standing still."

The fulfillment of a desire is not freedom from desire. Freedom from desire means to recognize the utter worthlessness, the uselessness of desiring in its totality. If a desire seems partially worthless, then a new desire will catch you. If desiring has become totally worthless, then a new desire cannot catch hold of you.

Such a state of mind, where desiring becomes futile, is not a state of frustration. This is not a state of dissatisfaction. Because where there is frustration, it is not yet known that the desire is worthless. The meaning of frustration is that a desire wanted to be fulfilled, it has not been, but even now there is still hope in the mind that it can be fulfilled. I wanted to be successful, but did not become successful, and even now there is hope in my mind that if I had tried differently, success was possible.

Only those who are unsuccessful but their hope does not die get frustrated, their minds become sad. But, the ones who are unsuccessful and whose hope also dies do not get frustrated: they attain desirelessness. They stop moving, saying that running is futile; they have searched by running, and now they will remain unmoving and attain.

The strange thing is, that which was never attained by running is attained as soon as you stop moving in search of it. Because the one we are searching for is within us, the one we are searching for is with us, the one we are looking for has always been with us.

Hence the more we run, the more we miss that which is already there.

We have to stop running around in order to see inside our own house; we have to give up the outer journey of desire to see within ourselves. To see our own godliness, we have to turn our gaze inward. To find out what is in our own hands, we have to stop trying to open the closed palms of others.

The depth of experience is not the satisfaction of desire. If desires could be satisfied, Mahavira was a fool. If longing could be satisfied, Buddha was mad. If longing could be satisfied, Jesus needed psychoanalysis. Desires can never be satisfied. Buddha said that they are impossible to fulfill, they can never be finished. This experience itself can take one beyond desire. And what is not attained by longing is achieved by desirelessness. The experience is total only when passions and longing have become completely worthless and the flower of non-possessiveness blooms.

The flower of non-possessiveness blooms within a man whose passions have fallen away, whose desires have fallen away. Such a person does not run, he stands still. Then home is not far away, it is under his feet. Then there is nothing to achieve in the world outside. The possessor becomes the possessed, the seeker becomes the seeking, the seeker becomes the sought.

Whoever looks within discovers that he was only seeking himself. He was looking into mirrors, seeking in many mirrors, but he could find nothing. Now he discards the mirrors and looks within himself. He realizes that nothing can ever be achieved by looking into a mirror because only a reflection is there. In the mirror there was only an illusion of virtual space, an illusion of a false sky. What was seen in the mirror was nowhere – it was nowhere in the mirror. If it was anywhere, it was outside the mirror. But if someone is searching for it in the mirror…

We are all searching in the mirror as long as we are searching for desires. The day we turn our backs to the mirror – after having broken many mirrors, bloody all over with broken skulls from colliding with the mirrors – and assert that we have looked enough into the mirrors, that day we will no longer seek in mirrors. That is the day we come to realize that where we were seeking was just a reflection.

We are holding on to our own images in the mirrors of desires. We are searching for our own selves in the mirrors of desires. Every person is seeking his own self, but he is seeking where there is only its reflection, not the reality. The reality is here and he is seeking there. Reality is now and he is seeking in the sometime. Reality exists in each moment and he is seeking in the future. Reality is inside and he is seeking outside. Realization of this is the depth of experience.

Desires are circular; they are never satisfied, but after much chasing, the chaser experiences this and stops. He jumps out of the circle. He steps away from the circular desires.

And the day someone stands in desirelessness, nothing is left for him to attain. He has attained everything.

Question 3

Osho,

One more thing from the first question. How do objects, possessions, hypnotize and possess their owner, the possessor?

The seeds of slavery are hidden in the desire to possess, to be a master. We become slaves to those we possess because our ownership depends on those whose possessors we become. When the possession depends upon someone else, how can we be the owner? The one upon whom the ownership depends becomes the owner.

If I have ten slaves, I am the owner of ten slaves and my ownership depends on having those ten slaves. If I lose the ten slaves I lose my ownership also. The key to that possession is not with me, it is with the ten slaves. In a deep sense those ten slaves have become my masters. I cannot be the master if they are not there – how am I to be the master of those without whom I cannot be a master?

Knowingly or unknowingly we have become slaves to possessions; we are chained to them because without them our ownership disappears. And the interesting thing is that a slave will also desire to be free because no one wants to remain in bondage. So when the master dies, the slaves are happy – but if a slave dies, the master weeps. Now which of the two is the slave, the one who weeps or the one who laughs?

The desire to possess makes one a slave. In this world, only the one who does not want to be the master of anyone is a master. How can you end the masterhood of someone who has never made anyone a slave? His masterhood is independent. If his masterhood is dependent, what kind of master can he be? Even inanimate objects can become our masters, they begin to rule us. The possessor becomes the possessed.

Taking care of his possessions, the owner forgets by and by that they were meant to serve him, and it does not occur to him that he has started to serve *them*. He does not realize it because those possessions did not come to him; he went out of his way to possess them. And slaves always go to their masters, never the other way around. Whoever you go to, ownership goes into those hands. Things never come to you, you go to them. Man is in search of things; things do not go in search of man. Whatever you search for, whatever you toil for, whatever you take trouble over, whatever you attain with great difficulty, it will be no surprise if you hold it to your chest to keep it safe, and then get crushed under it. The cause is your fear of losing it.

I have heard that one night a thief entered the hut of a Zen monk, Ryokan. Ryokan stood with hands folded in greeting before the thief and said, "Forgive me, you have come to the wrong place.

You have traveled such a distance and there is nothing in this poor man's hut. There is only this blanket – take it." And he gave his blanket to the thief.

Ryokan had only that one blanket and now he was naked in the cold night. The thief said, "What are you doing? You have nothing else and still you are giving me this blanket!"

Ryokan said, "Remember, today you have entered a master's dwelling. Up to now you have been entering only slaves' houses. They could not have given you a single thing. Those you think have got much could not have given you a single thing. But now remember, there are also masters who have nothing. In fact, they are masters just because of the fact that they have nothing. Take the blanket with you."

The thief went away with the blanket.

That night was a moonlit night, just like tonight. Ryokan sat in front of his door. In the cold night, with the rays of the moon and the cold breeze, he started shivering.

Had Ryokan been a slave, he would have said, "It is too bad that the blanket was stolen, or that I gave it away." But he was a master, and in spite of that cold night, the idea that it was bad the blanket was gone didn't even come to his mind.

That night he wrote a song: "I wish I was able to give this beautiful moon as well to the thief! The poor thief – so busy in stealing, he is not even able to look at the moon."

This is a master!

You are seen covered in a blanket, but don't be mistaken – often it is the blanket that is covering itself with you. You are seen wearing diamonds and jewels around your neck, but don't be mistaken – often it is the diamonds and jewels that are wearing your neck. You live in a big house, but don't be mistaken about it – when houses gossip among themselves, they tell each other in whose inside they are living. Your living in a house is not possible because the house lives in you so much, so how can you live in the house?

The possessor becomes the possessed. The owner of things becomes a slave to the things. But don't think that the possessions are doing something wrong in this: it is completely a one-way affair. It is you who becomes the slave. It is your views and your way of thinking that bring slavery to you; the possessions have no hand in it. How will possessions make someone a slave? Things don't even come to know which man had the illusion of being a master and which man had the illusion of being a slave. We are encircled and bound because of our own ideas. One man can be free in spite of his hands being in chains, and another laden with gold ornaments can be in prison.

Life is amazing! And there is no other being except man who walks such crooked walks. He does such strange things. He changes the name of *slavery* into *mastery*; he changes the name of *chains* into *ornaments*; and even when he is inside a prison, he decorates it so much that it feels that he is sitting in his home.

We have all decorated our prison walls so well. We have given them beautiful titles, and we are lost among those beautiful names. But reality cannot be changed just by giving a beautiful label to it. Realty is realty. And the beginning of religiousness is knowing the realty in its naked form.

Non-possessiveness is a fundamental element of religion. Non-possessiveness means knowing the truth that: as long as there is desire for things in my heart, I cannot be the master of things. As long as I desire things, I am destined to remain in their slavery. I can be master of things only when the desire for things has disappeared from within me.

You may have heard the following story…

One night a sannyasin arrived at a palace. His master had sent him there to gain insight from the king's court. Before he left his master, the sannyasin asked, "What insight can I get from the king's palace that I can't learn in the ashram from the world of meditation?" The master told him not to argue, and to ask the question to the king.

When he reached the palace, he saw the courtiers drinking wine and courtesans dancing. He asked himself, "What kind of trouble have I been caught up in? The master has played a practical joke; he has made a fool of me. Perhaps he wants to get rid of me. But it is not right to return now."

The king received the sannyasin with great affection and asked him to stay in the palace. The sannyasin replied that it was meaningless to stay.

The king said, "Then stay tonight, and go back tomorrow after a bath and food."

The sannyasin stayed but he did not sleep the whole night. He thought, "This is madness! How can I learn from a palace where wine is drunk freely, courtesans are dancing, wealth is displayed everywhere: where there is so much indulgence? I am a seeker of the highest knowing, I have wasted this night."

When he got up in the morning, the king invited him to bathe in the river behind the palace. While they were bathing, they heard a loud noise: the palace was on fire. From the banks of the river, flames could be seen rising high in the sky above the palace.

The king asked the sannyasin, "Do you see that?"

The sannyasin immediately came out of the river and shouted, "What are you talking about? What is there to see? My clothes are there on the bank, they may catch fire!" But as he ran toward his clothes, it struck him that although the king's palace was on fire, the king was still in the water – but *he* was running to save his loincloth on the bank.

He returned and fell at the feet of the king, who stood there laughing. He asked, "How is it that you are standing here even though your palace is on fire? I don't understand."

The king said, "I could not have stood here if I had ever considered it to be *my* palace. The palace is a palace, I am I. How can the palace be mine? When I was not yet born, the palace was there; it will be there even after I am gone. How can it be mine? You considered the loincloth yours, but I know the palace is not mine."

It is not a question of possessions, or to whom they belong. The question is of our attitude, our behavior, our way of thinking, and our way of life. Everything depends on how we live. If we are attached to things, it doesn't make any difference whether the thing is a palace or a loincloth. And if we are not attached to things, then it also makes no difference if we have a loincloth or a palace. Man becomes a slave because of his attitude, and he can also be free by breaking this attitude, by changing it.

Question 4

Osho,

In the second talk on non-possessiveness, you said that Mahavira became an emperor when he began the life of a sannyasin, but his elder brother remained a pauper and a slave in spite of living amid affluence. Wasn't this a one-sided, lopsided life for Mahavira, attaining spiritual wealth while avoiding material affluence, in other words keeping himself free of possessiveness? Why was he unable to accept both the inner and outer richness together?

Mahavira renounced everything and left, not because there was affluence but because it was not real affluence. He didn't leave because there was something worth renouncing but because there was nothing there worth holding on to. But it appears to us that he left the palace, he abandoned his diamonds and jewels, he left his wealth behind. This is how it appears to us, but for Mahavira, nothing but stones and pebbles were renounced. These things appear to us as diamonds and jewels, but Mahavira saw only stones in those diamonds and jewels, nothing but stones.

Those who wrote about the life of Mahavira said that he renounced so many diamonds, so many jewels, so many pearls, so much wealth. But if someone had asked Mahavira, he would have said, "Are you mad? You have simply given beautiful names to stones!" Yes if Mahavira *had* renounced stones, we too would have not said that he had renounced stones. We have all renounced stones: all children collect pebbles and stones, and a day comes when they outgrow them and drop them. But we don't write about the life of a child, that he has renounced pebbles and stones, because we know they were only pebbles and stones. When we realize that Mahavira had only renounced stones, we will no longer say that he renounced something.

No, it is not surprising that Mahavira renounced. What is surprising is how we fail to renounce. If someone asks Mahavira, he will not say that he renounced something, because only something that has value can be renounced. Mahavira will say, "I have not renounced anything because it is pointless to talk about renouncing something that had no value."

Every day you throw garbage out of the house and you don't publish in the newspaper that you have thrown away so much garbage. Mahavira is entitled to renounce at least whatever has become garbage for him! Are we not willing to allow him even that much?

Yes, we have difficulty because we don't see it as garbage. Try grabbing a stone away from a child, then you will know: he will cry the whole night, he will shout out in his dreams. You have taken away all his possessions that he had collected from the banks of the river! You will say he is mad because they were only pebbles and stones. They may seem to be stones and pebbles to you, but to the child all colored stones seem more precious than diamonds and pearls.

In fact, the difference is in your level of consciousness compared to the child's. You see them as stones; children see them as precious stones. You insist on throwing them away, the child insists on keeping them. The difference between Mahavira and us is the same as between the adult and the child. A new consciousness has arisen in Mahavira. Everything in this world has becomes valueless for Mahavira: all its value has been lost, it has become completely without value.

Mahavira didn't renounce anything, things simply lost their value for him; they dropped away from him. It is very difficult to carry the burden of things that have become meaningless. Mahavira didn't renounce and leave; he just went away, and those things were left behind. Mahavira's elder brother remained in the palace and he was unhappy, thinking that his younger brother had made a mistake: he had renounced precious stones, wealth, fame, all the luxuries, and had gone away. The difference between the two brothers is that of a mature mind and a childish mind. Mahavira's elder brother is unhappy that Mahavira had chosen to remain unhappy. But Mahavira has not chosen to be unhappy: he is so filled with bliss that there is no longer any way to be unhappy.

I told you the story of the king who lived in a palace but was not attached to it. So why could Mahavira not live in the palace in the same way? The situation changes from person to person; it depends on the type of individual. Mahavira could not live there.

Krishna could live there, Janak, the enlightened king, could live there but Buddha could not. This is a personal matter in which each individual has absolute freedom. The rules for one cannot be imposed on another. Whatever potential Mahavira possessed was actualized, and the flower that could bloom in Mahavira blossomed. There was a unique blissfulness in the blossoming of that flower. To live in a palace and yet not be attached to it has its own blissfulness. To live under a tree, out in the open, and not in the palace also has its own blissfulness, and there can be no comparison between the two. It will depend upon the individual.

What bliss could there be in sitting, resting, and sleeping under the trees, in wandering from village to village with a begging bowl in your hand? It is important to understand this because it is a very valuable and deep point about the phenomenon of non-possessiveness. For Mahavira this way is natural: just as breathing in and out is normal and natural and not one's own doing; just as the cycle of birth and death continues. So why should Mahavira take the responsibility of managing his life? He leaves that for existence to take care of. This is a sign of the deepest religiousness; it is absolute trust.

Will there be a sunrise tomorrow? Tomorrow morning, if the sun does not rise and if it sends its resignation during the night, or if tomorrow morning it goes on strike and does not rise, then what can we do? If tomorrow the oxygen disappears from the air and life becomes impossible, what can we do? What security have we created? What arrangements have we made? If tomorrow the earth becomes cold or the earth disintegrates – many planets have disintegrated, some are disintegrating, many suns have become cold, many more are becoming cold – if this happens tomorrow, what arrangements have we made?

What arrangements or power do you have to make sure it will happen or not happen?

Mahavira's thinking is that in this vast cosmos, none of the arrangements or systems for its smooth running are in our hands. What sense does it make for this man called Mahavira not to trust in existence and try to make arrangements for a shelter? What is the point of going into this mistrust? Mahavira says why even arrange this much? When one has to endure so much chaos, he adds a bit more of chaos to it. In such a cosmic chaos, in such cosmic insecurity, what kind of security can be managed by having a bank balance?

So Mahavira drops this unnecessary burden from his head. He says, "The source from where all breathing originates, all sunrises come, from where all the roots will derive their life juice tomorrow, and all the flowers will bloom, and all the birds will sing their songs, that same ultimate source will also keep this body alive if it wants to do so. And if it does not want to keep it alive, then Mahavira does not want to go against that either."

Leaving all possessions behind is Mahavira's declaration of this very fact: "Now I am not living on my own insistence. If existence wants to keep me alive, that is its business. Now I am not going to live according to my own desires."

That is why Mahavira observed a small and amazing rule which I should share with you. Perhaps no other sannyasin in this world has ever observed such a rule; the truth is, it is very difficult to find a sannyasin like Mahavira. Before going to beg for alms each day, he would decide during his morning meditation to accept alms only if a certain condition was fulfilled; otherwise he would not accept them. Beggars never impose conditions. How can there be any conditions for beggars? They beg without any precondition. But Mahavira begged according to his own conditions because he was not a beggar. The conditions related to whoever was giving him alms that day. It was not revealed to others, so a suitable arrangement could not be made. He alone knew the condition.

For example, in the morning he would make a condition in his mind that if a fair-skinned, one-eyed woman in black clothes offered alms he would accept them; otherwise he would not accept anything. He did not know the town and he had arrived during the night. Now, according to the condition he would only accept alms given by a one-eyed fair-skinned woman in black garments; otherwise, after wandering in the town he would return. He would say, "Existence did not want it, so let it be," because he had no desires of his own in his life. He wanted neither to die nor to live. From his side, Mahavira had no lust for life. If existence wants, it will keep him alive; if it wants, it will take him away.

Once it happened...

Mahavira went to the same village every day for months and could not receive any alms because of his condition. The villagers tried many things, but they had no way of guessing the condition – it was so difficult to know what was in Mahavira's mind. The condition was that he would accept alms only if a princess bound in chains offered it with one foot in the house and the other outside, tears in her eyes and a smile on her lips. He couldn't receive alms for months and yet he continued to beg and to go back happily. The entire city was in anguish, crying, begging Mahavira to accept alms but Mahavira would say, "It is not the will of existence."

One day it happened. An imprisoned princess offered him alms. She had tears in her eyes because she was in prison, and there was a smile on her lips because Mahavira had come to her door for alms. One of her feet was inside the door because it was chained, the other foot could step outside. Mahavira accepted the alms.

Now, even existence cannot place the responsibility for such an event on Mahavira; only existence itself can be responsible for it.

This is ultimate surrender to existence; this is the ultimate stage of sannyas – where an individual does not take even a single breath on his own. Hence Mahavira can say, "The fruits of my karmas are not for me, and the results of my karmas are not tied to me. I am not responsible. Now I am not doing anything. Now whatever is happening is happening on its own. Doing is not in my hands. I am not doing it: I do not have any desire.

This is Mahavira's individuality. It is a mistake to start comparing any two people. If we compare Janak and Mahavira, it would be wrong. Janak has his own bliss. Mahavira says, "If existence wants me to continue living, it will arrange it in one way or another." Janak says, "If existence has given me a palace, who am I to renounce it? If existence has given me a kingdom, why should I bother to leave it?"

Now, who is right and who is wrong? Both have their own way of looking at existence. Both are right. There are a thousand types of people: Jesus is his own kind of man, Buddha is his own kind, Mahavira his own, and Krishna his own. Whenever we compare we make a mistake because in comparing, we lean toward the one whose type resonates with our own. Then we start to see the other as wrong.

No, there is no reason to compare. Millions of individuals have flowered, and there is a possibility for millions more to flower. There is no reason for comparison. But if one looks in a deeper sense, the two are one and the same: Janak is in the palace because he says,

"When existence has given me the palace, why should I renounce?" and Mahavira is in the jungle, but he says, "If existence wants to keep me alive, then even in the jungle it will keep me just as if I am in the palace. Why should I worry?" They are saying the same thing, but the way of the two individuals is different. The same thing becomes a different song in these two individuals; the same thing takes a different note in these two people. The same thing takes a different meaning in them. But it is one and the same.

It is about total surrender to existence. If we can understand this, then we must try to understand each individual the way he is in his totality, without comparison. One day we realize that although there may be thousands of flowers there is only one beauty, that although there may be thousands of lamps there is only one light, and that there may be thousands of seas but their water is salty throughout. The day this is clearly understood, the individual disappears and the essential truth is realized to its very roots.

Question 5

Osho,

Another difficulty has arisen today. You have talked about non-possessiveness from a profound perspective, and it is clear that what you call non-possessiveness means freedom from all desire. It sounds very positive listening to you but people can take it in a negative sense. Then all scientific endeavor and search, even the inspiration to action would be lost, and all progress would be hindered. Please clarify this.

One further question: Mahavira was a mahavira, Buddha was a buddha, Christ was a christ. But their followers could never reach the same heights as they themselves had. So a kind of inertia spread among their followers. The result was that although they could not touch those same spiritual heights, they also spurned the material world. What do you have to say about such a situation?

Non-possessiveness can become a defense of poverty; it can be in opposition to progress. It can be an obstruction to the pursuit of prosperity in life. Anything can produce contrary results if it is understood in a wrong or mistaken way. Anything taken the wrong way will not bring any benefit to life, rather it will do harm. And there is always the possibility of misunderstanding. I shall try to explain this by telling you a short story…

There was a town in which a very wealthy man lived. He was a miser just the way wealthy people are. He would not give a penny. A temple was being built in the town and people went to him many times for contributions, but to no avail. New beggars who arrived in the town were informed by the old ones that they should not go to that man's house because no one had ever received anything from there.

A small temple was being built in the town and even the poorest man had given a small amount to the temple fund. So the townspeople decided that a list should be drawn up, showing the contribution of each man. Some had donated one thousand rupees, some had donated ten thousand, some had donated five rupees, and some had given one rupee. But there was not a single person who had not contributed something. With that list, about fifty of the town's leaders went to the house of the rich man. They expected to return with something from him because seeing the list, he would certainly be impressed. If not impressed, he would at least feel ashamed.

They began reading the names from the list out loud, saying so and so, who is not so wealthy, donated ten thousand rupees, someone else who is poor gave one thousand rupees, and another person on a daily wage gave five rupees. They were reading aloud and watching him to see what effect it was having on him. The rich man was getting more and more eager to know the names and appeared to be very impressed.

The townspeople thought they would succeed in their mission. After hearing all the names, the rich man stood up at once. He said he was very impressed.

The people thought they would not go empty-handed that day. They said, "If you are so impressed, give us your contribution."

The wealthy man spoke, "You have misunderstood the meaning of my being impressed. I am impressed, so I am thinking to go round the town from tomorrow to beg for alms. It is a big mistake not to beg in a town where everyone is willing to give."

This is how man gets impressed. Mahavira left his palace and went out on the road. Seeing this, those who had palaces could have become aware that they were engaged in a meaningless race because someone who had a palace had become a renunciate and was standing on the road. No, this did not happen. What happened was that those who lived in huts started thinking that, when the owner of a palace is renouncing it, why should we make an effort to build a palace? But when a poor man accepts his poverty, he is never able to attain that state reached after experiencing wealth. He simply remains poor.

Seeing Mahavira begging for alms, other kings ought to have felt ashamed. They ought to have thought, "Something that this man could not find as a prince, he is finding in begging." No, the kings did not think like this. But the beggars took pride in themselves. They said, "Look! When he could not find what he was looking for in the palace, he came outside to beg, which we already are doing. So God looks somehow more kindly on us."

People do think like this. So there is truth in the thought that people who were influenced by Mahavira – remember, not Mahavira himself – have their hand in preserving India's poverty. People influenced by Buddha and Mahavira – remember, not Buddha or Mahavira themselves – have their hand in India's lack of science, in India's lack of progress.

But it is very complex. How can Mahavira be blamed for it? For example, take fire: it ignites your hearth and it gives light in the darkness of the night. But if you want to set fire to someone's house, it serves that purpose also. How can the person who had discovered fire be blamed?

Then there is the atom bomb: Can the scientists who made the atom bomb be blamed, held responsible, for Hiroshima? No, they can't be. Because atomic energy can also bring a thousand times more yield to the crops. All the machines in the world can be operated by atomic energy and man can be freed of work. Atomic energy can remove poverty and wretchedness forever. Atomic energy can bring longevity to man. Atomic energy can get rid of man's fatal diseases.

But none of this happened: people are dying of starvation and there has been no growth in the yield of the crops. People are dying of cancer and no cure has been found through atomic energy. Children die untimely deaths and nothing has been discovered through atomic energy to save them. Instead, an atom bomb has been dropped on Hiroshima so that hundreds of thousands of people were turned into ash. What can be done?

There is an Arabian proverb that whenever some new discovery is made, the Devil takes control of it first. Mahavira's discovery is great: the Devil took control over it first. Einstein's discovery is great: the Devil took control over it first.

So there are only two ways. One, not to discover anything at all: out of fear of the Devil taking over, beneficial things are not created; out of fear of potential exploitation, no charity is asked for; out of fear of bad outcomes in the end, nothing good is done, because good works can decay and be turned into bad. But then too the outcome will be evil. Because if no good is done, then only evil will remain.

The second way is that the risks have to be taken. If man misuses things, let him. What is right must continue to happen. If not today then tomorrow, he will realize his mistake, his suffering and pain. He will realize that what could have been used to create paradise, he has made hell out of.

Mahavira is no supporter of poverty; he only proclaims the futility of wealth. And these are two very different things.

The second thing that was asked is that the followers of Mahavira could never reach the height of Mahavira, Christians could not reach the heights of Christ, and Buddhists could not reach the heights of Buddha. Mahavira's followers could never reach the heights of Mahavira: there is a reason why the followers of Mahavira could not reach his level. A follower can never reach those heights; a follower can never reach the same heights because whoever follows another is in fact losing his own self. Following someone else, a person destroys himself. To follow another, we have to eliminate ourselves. To put on another's clothes, we have either to shorten or lengthen ourselves. To adopt another's individuality, we have to suppress our own selves. A follower can never reach the same heights because someone who has decided to be a follower has decided to commit suicide.

I do not advise you to become a follower of Mahavira. I do not say to become a follower of Jesus. It is enough to just understand Mahavira and let go of the rest. It is enough to understand Jesus and let go of the rest. If possible, be yourself. There is no way for you to become Mahavira or Jesus. This does not mean that you cannot reach the same height that Jesus reached. You too can reach it, but only if you become yourself. Whoever tries to be a carbon copy cannot achieve the clarity of the original. And if it is an Indian carbon copy, it is even more difficult! Then it is very difficult even to understand what is written underneath. Can a copy be any better than the original? Two thousand five hundred years have passed since Mahavira's death. In these two thousand five hundred years, thousands of people have copied him, and you are coming after them. Thousands of copies have been made of the original. Now, nothing can be understood from those copies, but you go on as if you have understood, you go on following.

A follower can never be a spiritual person. In reality, a follower is saying, "I would like to drop the responsibility of being myself. I would like to follow someone. I am ready to be blind. I will walk with the help of someone's hand. Let someone take me to the destination; I refuse to take the responsibility of walking by myself."

One who denies his own eyes, one who refuses his own feet, and one who refuses to take the responsibility for his own awareness, can never evolve. He has chosen all the ways not to evolve.

But we have always been taught to follow someone, be like someone. This is a dangerous teaching: nobody can be "like somebody." So far, no one has become like someone else, it has never happened. Many people followed Mahavira, but who could become a Mahavira? It is not that the followers made any less effort, that could not be said: they made a great effort. Sometimes it seems that the followers of Mahavira made greater efforts than Mahavira himself. The truth is that for Mahavira to be a Mahavira, no effort is needed. It is spontaneous. It takes no effort for each person to be himself, only to be another needs an effort. Effort is needed only to be someone else.

If Rama's wife Sita is lost, Rama does not have to make an effort to cry. But in Ramaleela, when the story of Rama's life is enacted, Rama has to make an effort as tears do not come naturally. Maybe from behind the stage he wets his eyes before coming out onto the stage. Perhaps he has put chilli powder in his hands to make the tears come. So when Sita is lost in the play, he quickly rubs his eyes to make the tears come. Since it is not that easy to make the tears come in Ramaleela, one needs to help them to come. Would Rama also have needed to make this effort for tears to come? No, it is spontaneous, natural for Rama. It is his authentic inner state.

Mahavira's renunciation and his nakedness were natural. Someone else can be naked only by making an effort and when he does so, his nakedness will be more of a circus – it cannot be his spiritual journey. It will only be a borrowed thing, imposed by someone else. At the most he can imitate Mahavira, he cannot *be* Mahavira.

Those who follow Jesus, Buddha, Krishna, or Rama are simply acting. They have refused to have a real, authentic self. There is one thing worth remembering: existence has given each person the right to be his own self, and whoever forsakes this right, forsakes the greatest gift of existence. Such a person is deceiving himself. Such a person says to existence, "You have thrown a very great responsibility on me. I am not up to it, let me follow somebody. I cannot be an engine, I am only fit to be a carriage attached to an engine, shunting here and there." Such a person will spend his whole life like this.

Each individual is born to be himself; he is incomparable, he is unique. There was nobody created the same in this world in the past, and there will not be in the future. Existence is not a mediocre creator; it is not an ordinary creator who creates the same person a second time. It creates new people every day.

I have heard a story…

Someone bought a Picasso painting for a million dollars. The buyer asked Picasso's wife if the picture was authentic, if it was painted by him.

Picasso's wife replied, "Don't worry; you can buy it because Picasso painted it in front of me." So he bought the picture and went to tell Picasso. He showed him the picture and told him he had purchased it for a million dollars.

Picasso looked at it and said it was not original, it was not authentic. The man was puzzled, he became nervous. He had paid one million dollars and Picasso declared that it was not original.

The man asked, "What are you talking about? Your wife assured me that the picture was painted in front of her."

His wife was present. She said, "What are you talking about, have you forgotten? You painted this picture. I was there!"

Picasso replied that he himself had painted it, there was no doubt about that. But still it was not authentic. Now they were even more confused. If it was painted by Picasso, why wasn't it authentic?

The purchaser said, "Are you joking?"

Picasso replied, "I am not joking. The picture was certainly painted by me. But I also painted it earlier, so this is simply a copy. It is not the original. I have already exhibited this concept of mine once before."

Existence does not repeat a concept or a picture that it has created before. Buddha was created once, the matter ended there. Mahavira was created once, the matter ended there. You will not be able to find even a single piece of stone similar to any other in the whole world, so what to say of human beings? If you tear one leaf off a tree and try to find another like it, you will not. Compared to that, the question of humanity is far greater.

Man is the evolution of a very complex consciousness. In this world, each individual is the highest, the supreme. No man has the right to copy another. This doesn't mean that he should not try to understand Mahavira. Actually a follower never understands. It is not even necessary. In fact, the follower follows just to save himself the trouble of understanding. Someone who doesn't follow anybody will have to work toward understanding.

Those who have known music have also inspired it in the lives of others. Those who have plucked the strings of life have ignited the lamps of knowing and wisdom in others; they have encouraged the sweet fragrance of the self and the dance of existence to arise in the lives of others.

The authentic seeker will try to understand Mahavira or Buddha, but will not try to follow them. In seeing how those beings evolved and developed, a thirst of his own is created – so that his own bud may also open and yearn to become a flower, so that listening to the harps of others, the strings of his own harp may also be stirred and he may be inspired to sing his own song. Perhaps the sound of their ankle bells becomes a challenge for his own bells to dance.

But you do not need to understand to follow someone. To follow someone, you do not need to understand. Put a blindfold over your eyes and walk. To follow someone, the greatest qualification is to be blind. Understanding is a totally different thing.

If you want to take your life toward truth, if you want to grow, then never make the mistake of becoming someone's follower nor let someone else become your follower. Both are dangerous. Rather, understand others and if your life comes to a flowering, then keep your flower on the road in the center of the marketplace, so that others can see. Perhaps their buds too may take the challenge to flower.

But when their buds flower, it will be like them, not like yours. And when their veena resonates, the music will be of their own, not like yours.

Each person needs to offer his own self at the altar of existence. Each person has to offer his soul at the altar of existence. One cannot go to the altar of existence on a borrowed soul. There, you will be asked, "Is it authentic? Have you brought your own self? You haven't come wearing someone else's mask?"

You cannot cheat at the door of existence. It may be possible to befool here on earth: a man standing naked may seem exactly like Mahavira. A man wearing saffron clothes may look exactly like Buddha. One can be befooled on this earth. But in front of existence, all the clothes will drop, all the layers will be uncovered. In front of existence – when everything will be naked and appear in the mirror of existence, when one's total nakedness will be visible – then nothing else will be seen other than what you are. There, you will not find what you had covered yourself with; there, you will not find what you had arranged, you will not find what you studied. There, only what you are is seen. That day you will be sad and miserable that you spent so many lives following, copying.

Life's meaning is not in following someone else, it is in the unfolding of one's own self. It is not a process of becoming like someone else, it is to *be* oneself. Whoever accepts this challenge to become himself will not be a copy but will reach the same height that Mahavira reached, will reach the same place where Jesus had reached, will reach the same place of liberation and nirvana where Buddha arrived after his enlightenment. Everybody can enter that very nirvana, that ultimate liberation, that heaven, that kingdom of godliness. I repeat again this ultimate truth: there is no other way but to offer the flowers of one's own self at the altar of existence.

Enough for today. There will be more tomorrow.

9

Uncovering the Original Face

Question 1

Osho,
Concerning non-theft, you have said that to copy or follow anybody on the physical, emotional, or mental level is theft. But life is a network of interrelatedness, we are all connected. So how is one to separate one's pure individuality from outside influences and protect oneself from them?

Life is a network of interconnected relationships, but it is not only that. Every individual must interrelate, but even interrelationship is a relationship between two individuals; two individuals are necessary to establish a relationship. So, seen from outside, life is interrelated – but it is also interrelated from within. If the individual is not there, all interrelationships become false.

Love is a relationship and the presence of the lover is necessary. But if individuality is borrowed, it is not true individuality at all. Individuality is always one's own, it cannot be borrowed; otherwise it is a deception. A borrowed personality is an assumed face to show others; there is nobody beneath the facade. It has no individuality, no vitality, no originality.

In fact, what we ordinarily call an individual is not an individual but a personality. What we ordinarily call an individual is not original, it is a collection of clothes. It is like an onion. If we go on removing the layers of an onion, it seems we will get to the onion after each layer. But we only get more layers and never the onion. Similarly, we are like a bundle in which all manner of borrowed things have been collected. No matter how deeply we delve into this borrowed individuality, we get nothing at the end. If there is no soul, no originality, then our whole life becomes false.

The greatest theft in life is copying or following. If someone is only interested in becoming like someone else, he is a thief in the real sense of the word. When somebody assumes the personality of someone else, it is an imitation, and he ceases to be original. His authentic originality is lost. This does not mean that we should not accept others' thought processes or stop relating to others. We should certainly relate with others but we should protect our being, the self.

Thought processes *will* come from others and you will have to receive them – do so by all means – but do not get identified with them. Receive them and share your own also. But you should remain beyond them, untouched, unidentified. Something in you which is beyond all receiving and sharing should remain intact.

There is a word in the English language, *ecstasy*. We have a word, *samadhi*. When *samadhi* is translated into English, the word *ecstasy* is used. *Ecstasy* is a very special word: it means to stand outside. The meaning of *ecstasy* is to remain outside and yet be constantly in the midst of the flow of life. In spite of being in the world, something within us remains that is not of the world: our originality. This is what becoming yourself means. If we are totally immersed in life and there is nothing left except our outer relationships, it means we have lost our souls. The meaning of the soul, the self, is that there is something within us which is untouched and separate from the outer world, while everything on the outside continues.

When you are walking on the road, there is someone within you who does not walk. When you are angry, there is someone within you who sees that anger. When you are eating, there is someone within you who does not eat but is aware that food is being eaten. At every moment in this interrelated network of life, if you can hold that "someone" within you who is safe, who remains as your original self… One who does not own this original self has no right to be called a man, a human being. He has no soul, he has lost it.

Very, very few people among us have a soul in this respect. We are simply a collection of layers, a collection of clothes; there is nothing beneath them. I call this stealing also. It *is* stealing. To steal someone's wealth is not a great theft, but to assume someone's personality is a very great theft. To steal someone's clothes is not a great theft, but to lose oneself in trying to imitate someone else is a very great theft. I am not saying that to take someone's house by force is not stealing, but it is not as great a theft as losing the self by becoming a shadow of someone else.

I have heard a story…

God was upset with a man and placed a curse on him. It was a strange curse: from this moment on he would lose his shadow.

The man laughed when he heard this and said, "What use is my shadow to me? When I am saved, how will the absence of my shadow affect me? I never cared before whether I had a shadow or not. Isn't it crazy to curse me like this? And if you are really upset, this is not such a terrible curse."

Hearing this, God laughed. God was wiser than that man.

The man returned to his town laughing and thinking that God was crazy. What did he lose by losing his shadow? But when he went into the town he realized that God was not so crazy – because he got into a lot of trouble. Whoever saw that he had no shadow was afraid of him and ran away. His wife closed the doors on him.

His father said, "Get out of here! Don't ever come to me. What are you? Are you a ghost, a spirit?" His friends shut their doors when they saw him. Customers stopped going to his shop.

When he was walking on the road, people called their children indoors. He had no shadow. It became difficult for him to live in the town. Finally the townspeople, who had never heard of someone without a shadow, decided that he was very dangerous and drove him out of town. Then he realized how much he had lost by losing his shadow.

Never mind this man, we are all just shadows. We have lost our souls, our selves. We are just shadows. It is very difficult to comprehend, to estimate how much we have lost. That man only lost his shadow, and he ran into so much trouble. But we have lost our souls. But because everyone's soul is lost, no one drives us out of town. If a shadow is lost, others will know about it, but if the soul is lost, only the self will know about it. Others will not be aware of it because it is not an outer event.

So to understand the meaning of non-theft correctly, we should constantly ask ourselves: "Do I have anything within me which I can call my own – my originality – that I brought with me at birth and which I have not acquired in life? Do I have anything that was my own even before I was born?"

If you can remember that which is within you, which was with you even before you were born, then you can understand that something will remain even after death. If you think that all that you are came after you were born, death will snatch everything away. If you have at least something of the nature you were born with, which you feel has not been learned during your life, or taken or acquired from life, then there is no reason to be afraid of death. Death cannot snatch away what you have not obtained from life.

But we are all afraid of death, not because it is frightening, but because there is nothing within us from life that can be saved, that can remain with us after death. Death will take away everything that we have gained from life and from others. It may be fame, wealth, knowledge, or character. It may be anything which we have acquired from others, which we have stolen. This kind of stealing is not recognized by the courts. It is subject to the supreme law called religiousness. It is only in the court of existence that this stealing is recognized.

Do you have anything that you can call original, not obtained from anyone else? If not, you are living a stolen life. And you do not have anything. If you remember just once that you have nothing which you can call your own, a revolution will begin to take place in your life. So don't start thinking that if you haven't stolen even a penny from someone else's house, then you have never stolen anything. That kind of theft has nothing to do with religiousness. We are concerned here with a special kind of theft which is beyond the jurisdiction of the law, which cannot be decided by the courts, which is beyond the scope of judges. Religiousness is concerned with a kind of theft which is related to dignity and honor, which is a theft of individuality, of our faces – and all of us live with stolen, borrowed faces. In the way we live we are not ourselves, we are someone else.

I have said in this context that non-theft is the path toward attaining one's own individuality, one's soul, and theft is the highway to losing the soul. This theft can manifest itself at the emotional level, at the mental level, and at the physical level. Even our way of walking is learned from others. We do not even think in our own way, we learn that from others. We don't even feel in our own way, we learn how to feel from others.

For example, consider a man who reads a newspaper in the morning, and then talks the whole day about some news item or other. It does not even occur to him that what he is talking about contains nothing of his own. He reads the Gita and goes on repeating it throughout his life, and he never reflects on the fact that there is nothing of his own in what he is saying. In all our activities – speaking, thinking, moving here and there – everything is learned from others. There can be no showers of joy in such a life, not even a drop of nectar. Such a life is like a dry desert, where streams never flow, where no greenery exists.

Whoever lives through these borrowed sources lives like someone who considers the homes of others to be his own, considers others' eyes to be his own, considers others' thoughts to be his own. A man who collects scraps of information from the scriptures considers himself to be a person of discretion and thinks he has acquired knowledge. Such a person lives in a delusion and goes through his whole life uselessly. We all waste our lives like this.

But if this question, "Am I really a thief?" arises in you just once, it will haunt you forever. And if it does, you will notice that your laughter was learned from the lips of someone else, that the tears you were shedding were not real, and that your bows of respect were devoid of sensitivity and sincerity. You will see that there was no love in your lovemaking, it was learned from some play in the theater, and that your whispers of love to your beloved were nothing but a repetition of some dialogue heard in a movie. If this question arises in your life, you will begin to be free of theft – if not today, then tomorrow. Your individuality will begin to evolve, and you will laugh in your own unique way.

If people in this world were to laugh, weep, and think in their own unique ways, the world would be a wonderful place to live in. Then the world would be really vital and full of life. At present it is not like that. It is a collection of dead bodies, where we live as if dead and yet do not know it because there are dead bodies just like us all around. We read the morning newspapers, the neighbor also reads them; he repeats the news and we do the same. We read the Koran, he also reads it. He recites from the Koran, we do the same. What we have learned, he has learned from the same source; our opinions agree with his opinions, and it seems everything is going along well. But nothing is going well. If it were, there would not be so much unhappiness around.

Even if there is nothing left in your life, the realization of the self is quite enough. Then even if you have nothing left, your joy cannot be snatched away. Everything can be taken away except your joy, and there is no greater joy than that of the self. When a flower blooms in all its totality, the fragrance of its joy spreads all around. The complete blossoming of its flower *is* its joy. Life becomes full of ecstasy when the flower of individuality is fully blooming, and then someone becomes fulfilled, fully satiated. Then, even if you have nothing – no wealth, no position, no fame – then too you have everything. Otherwise, even if you have everything – wealth, position, fame – but no individuality of your own, you are nothing. You are utterly empty within.

There are great discussions going on in the West about the word *emptiness.* It is discussed by thinkers like Sartre, Camus, Marcel, and Heidegger. They say that we are empty, there is absolutely nothing within us; we are just like empty containers or boxes. In the West, great discussions are taking place about emptiness and it should not be so. Why are they saying all this when there is so much wealth, more than the world ever had before? We have palaces that are like skyscrapers, before which the palaces of Ashoka and Akbar seem like small huts. We have the power and the capacity to reach the moon; we have weapons that can destroy the whole world in a moment.

So what is this emptiness within? It means that everything is outside, nothing is inside. We have no individuality, we have no soul. Everything is available – we have the capacity to reach the moon, but not the strength to reach our own center. Wealth is plentiful, but there is no *being* at all. Our houses are very large, but the people residing in them are very small and insignificant.

This state of affairs is the result of theft. The West will have to learn non-theft in order to destroy this emptiness. People like Marcel, Camus, and Sartre will have to learn, will have to search for the means to awaken individuality. When all material wealth is attained, only then do we realize that we are nothing. No poverty in the world can create the anguish that grips us when that happens.

Non-theft is the key to attain individuality, and theft is the means to lose it.

Question 2

Osho,

You have said that to be a Hindu, a Jaina, or a Christian means to follow somebody; hence it is theft. So are these all borrowed personalities? Aren't these various cultures based on eternal laws? Cannot an authentic life be lived in the midst of these different cultures? How do you see theft in all this?

Mahavira is not a thief; it would be difficult to meet a more non-thieving person than Mahavira. But Mahavira is not a Jaina, he is a *jina*, a conqueror. It is necessary to understand the difference in meaning between the words *jina* and Jaina. A *jina* is one who has conquered the self. A Jaina is one who follows the conqueror.

Gautama Buddha is not a thief, it would be difficult to find a more non-thieving person than Buddha. But Gautama Buddha is a buddha; he is not a Buddhist, he is a buddha, an awakened or enlightened soul, a realized soul. And a follower of the awakened one is a Buddhist.

Similarly, Jesus is not a thief, Jesus is a christ. *Christ* means one who was crucified on a cross and attained the destruction of the "I" – the ego. But Jesus was not a Christian; a Christian is one who follows the crucified Christ. There is a great difference between the two. Jesus' neck was hanging on a cross, while a small cross hangs around the neck of the Christian. But crosses do not hang on necks – necks hang on gallows or crosses. Jesus dies on the cross, he is a christ. But the Christian hangs a small golden cross around his neck. Remember, a cross is not made of gold, nor is a gallows made of gold. If gallows were made of gold, what would thrones be made of? And remember, gallows are not hung from necks, but vice versa. So the Christians are thieves.

Mohammed is one thing, and a Mohammedan is a different matter. If Mohammed comes into the world, it is a matter of rejoicing and happiness and beauty – but if a Mohammedan is in the world, it is dangerous. If Mahavira is in the world, he is worthy of a welcome, but if a Jaina is there, it is dangerous. Buddha has his own uniqueness, he has a special fragrance – but a believer in Buddha has an unpleasant odor, he is not fragrant. And there is a reason for this.

First, as soon as someone decides to follow another, it means he is willing to lose his own individuality. Following someone else has no meaning. In fact, to follow someone else means that the follower wants to save himself from the realities of life. One who doesn't want to be a *jina* becomes a Jaina; one who doesn't want to be a buddha becomes a Buddhist. One who does not dare to be a christ becomes a Christian. He knows there is nothing special or particular in being a Christian – but any attempt to become a christ will endanger his life. What does one do to be a Jaina? Becoming a *jina* requires great spiritual discipline; a Jaina has simply to follow the *jinas*, it is just a game. In becoming a *jina*, one has not to follow, but to work hard toward fulfillment – to practice spiritual discipline. Spiritual discipline entails difficulty; it requires hard labor and firm determination.

In fact, people who don't want to work hard toward self-fulfillment are playing a game of self-deception and resort to a kind of worship. They play the game of following someone else to avoid realizing their own individuality. No one can achieve individuality by following another; the other is always the other. I may follow another and roam the whole earth, yet I will not reach within myself. If I want to reach within, I will have to cease wandering. To follow always means to move around on the outside.

Mahavira did not follow anybody, Jesus did not follow anybody, Krishna did not follow anybody. It is interesting to note that innumerable people become followers of those who have not followed anybody. Buddha followed no one but thousands follow him.

To learn from Buddha himself, we need to learn that we should not follow anyone. To learn from Buddha himself, we must learn that we should not follow anyone. If anything is to be learned from Mahavira, it is that nothing will be gained by worshipping somebody. Mahavira is not in favor of worshipping anyone. If we want to learn something from Jesus, we should bear in mind that christhood can be realized without becoming a Christian; Jesus was not a Christian. If we want to learn anything from Mohammed, we should understand this very firmly: that godliness has nothing to do with Mohammedans. Mohammed was not a Mohammedan but he could encounter godliness.

These individuals who did not follow anybody are now followed by us in the hope that we may also attain what they achieved. But if we see there has been a mistake in the science of it, there has been a mistake in calculation somewhere… They achieved because they went within themselves, and we want to achieve the same by following someone. To follow is to go outward. Therefore, I consider all forms of following to be theft.

This kind of following has not produced any civilized culture. In every civilization this concept of following has created the opposite. It has not produced a civilized culture, but rather the opposite because all these followers do nothing but fight and murder each other. The church, the temple, the mosque, and the gurdwara have become the centers and the means to fight one another. Human history is full of religious wars. These followers who believe in following Mohammed, or Mahavira, or Krishna, or Christ, could not develop any system that would help them become krishnas or christs themselves, but they developed great skills in annihilating one another.

There are many kinds of killing. Some leap into the battlefield with sword in hand, and others go out fighting with ideas and principles. The Jainas try to twist the principles of the Mohammedans, the Mohammedans try to pervert the principles of the Hindus, the Hindus misrepresent the principles of the Christians, and the Christians distort the principles of Buddha. Then when they get tired or are not satisfied with fighting with ideas and principles, they draw their swords instead.

Humanity should have been greatly blessed to have Buddha, Mahavira, and Christ among it, but on the contrary many troubles have been created because of them. Bertrand Russell has written: "What harm would there have been if God had not sent Jesus here?" At least there would have been no Christians – and in the Middle Ages, the Christians covered the whole of Europe with corpses. So a famous man like Bertrand Russell had to ask: "What harm would have occurred if God had not sent Jesus here?" The world would have been a more peaceful place if this one man had not been sent. At least the fighters, the murderers would not have been Christians.

This is something important to think about. The world should not have become a horrible place because of the birth of Jesus – his coming should have increased the fragrance in the world. The world should have been lucky to witness the birth of Jesus. But it did not turn out to be so because his birth gave rise to Christianity. Whatever was given by Jesus has been destroyed by the Christians.

Jesus says, "Love thy neighbor as thyself," but the Christian keeps his sword sharp for his neighbor. Mohammed says, "There is only one God, and all are his children," but the Mohammedan goes out to kill those children. The Hindu says everything is *brahman*, godliness, and in spite of this he conveniently forgets this great Vedanta principle when he has to touch a sudra. It happens to even the greatest so-called pundit: someone who was saying that *brahman*, godliness, exists in all moves a little away when he sits next to a Mohammedan. Suddenly he finds out that godliness is afraid to reside in a Mohammaden!

The world was fortunate to have Jesus, Krishna, Mahavira, Buddha, and Confucius, but a flood of disasters and chaos have followed them. Institutions have been created which are nothing but instruments of war. Whole armies of believers get together and religion is turned into politics. Religiousness becomes an organized institution as soon as it falls into the hands of these followers, and then it is turned into politics.

Religiousness is not an organized institution, it is a principle. But when believers create an organized institution for religion, that institution assumes great importance, and those who are not a part of that institution are looked upon as enemies. Then the members of the institution are regarded as "us" and non-members as "them," as aliens.

Thus every religion goes on dividing people into different factions. There are some three hundred religions on this earth, so mankind is divided into three hundred factions. Real religion is to unite people, not to divide them. Who made this division? Did Mahavira do it? Did Mohammed do it? Only one of them can be right. Did Mahavira himself create this division or was it Jesus? Either Mohammed created it or the Mohammedans. Either Jesus or the Christians were the troublemakers. Mahavira, Jesus, and Mohammed were great messengers of peace because those whose troubles have fallen silent cannot be troublemakers in other people's lives; they can only be messengers of peace. But something else happened when their followers created organized institutions after their deaths.

There is a mystery with the followers. It is interesting to note one truth about followers generally: those who are at the opposite pole to the principles adopted by the master become his followers. Mahavira renounced everything, but people with plenty of everything go to bow and fall at his feet. Voracious eaters, who think of nothing but food all day, are the first to be impressed by him since, "This man does not eat any food for months! He must be a great ascetic!" They fall at Mahavira's feet. Mahavira stood naked, so those who love clothes and who are unable to bare their bodies even a little are impressed by Mahavira: "He is no ordinary man." So it is not surprising that thousands of followers of Jainism run cloth shops across this country. Is Mahavira's nakedness responsible for this? It is something to think about.

Jesus said that if someone slaps you on one cheek, offer the other cheek. If somebody steals your coat, give him your shirt too. If someone asks you to carry his load for one mile, carry it for two miles. It is no wonder that the Christians plundered the whole world. The Christians spread slavery throughout the whole world; they will not only steal your coat, but take your shirt too; they will make you walk for two thousand miles instead of two; they will slap you on one cheek, turn the other cheek and slap you on it! Jesus could not have imagined all this, but such were the people who flocked around him.

The fact is that opposites attract each other. Just as a man is attracted toward a woman, a woman is also attracted toward a man. In a similar way all attractions are to polar opposites; all attractions involve the opposite. Pleasure-seekers always gather around someone who has renounced everything. Those who cannot themselves be ascetics fall at the feet of the ascetics. Crowds of people clinging to worldly things gather near those who have found godliness – these are the people who then become followers. This is how everything becomes perverted. Jainas pervert what Mahavira said, Christians destroy Jesus' words, and Muslims do the same with Mohammed. This is very unfortunate, but it is so. Opposites attract. Those followers should all disappear. Mohammed should be there, Buddha should be there; their spirit, fragrance should exist but there should be no followers in between. People should understand what Mahavira said but no one should profess to be his follower. You can read, understand, contemplate, be happy, remain blissful, dance, but do not cling. You have been clinging long enough, and not remembering this fundamental principle has created great trouble.

The fact is that opposites attract and we gather around the opposite. And this gathering of opposites immediately puts things in the hands of the enemies. This rule in life is almost like when you put a stick in water it immediately starts to look bent – it is not, but it looks like it. The rules of water and air are different. As soon as the stick comes into the air, it becomes straight again. Put it in water and it looks bent again. The stick which is straight in Mahavira seems crooked in Jainas. The life of Buddha which is very simple becomes very complex and crooked in Buddhists. The love in the life of Mohammad becomes hate in the life of Mohammadans. The surrender in the life of Jesus becomes aggression in the disciples of Jesus. We have enough credible history to be wary of the disciples.

This does not mean that I am an enemy of Mahavira. His disciples are the enemies. This does not mean that I am an enemy of

Jesus. His disciples are the enemies. If one wants to save Jesus in his purity, then one has to remove the hurdle of the disciple.

And one does not gain anything by making someone a disciple; the follower only corrupts the great principles of the one he is following. He is not able to transform his own life.

A while ago I was reading a short story…

A child was talking to his father. He had read a proverb in his book that said a man is known by the company he keeps.

The boy asked his father, "Is this true?"

The father said, "Yes, it is true."

Then the boy asked, "Say there is friendship between a good person and a bad person, who would be known by whom? The bad person is with the good one, so should we consider him a good person? Or the good person is with a bad one, so should we consider him a bad person? Now who should be known by whom?" The father was perplexed.

Jesus is known through the Christians, so it has become difficult to know Jesus accurately. Mahavira is known through the Jainas, so it has become difficult to know Mahavira. If the followers are removed, the flowers of these great masters will blossom in their perfect beauty; their lamps can shine at their brightest. Then we will reclaim the spiritual wealth of the whole world.

At present the believer in Mahavira thinks that Mohammed is not part of this wealth, and the Mohammedan thinks he has no relationship with Buddha; he is from someone else's estate. If at some time there are no followers in this world, every individual will own the heritage of the whole world. Then Socrates will be ours, Mohammed will be ours, and Mahavira will be ours. We shall be more prosperous, and a true civilization will be born. Up until now, civilization has not been able to take birth; right now there are so many distortions and those distortions we call our civilization. Humanity's civilization will arise the day everything in the world will belong to everyone. Think about it. I will give one more example to explain this. If there are twenty-five different schools of thought in the field of science, will science progress or will it be destroyed? If the followers of Newton make their own circle and the followers of Einstein make another circle; and if the followers of Newton declare that they don't believe in Einstein because he has said some things which do not agree with him; the followers of Max Plank make another circle; the followers of Fred Hoyle make another circle; there will be many schools of thought in science. Now, there have been around fifty famous scientists during the last two or three hundred years, and if there were fifty different circles, would science progress or die?

Science can advance because there is no such division in the field of science. Whatever scientists have given to the world is the common heritage of all mankind. Religion could not create civilization because there are so many different religions or circles. There are nearly three hundred such groups in the world at present, so how can we expect or hope to create a true religion? These groups should be destroyed.

Mahavira saw the truth from one angle. Buddha saw the same truth from another, Mohammed from a third angle, and Christ explained the same truth from a fourth perspective. All this is man's heritage, and if all these are united and we become their inheritors, then a true civilization will arise in the world.

Right now there is no civilization, only fragmented distortions. A religious mind will only be created when this whole heritage becomes ours. Today we have only the sectarian mind; the religious mind does not exist in the world. When a truly religious man comes into the world, he is immediately surrounded by sectarian people, and within a few years they pervert and destroy whatever he achieved through his whole life's work.

Mahavira belongs to no one, Buddha belongs to no one; they belong to everyone and everything. No one is their master, no one can claim them – or you can say everyone can claim them.

If such a situation takes place, then religion will become a science. Religion is certainly a science – and according to me it is the supreme science – but it has yet to achieve that status. When religion becomes a science, our life will become refined and progressive. But at present, religion is distorted. At present it is only founded on sects.

Who is responsible for this? The follower is responsible. If the follower had achieved something by doing all this mischief, we would be satisfied. But it has taken him nowhere because he has forgotten all the basic principles. It has taken him nowhere. Each individual has to discover the truth for himself; he has to travel within himself to find it. Whoever follows another loses himself; he cannot reach the self in this way.

Question 3

Osho,

When you gave the illustration of an onion, you said every individual has many faces, many masks, that are stolen, and these masks will always be there in all circumstances. We must distinguish between an authentic face and a false face. I hate somebody, but when he comes to see me, I smile and welcome him. This is my false face, which I show to him. If I have great sorrow in my heart and yet I smile, then this face of mine will be a mask – a false face.If you have understood what death is, if you have known the secret of death and you are living your life, isn't this also a kind of mask? If you have attained victory over untruth and you are proclaiming the truth, isn't this also a kind of facade? I may add one more example: a flute attracts people by its tune. Isn't the tune only a visage of the flute? The ornaments for the ankles produce a musical sound. Isn't that musical sound only the visage of that ornament? If this is a fact, a distinction will have to be made, so please explain the difference.I have one more question to ask. If life is one grand, interconnected relationship, individualities will be created in many forms and ways. How can you call this individuality a false face? When a child is born, he comes into this world with impressions from a series of previous births. He receives love and affection from his mother, acquires knowledge and language from his teachers, and inspiration to think and experience from wherever he roams in this world. Is all this acquired experience to be looked upon as stealing? If so, the individuality will have to be split and made separate. How can we create our own individuality when we do not accept the experiences received from others and do not turn them into our own impressions?

I think the meaning of *mask* has not been correctly understood. Your face is not your mask. In a drama you put another face over your own – for example, the face of Ravana – and that borrowed face is a mask. Your own face is not a mask, but when you put on another false face whose roots are nowhere inside you, with which your life has no relationship, which is simply hanging on a string from your ears, which has no bridge connecting it with the throbbing of your heart, then and only then is it a mask.

Your real face is not a mask; it is the false face which is a mask. So understand its correct meaning. But a false face does not need to be of paper or plastic. You are very successful in covering your face with many masks. As you said, you put on a mask when you smile and welcome someone you hate from the bottom of your heart. Then it is a false face and such a false face is very harmful, although it seems to be useful. It prevents you from showing or exposing your hatred. But the hatred doesn't disappear. The danger is that as well as deceiving that man, you also slowly begin to deceive yourself. Then that oft-repeated smile goes on suppressing your hatred within, and a day comes when you forget that you are hateful. You will smile, while at the same time your hatred remains hidden inside.

If a religious person feels hate, there are two approaches to it. If hatred is not there, he should smile. If the hatred is there, at least he should not smile; he should expose that hatred on his face. This behavior has two advantages. If he shows hatred on his face, he has to suffer the harm which results from expressing hatred. He needs to have the courage to face the harm. The pain he suffers will become the motivation to transform the hate – otherwise why should he change? The harm and the obstacles that hatred brings to his life will be a good reason to change it. They will compel him to think about transforming or dropping his hatred because they lead him to hell.

We put on smiles and try to create heaven on the outside, but hell is growing within. Then how is that hell to be destroyed? The pain of that hell is not fully felt, and so lies hidden within us, beyond destruction. There is an interesting point here. By smiling, we think we welcome another person, although there is hatred inside us. Those smiles are full of poison, and the other person can clearly see that our smiling face is a mask. It is very difficult to hide the hatred that is arising from within. It shows itself through the lips, through the eyes, in the way we stand or sit, and in all our activities. So a false smile only suppresses the hatred; this way, we cannot establish any communication with others and it doesn't make the other happy. The other will often be happier if you are authentic.

If you are angry with somebody, say clearly that you are angry. If you get angry and suffer the pain of it, then soon this fire of rage will be the means to take you out of your anger. Otherwise there will be anger inside and a smile outside, and once that anger builds up inside it will burn you. The false smile, the dry smile, the futile smile will spread with no result.

When there is complete individuality and utter sincerity in our smiling, it touches the other's heart. The whole of existence laughs along with that smile, and only then is the smile alive. When every fiber of our body laughs too, only then does the smile become a gift from the eternal, otherwise not.

A religious person talks of removing these masks: non-theft means to tear them off. It is difficult. That is why meditation requires discipline. To stand in the hot sun is not spiritual discipline. The meaning of spiritual discipline is to have the courage to withstand all the heat of life. When you are angry, admit that you are angry; and when there is hatred, say that you are full of hate. At least be sincere, be honest. Express what is there. Feel the pain of it, live that experience. You will burn your hand living like this, and burning your hand will cause you to prevent that pain in the future. The next time, the person with whom you had been angry – to whom you expressed your anger and hatred – will be convinced of your love when you laugh with him and love him.

Everything is dubious in the life of someone whose hatred is false, whose laughter is false, and whose anger is also false. If a father has not really been angry with his son, remember that the son will not be able to trust even his father's forgiveness. He knows that his father is not honest, so you don't know if even his forgiveness… If a wife curbs and conceals her anger when she is angry with her husband, it will be very difficult to trust her even when she smiles – because she has no authentic individuality of her own. Even the possibility of her love being true becomes less every day. If her hatred is false, how can her love be true? One whose anger is false, his forgiveness cannot be true. How can you trust the tears of someone with a false smile? Then such a person's whole life is a tale of falsehood.

Religiousness is a revolt against this. Religiousness is rebellion, it is the opposite of insincerity. It is a challenge to be authentic, to be true, to be against insincerity, against untruth. Religiousness asserts: weep if there are tears, laugh and smile if there is pleasure. If someone is true to his feelings, he cannot entertain hatred or anger for a long time – and there are reasons for this.

Authenticity is such a great phenomenon in someone's life that it becomes impossible for the thorns of hatred to grow in someone in whom insincerity does not exist, in whom it has been dispelled. That is because inauthenticity is the seed out of which all these things grow. If that very seed is destroyed, then these other things start falling away on their own.

Authenticity means someone is true to himself, and cannot entertain anger for long – because such a person will soon see that anger brings pain upon himself. Somewhere Buddha has said jokingly, "I laugh a lot when I see someone angry because this type of person is punishing himself for the faults of others."

Somebody might say, "I am angry because that man abused me." Someone else has abused him. It is someone else's fault, but he punishes himself. No fire rages in his skin and bones, but the fire of rage burns his soul, burns everything within, turns everything to ashes. Someone will pull his hand back after putting it into the fire, but why does he dare to put his hand into the fire of rage? He does so because he cannot really see that he is putting his hand into fire. When he puts his hand into the fire of rage, he pretends he is touching flowers. He is burning with hatred inside but holds a smile on his lips. If he looks deep within, he will find that his hands are burning with the fire of that hatred, but he remains caught up in the smile.

If you don't laugh a false laugh and sincerely try to understand your weeping, your miseries, and your pain, you will soon see this fire burning inside. There is no greater fool than the one who holds onto hatred even once he has understood what anger and hatred are. It is an impossibility; he comes out of it.

So when I said you are stealing when you put on a mask, I do not mean to say that every time you smile it is false. I do not mean that. Your smiling is a mask only when it does not arise from within, when it is all on the outside. Your weeping would be a mask when there are no tears within, when they are only in the eyes. Greeting your guest is a mask when you say to yourself, "What a disaster, this guy has come!" and you actually say, "A guest is to be considered as a god, you are most welcome, please be seated." In that situation, the guest is certainly dishonored, and the god within him is certainly ignored.

Always say what is in your heart. Tell the truth. It is very difficult; it has to be, because only afterward is there liberation from those false masks. You will find it difficult to say to the guest who has come to your house, "You have put us to great inconvenience, and you do not look at all like a god." But if you are that frank and overcome this difficulty, you will soon be able look upon the guest as a god.

But a cunning person who says to himself, "Why has this awful fellow come to my house!" and outwardly says, "You are a god, you are most welcome, your arrival has filled my house with joy," can never regard a guest as a god. He deceives himself so badly that this cunningness will make him crooked, complex, and dishonest.

Throughout our lives we accumulate cunningness and dishonesty, and everything about us becomes false and untrue. A religious person declares that he will give up this dishonesty; he will be innocent and frank-hearted. He will be what he is; he will show himself as he is. Then the masks disappear and his true face appears.

Everyone has a true, original face but we have covered it with so many masks that we ourselves do not know which is real. When we stand before a mirror and are pleased with what we see, there is a ninety-nine percent chance of that face being a mask. Even in a mirror we are not who we are. We would like to be seen how we imagine ourselves to be. That's why people stand in front of mirrors with all their make-up on.

I have heard about an ugly woman. She would break a mirror if someone held it in front of her. She would say, "Where did you get such a horrible mirror? It makes my face look absolutely ugly."

We also like to break mirrors; we are not prepared to change our faces. But our faces are not changed by breaking the mirror, life is not changed by breaking mirrors. What I mean by a mask is that we should not cover our real face with false ones. It doesn't mean that we do not change our expressions. They are changing throughout life all the time, but those changed faces will be ours.

When there is darkness in our life, tears will certainly come to our eyes. If a friend dies tomorrow, tears will flow. If we meet a long-lost friend tomorrow, our hearts will certainly throb with delight, and we might sing and dance. Our expression should change every moment, it should be responsive – but that face should be ours. I am not saying that we should maintain only one face throughout. If we did, it would be a face of stone. Then you could not continue living, then you would need a face that is of stone.

I have heard…

Somebody approached an American millionaire for alms. The man asked for a small gift but the millionaire said, "I have made a rule about giving alms and gifts. One of my eyes is artificial – it is made of stone – and the other is real. And I only reward the person who can point out the artificial eye. But so far nobody has been successful in this test. You can try."

The man looked into the eyes of the millionaire and said, "Your left eye is artificial."

The millionaire said, "You surprise me. How did you know?"

The man replied, "Your left eye shows some mercy in it, so I thought that must be the stone one."

Faces may change but they cannot be expressionless. Only dead people's faces can be without any expression, those of the living cannot be. If you observe children's faces, you will see that they change as quickly as a gust of wind. And if you examine the faces of older people, you will see that they have become stony, meaning everything is fixed. There is no liquidity.

When I tell you not to change your face, I do not mean to say that you should make your face expressionless. I am simply asking you not to put on false faces. It should be your real face, and it will change every moment. When the moon rises in the sky it will have a different expression, when it is a dark night it will be different; when the flower blossoms in the morning it will be different and when the flower withers away in the evening it will be different; and when it sees a beggar on the road it will have a different expression. It should respond to every mood and express itself as the situation demands. It must be so. Life is responsive so your face should have liquidity. But the face must be yours; the liquidity should be yours. There will be change every moment, as everything in life is changing every moment. When the winds come then the dry leaf will fly toward the East, when the winds come the leaf will move to the West, when the winds stop the leaves will stay where they are. Nothing is fixed, everything is undergoing change. Life is like the shimmering leaves of a tree; they tremble all the time. Nothing in life is permanent except change. Change itself is the only thing in life which does not change.

Heraclitus has said: "You cannot step into the same river twice." Even in the same moment you cannot step twice. Life is like a river in which everything goes on changing. But whatever is going to change should be yours; that face should be yours, it should be authentic. If you are yourself, you will go on changing.

Change is life, and if you can remember during all these changes that there is someone within who sees these changes, you will attain enlightenment. The face should be yours, and you should also be the witness who stands behind this flow of changes and observes them. When the moon is rising, your eyes are smiling; when there is a dark night, your tears are flowing. Smelling the flowers, your heart is dancing; when they wither, you are sad. When you meet loved ones, there is joy; and when you separate, there is pain – and behind it all you are observing all these changes. But the changing face you are observing should be yours.

What is there for the witness to observe in a false, plastic face? It does not change. When you assume a false, artificial face, you have to change your face [mask], remove one and put on another. But when your own face changes, it becomes fresh with all the changing circumstances and in every new turn of life. The face is the same but the new responses to life make it fresh. If the awakened being within is watching, the changing faces become meaningful, and the unchanging witness is like *brahman*, godliness. Then you go beyond yourself – and when that happens, you become godly.

Question 4

Osho,

You have said that to assume a false personality or a false face from the outer world is a subtle form of stealing and leads to hypocrisy and non-religiousness. But I see that many new sannyasins are now gathering around you and without any special preparation or maturity, you go on admitting them into this new sannyasin way of life. Are you not harming religion to a great extent by acting in this manner? Please explain this.

The first thing is this: if anyone tries to be like me, I shall stop him. I shall tell him that it is suicide to try to be like me. But if a person starts his journey to try to be himself, I will wish him the best of luck. I have no objection to becoming a witness for those who want me to become a witness to their journey toward godliness. But I am not their guru or master.

Nobody is my pupil, I am simply a witness. I do not have any objection to being a witness if someone embarks on the path of sannyas in front of me, but I would object strongly if anyone were to ask me to become my pupil because I am not a guru. If anyone wants to follow me I shall stop him. But it is impossible for me not to offer my good wishes to someone who begins his own journey toward godliness. There is no reason to believe that the sannyasins you see around here are trying to imitate me. I do not wear red or orange clothes. I do not have a *mala* around my neck.

You tell me that I accept and approve sannyas for anyone without considering his or her worthiness. When existence itself accepts us all without any conditions, who am I to reject? There is only one way of being worthy of sannyas, that a person feels his unworthiness in total humility. This is the only way of being worthy.

If somebody says with folded hands, "I am worthy. Please give me sannyas," I will immediately say, "Goodbye, please forgive me." There is no need for a worthy person to become a sannyasin. And someone who thinks himself worthy will not attain sannyas because what sannyas requires is the flower of humility, of humbleness. It blossoms in humility. If you stand before existence with a certificate of worthiness, you will find the doors closed to you. The doors will open for one who stands at the doors with tears in his eyes and says, "I am unworthy. I am not worthy enough to ask for the doors to open, and yet I am trying. I have a great desire, a single-pointed thirst for truth, an intense longing to see reality."

It is enough for me that someone comes to me and expresses his or her desire to be a sannyasin. I never examine the worthiness of that person. Is his longing not enough? Are his keen thirst, his prayerfulness, and his request to be a sannyasin not enough? And what is the test of worthiness? What can anyone do except express his thirst or his prayerfulness? What can anyone do except surrender completely? Is any qualification or certificate required for surrender? Someone who is worthy cannot surrender because he thinks he has the right to receive sannyas. Only those who are fully aware of their unworthiness can surrender.

The doors of existence are always open for those who are helpless, inadequate, vulnerable, and unworthy – whose hearts are full of prayer. But those who are competent, certified, and worthy, hold degrees from Kashi, or are experts on the scriptures, are full of ego and vanity. They come with a list of fasts and disciplines observed. There is no greater disqualification for sannyas than ego and vanity. All those who consider themselves worthy are full of ego.

Only people who consider themselves unworthy are able to choose the path of humility, so I cannot question their worthiness. Moreover I am not their master, so who can inquire about their worthiness? They have come to me only with the intention to take me along as their witness. I shall say more about this…

According to me, sannyas is a direct relationship between an individual and existence. There cannot be any mediator. Sannyas is a direct surrender by an individual. When godliness surrounds you on all sides, there is no need for anyone to be a mediator between you. If a person wants to surrender to existence, he can. An unworthy person begins to be worthy by surrendering himself to existence. Moreover, worthiness begins with the determination, the surrender, and with the prayerfulness of the unworthy.

A sannyasin is not a self-realized person; he has simply become firmly determined to begin the journey toward self-realization. Sannyas is simply the starting point of that sacred journey, it is not the end. It is only the sacred beginning. It is a milestone on the way, it is not the destination. If one has already reached his destination, why should he go further? And how can someone who has not reached his destination show that he has reached it? The first step toward that destination happens when someone considers himself unworthy, and when that step is taken, it should be regarded as great worthiness. When a person dares to take that first step, he shows great determination.

I look at sannyas from a special point of view. According to me, sannyas is only remembering: "I now dedicate myself to the whole of existence. Now I dedicate myself to the search for truth. I am courageous enough to say that I shall try to live with a religious consciousness. These orange clothes which you see are to remind me that now I am not who I was." Even other people can remind them that now they no longer are what they used to be. Nobody can become a sannyasin by merely changing clothes, but a sannyasin can change his clothes. No one can become a sannyasin by hanging a *mala* around his neck, but a sannyasin can put on a *mala* and use it. The *mala* around his neck is a reminder of the transformation in his life.

When you go shopping in the market, you tie a knot at the end of your handkerchief or clothing. Whenever you touch the knot, you are at once reminded of what is to be bought. The knot is not the item itself, and it is also not certain that the one who tied the knot will definitely bring it. He can still forget what it is. He ties the knot and ninety times out of a hundred, he will bring home the item for which the knot was tied. These clothes, this *mala*, are only outward changes, they are not sannyas itself. It is just like tying a knot to remind yourself that you have begun the journey into sannyas. This is a remembrance, a very helpful reminder for your consciousness.

10

The Greatest Truth of Life

Question 1

Osho,

So that the disciplines of nonviolence, non-possessiveness, non-stealing, non-desire, and awareness come to fruition, and there can be development of the individual and society, what can be the contribution of neo-sannyas as proposed by you? Please explain this in detail.

Nonviolence, non-possessiveness, non-stealing, desirelessness, and awareness are the fundamental aims of the art of sannyas. Sannyas is an art, like life. Only sannyasins can be experts in the art of living; in fact the art of sannyas goes beyond life. Only those who can experience life in its totality are able to enter sannyas; it is the next step of life. Godliness is the peak which is reached by ascending the ladder of samsara, worldly life.

So the first point I would like to make clear is that there is no opposition, there is no conflict between worldly life and sannyas. They are two stopovers on the same journey. Sannyas evolves and blossoms in worldly life. There is no conflict between sannyas and samsara; on the contrary, sannyas is the fruit of a deep and wide experience of worldly life. In fact, the depth of sannyas is directly proportionate to the experiences of life. Only those who do not understand life, who cannot go deep into all the experiences of life, stay away from sannyas.

According to my view, the flowers of sannyas bloom in the midst of the world and go beyond; sannyas means going beyond worldly life. In his search for happiness, someone finds that he is going deeper and deeper into unhappiness. In spite of wishing or longing for peace, he finds anxiety. Running after wealth, he sees his inner poverty more solidly. His eyes open and he begins to look beyond the activities of his life.

Hence these five aims that we are discussing here, if understood properly, are the aims of sannyas. And for those whose eyes have not begun to look beyond the activities of their lives, these aims are not for them.

Some people have told me that they find this subject difficult to understand, that it goes way above their heads. My advice is to raise your heads. That will enable your raised eyes to look into the world of samsara, and these words will enter your heart. This subject is high rather than deep. In reality, the height itself becomes the depth. And what I am speaking of is not really high in itself: we feel the subject as high above us because we are standing so far down in worldly life. But the height is relative.

One more thing needs to be remembered: you do not need to rise beyond the world, but just to look above the world. There is no harm remaining in the world; then one is able to see the stars even while standing on earth. Remaining in the world, but with your eyes raised just a little, all these things will seem very easy.

Worldly life is bound to be complex and difficult because it results in nothing but unhappiness, ignorance, and darkness. Things appear to be one way, whereas in reality they are different. An illusion appears to be one thing but its reality is something else. But we are so lost in the world that we don't even imagine that there can be some other truth.

I have heard…

A man went to see the French novelist, Balzac. He began to talk with him about the characters in his novels. While discussing the characters, the talk shifted to other topics – political leaders and politics.

Balzac kept on talking for some time and then said, "Excuse me, let us come back to reality," and he began again to talk about the characters in his novels. To Balzac, the characters in his novels were reality, and the living characters on the stage of life were unreal. He said, "Let's leave these unreal subjects alone; we should get back to our talk about realities."

Balzac was a novelist, and to him the characters in his novels were true to life. We cannot see anything except this worldly existence in which we stand so deeply immersed. But it becomes unreal to those who raise their eyes and see beyond it. Sannyas means to raise your eyes. The world is not all; there is more beyond it. Sannyas is the search for what is seen beyond.

A few things will make this sannyas clearer. Sannyas is about to completely disappear from this earth because sannyasins so far have lived a life of renouncing the world. And now there is no future for this sannyas that lives by renouncing the world. Hence the sannyasin has disappeared from Russia, is being forced to disappear from China. Half of the world is without sannyasins. How long the remaining half can continue to live with sannyasins is difficult to say. If we fail to give a new dimension, a new meaning to sannyas, this century will perhaps be its last.

Why is sannyas disappearing? Until now, we have alienated it from the world, it was a hothouse plant, and so it is now unable to face the rough climate of the world. The society that had disconnected the sannyasin from the world is itself on the verge of disappearing. So now the system and tradition of sannyas created by that society cannot survive. If the society itself is changing, then its entire way of functioning and all its dimensions disappear. The societies in which there were kings and emperors are finished; those kings and emperors are no more. The poet who was nurtured in the courts of those kings and emperors has disappeared. The society which was there until yesterday, which has nurtured the sannyasin, is disappearing. That society is not going to survive and the sannyasin too will not be spared, if he cannot adapt to the new circumstances.

So, one thing that is very important in my view is to save sannyas. It represents the most fragrant quality of life. It is the greatest truth of life. So, it must now be linked with worldly life. A sannyasin cannot live now as an outsider in the world. He has to live in the midst of it, in the marketplace, in the shop, in the office; only then can sannyas survive. A sannyasin cannot live as an unproductive member of society. He has to be an integral part of the life around him. He cannot live as someone dependent on others. Now he will have to be self-reliant.

In my understanding, it is not necessary for someone to escape from the world, it is not that only then can the flower of sannyas blossom in his life. It is not essential. The truth is, the test of sannyas is in the midst of life: where life is a deep struggle, *there* is the joy of witnessing in sannyas. The fragrance of sannyas is only tested when its flowers bloom amid the foul odors of life. And the flower of sannyas can blossom in the world with great ease. Once we understand what sannyas is, there is no need to escape from the home, the family, the wife, the children, or work. A sannyas that can survive only by escaping is very weak: it cannot live long. Now a courageous sannyasin is needed, who can stand in the midst of life and yet be a sannyasin.

Wherever someone is, *there* is where he can be transformed. It is not the circumstances that matter but the mental attitude. Transformation comes from within and not from outside. The transformation is not of the relationships; rather it is of the person who relates.

A writer has narrated a small incident…

A man is on the point of death. His wife is beating her breast and weeping aloud; a doctor is standing near the bed. The man is respectable and famous, and a press reporter is standing there too, ready to send the news of his death to the paper. Along with the reporter, a painter is also present. He wants to see someone dying and to draw a painting of death.

The wife is weeping aloud. The doctor is standing dejected, crestfallen. For him, it is a professional defeat. He cannot save this man. The reporter is ready with his pen and notebook, to note down the time of death and then to hasten to the press office. The painter is standing there and thinking and observing.

Only one thing is happening in that room. A man is about to die, but it is not the same experience for the wife, the doctor, the reporter, or the painter. Four different events are taking place. To the wife, it is not simply somebody dying – she herself is dying. For her, this is not a scene happening outside, it is her very life. Now she can never be the same again. Something of herself will die, perish forever, and perhaps no new life will ever arise from it. It is not just her husband who is dying, a part of her heart is dying. She is completely one with the scene. The distance between the husband and wife is very small.

To the doctor, there is no death, no feeling of death inside him. He is sorry because he could not succeed in saving his patient. To the wife, something is dying in her heart; to the doctor, thoughts about the death are going on in his brain. He is wondering if the patient could have been saved if some other medicines had been given: "Have I made an error in the diagnosis? What should I do if another patient suffers from this same disease?" The doctor's heart is not at all affected by the death of the patient, but much activity is going on in his brain.

There is not that much activity in the reporter's brain. He keeps looking at his watch to note down the time of death and then to inform the office. There is nothing else going on. He is just working. He is standing faraway outside, with only a small connection. That connection is only that he has to report the news of this person's death. Then, after giving the news, he can go to a cafe or a hotel and have a cup of tea, or he may go to a cinema to watch a film. There the matter will end. The only relationship he has with the man is to see when he dies. He is just waiting for death to happen.

For the painter, whether the man is dying or not is unimportant. He is studying the darkness covering the man's face. He is waiting to observe the last flickering light of life on the man's face at the moment of death. He is watching the approaching darkness in the room. He is observing the shadow of death which has gripped the room from all sides. To him, the dying process is a play of colors which he examines because he wants to make a painting of death. He is totally an outsider; he has no other concern with this event. It does not make any difference to him whether the man dies, it makes no difference to him if the wife dies, or the doctor dies, or the reporter dies. Whether *A* or *B* or *C* or *D* dies does not matter to him. He is engrossed in catching the beauty of the colors of death; he has no relationship whatever with death itself.

There is only one situation, but four different mental attitudes. There could even be four thousand. Life is the same for someone living a mundane existence as for a sannyasin, but their mental attitudes are different. Whatever is happening continues to happen. The same shop will run, there will be the same wife, the same son, the same husband, but the mental attitude of the sannyasin is different. The sannyasin is trying to look at life from different viewpoints, different aspects. The mental attitude of the worldly man is quite different.

The world and sannyas are two different mental attitudes, so it is not necessary to escape from life, and it is not necessary to change the circumstances either. The amazing thing is that when your mental attitude changes, the circumstances are seen in a different way – because the circumstances take on the color of your mental attitude. Someone who escapes the world and becomes a sannyasin is still a worldly man because he still believes that a change of circumstances is the solution: "If I change the circumstances, everything will change." But no, he is a worldly man.

A sannyasin is one who says that if his mental attitude changes, everything changes. My emphasis is not on the circumstances at all, it is on the attitude of the mind. This kind of sannyas *can* be saved, and I want to emphasize that *this* sannyas is something worth saving.

The West has given science to the world; that is the West's contribution to humanity. The East has given sannyas; that is the East's contribution. It is the greatest thing that the East has given to the world, and the greatest people that it has given are Buddha, Mahavira, Krishna, Christ, and Mohammed. They all belong to the East; Christ too is not a man of the West. They are all people from Asia.

Perhaps you are not aware where this word Asia comes from. The word Asia originates from the word *asu* from the Babylonian language, which is almost six thousand years old. *Asu* means the place from where the sun rises. Japan is known as the land of the rising sun, and this is also the meaning of the word *Asia*. The world has received all its sannyasins from the lands of the rising sun. The opposite of *asu* is the word *ares*, an Assyrian word, from which the word *europe* originates. It means the place where the sun sets, the place of twilight, of darkness.

Just as science is the gift of the West – the countries where the sun sets – to the world, sannyas is the great gift of the East – the countries of the rising sun. The world has received two great gifts so far, and one is science. Naturally, science can only be born where the search is for the material. Naturally, sannyas can only be born where the search is for the immaterial. Science can only be found where one endeavors to go into the depths of matter. Sannyas can only be found where one endeavors to move into the depths of godliness. Those who want to fight with darkness will give birth to science, and those who love the light of the morning will set out on the search for godliness.

But sannyas, this contribution of the East, can be lost in the future because the kind of sannyas that existed up to now has lost its complete support system. It has to be saved. It *will* be saved, but not in the monasteries, in the forest, or in the Himalayas. The sannyasin in Tibet is also disappearing. Perhaps Tibet had the most profound sannyasins, but sannyas is disappearing there too; it will disappear, it cannot survive.

Now the sannyasin will survive in the factories, in the shops, in the marketplaces, in the schools, and in the universities. Now the sannyasin will have to be exactly where life is. There is no problem if the situation of the sannyasin changes, but sannyas itself should not disappear. That's why I'm in favor of an inward transformation of life itself into sannyas. An individual becomes a sannyasin wherever he is; he only changes his approach, his mental attitude.

Nonviolence becomes his mental attitude in place of violence, non-possessiveness becomes his understanding in place of possessiveness, non-theft becomes his bliss in place of theft. His vision goes toward non-desire instead of desire, and awareness becomes his discipline instead of non-awareness. Then his state of mind, wherever he is, is changed. And that changes everything.

Those whom I call sannyasins are not escapists from the world; they remain where they are. It's interesting that in the present situation it is easy to run away from the world, but very difficult to stay in the world and be a sannyasin. There is no problem in running away, but if a person is running a shoe shop and becomes a sannyasin, there are many difficulties. The shop is the same, the customers are the same, the seller and the buyer are the same; everything is the same. But the person who is running it has a totally changed state of mind. Everything else is old. He is filled with a longing to transform his mind, and it is very arduous to transform his mind in the middle of the same old surroundings. It is a profound spiritual discipline, and it is an amazing experience to pass through it. Remember, the cheaper you get sannyas, the less profound it is. The more you pay for it, the deeper it is. To remain a sannyasin in the world is a profound spiritual discipline. This is one point.

The second point is: up to now sannyas has been institutionalized. But sannyas can never be institutionalized and whenever that is done, all the beauties of sannyas, all the juice of sannyas, all its mysteries disappear. The moment sannyas is turned into an institution, it dies.

Sannyas is an individual experience; it flowers within each person individually, like love. No one can make love into an institution; love flowers and spreads between individuals. Similarly, sannyas is a love affair with existence; that also flowers and spreads in individuals.

Therefore there is no need for sannyas institutions; an institutionalized sannyasin is no longer a sannyasin. In fact, we create institutions for security, and a sannyasin is someone who has made the decision to live in insecurity, in danger. He is gathering the courage to live in insecurity. So in the future, sannyas cannot be tied down to any institution; it will be individual, it will be an individual joy.

Whenever sannyas becomes an institution, something very ugly becomes associated with it: there is an entrance into sannyas, but no exit. There is an entrance into the temple of sannyas, but no door to go out. And any place – even if it is a temple – which has only an entrance and no exit will very shortly turn into a prison. There is a bondage. That is why I leave the decision about sannyas up to the person himself. It is his choice whether he chooses sannyas or not. Later, if he wants to return to his original situation, original state of mind, then there should be no one in the world to condemn him. There is no reason for any condemnation; it was his personal matter, he made the decision and he can go back on it also.

This will have a double outcome. One, more and more people will be able to take sannyas. And later, if that decision doesn't suit them, they can go back to their old situations. And still later, if they feel that they have more courage and they want to experiment with sannyas again, they can return to it. When sannyas becomes institutionalized, a person is prevented from leaving it. And when he cannot leave, it becomes a prison for him. When he came into sannyas he didn't know much about it; most of it is known only when one is in it. And by the time he comes to know more about it, he has lost the freedom to leave. I know hundreds of sannyasins who are miserable because they cannot return to worldly life. Sannyas should not become a prison.

About this second point, I want to add something to the concept of the new type of sannyas. It has nothing to do with anyone else, nor should anyone else put pressure on any individual. It is his own understanding, his own insight. He can come in, he can go out at any time.

Along with this, I want to add one more point about periodical sannyas. I believe that no one should insist on lifelong sannyas. In fact, no decision about anything can be taken for a person's whole life. What can be guaranteed for tomorrow? What can one say about tomorrow? What seems right to you today may appear wrong tomorrow. If you take a decision now for your whole life, it means a less experienced person is taking a decision now for someone who will be more experienced in the future. After twenty years, you are more experienced; your decision of twenty years earlier will become a rock on the chest of the person you are twenty years later. A child's decision should not apply to someone who is now older. A ten-year-old child can take sannyas and the seventy-year-old man he becomes will repent for the rest of his life. No, there can be no lifelong sannyas. Everything in this life is only for this moment, and something as precious as sannyas can only be that.

A person enters sannyas to inquire into something, to know what it is, and if there is some juice in sannyas, then sannyas itself will keep him there. That is a different matter. But if he stays in it forcibly because of his former decision, that only shows that he has no trust in the beauty of sannyas. I believe that a person who enters sannyas will not leave, but that capacity has to be experienced within sannyas itself. It should not be only a vow, or a rule or law. A person should enter sannyas with the feeling that he is entering it in freedom: "If tomorrow I feel it was a mistake, it was a wrong decision, then I can leave it again."

Everyone has a right to learn from his errors. And we can learn only from errors. There is no other way of learning in this world. But if the error has to be turned into some kind of permanency, then he cannot learn from it. Then ignorance becomes enforced on the person instead of wisdom. That's why a lifelong sannyas might make a person more ignorant than wise.

There are two countries in the world where there are arrangements for periodical sannyas. Both lifelong and periodical sannyas are prevalent in Myanmar and Thailand. Anyone can take a vow of sannyas for three months of the year. So you will find hundreds of thousands of people in Myanmar who have been sannyasins, some for three months, some for six months, some for a year. And then, if it is convenient again in a few years, he can enter sannyas again for a few months.

If a person with forty-odd years of adult life experience becomes a sannyasin ten times, even for one month at a time, then at the time of his death he will not be like someone who has never tasted sannyas life. If a person becomes a sannyasin even for one month in a year, he will not go back as the same person he was, and the next eleven months will be quite different for him. After all, life is formed from what a person is inside. I believe it is not necessary to take a vow of sannyas for life. If it turns into a lifelong experience, that's a blessing. If it expands throughout one's whole life, that's by the grace of existence. But from one's own side, even a decision for one moment is enough. A decision for today is enough.

The third point is that up to now the various kinds of sannyas that existed in the world were all bound to one sect or another. So a sannyasin could never be free. Some sannyasins were Hindu, some Mohammedan, some Jaina, Buddhist or Christian. A sannyasin at least should belong only to religiousness. And that does not mean that he cannot go to a mosque or a temple. That is his choice. Whether he reads the Koran or the Gita is according to what he prefers. Whether he loves Jesus or Buddha is his personal matter. But the moment he becomes a sannyasin, he should not belong to any sect or religion; the moment he becomes a sannyasin, no particular religion is his. Rather, all religions are his.

So I want to add a third thing to sannyas: non-sectarianism. A sannyasin should be beyond sects. If we can create such a sannyasin in the world, who is not Christian, Hindu, Jaina or Buddhist, then we will easily be able to put the world on the path of religiousness. If sannyasins are no longer Hindu, Buddhist or Jaina, then so many causes which incite people against one another will collapse, and links to bridge people with each other will spread all over.

So I call a sannyasin only religious, not Hindu or Buddhist. He has no relationship with any religion because all religions are his. It's a different matter that if he loves the Gita, he reads the Gita. It's a different matter that if he loves Krishna, he sings songs of Krishna. It's a different matter if he loves Jesus and spends his nights in the church. This is a different matter altogether. These are his personal choices. But he is no longer a Christian, Jaina, Hindu or Buddhist. If a Hindu temple invites him, he goes there. If a mosque invites him, he stops by the mosque. Or if a church invites him, he becomes a guest at the church. If we can create even one or two hundred thousand of such sannyasins, who are beyond all religions on the earth, we will have taken the greatest step toward destroying all hatred and enmity between people.

I would like to divide this kind of sannyasin into three categories, which will make it easier for you to understand. Those who want to become sannyasins, leading their life where they are at present, should continue to stay and become sannyasins there. They have only to declare their sannyas to themselves and to the world. They can take a decision of sannyas as far as they themselves and the world are concerned. They don't have to make any change to where they are; they only need to start changing *what* they are.

But I meet many old people who are in difficulty in their homes because now they have no relationships there. The future generations have no interest in them; all the bridges between them are broken. These old people should certainly go to the ashrams, to the forests. Earlier on, there was such an arrangement in this country. After the collapse of that system, what we now call the generation gap was born. The generation gap is now found everywhere in the world. The old system in this country was that we would keep young people up to twenty-five years of age, as well as sannyasins after seventy-five years of age, in the forest.

The seventy-five-year-old sannyasins used to function as teachers and masters, and the young people were the students. That brought the new generation face-to-face with the old. A dialogue, a relationship would happen between the two. A seventy-five-year-old man would meet a young child and share with him what he has known and learned from life. There are many things which are not learned in universities. They can only be learned through life experience. Since we got the idea that all knowledge could be obtained in the universities, we have gained much knowledge but we have gradually lost wisdom. We can gain knowledge through universities, but not wisdom. Wisdom comes from the struggles and hits of life. It comes from living life itself.

So we used to bring our oldest people in contact with young children so that both generations, the coming one and the departing one, the setting sun and the rising sun, would meet each other – and what the setting sun found in its twelve-hour journey would be passed over to the rising sun. That relationship has been destroyed, and the results of that destruction are dangerous. The generation gap has increased; there is no dialogue between the old and the young, so neither do the children understand the language of the old people, nor do the old understand the language of the young. The old are angry with the young, and the young are laughing at the old – that is their way of expressing their anger. If there is no harmony in life and the generations face each other like enemies, then life becomes a chaos and loses all music.

So according to me there will be one kind of sannyasin that will live in the middle of his family responsibilities. But later on, many of them will no longer have those responsibilities. Many of them no longer have those responsibilities even today. Those who have no responsibilities become a burden on the family – because people who have always been active find it very difficult to remain idle. They start doing meaningless things that create disturbances in the world of the others. These old people should certainly move to the forest, leaving the crowd and marketplace behind. There they can meditate, they can search for godliness and also educate the children of the village who can come and sit with them for a few months or longer. My understanding is that it is these places that should become the universities. In this way, the older people can share all that they have known with the children.

There may be young people whose orientation means they simply do not want to be in the world. Then it is not necessary to force them to do that. There are lots of people whose journey of past lives has brought them to the point where marriage and family life make no sense to them. For them, worldly life has no meaning. Forcing such people into worldly life is as crazy as forcing someone who wants to marry and create a family into sannyas.

No, the people who have a natural fragrance of sannyas in their lives and want to live outside the marketplace should certainly move to the meditation universities. But those universities should be self-sufficient. They can be busy with agriculture or horticulture, they can run schools or factories or hospitals, but they should create something and live from that. These are the three categories of sannyas, and those who cannot be in any of these three can also do at least this much, that they go on a holiday from the world for two weeks every year to the forest universities.

The English word *holiday* is very beautiful; it doesn't mean vacation, it means a holy day. The Sunday, which is a holiday in the West, is a holy day because on that day even God stopped all work after creating the world. He rested on that day. For six days he created the world; on the seventh, he became a sannyasin! He rested on the seventh day.

Those who work six days should rest on the seventh; those who work the whole year around should go for a "holy day" for a month. They should forget the world, they should let go of the world. For a month, they should be submerged in some other journey. They should go back home after living in some forest university as a sannyasin for a month. Then they will return as different people; they will return a little more soulful, with some experience of the inner. The world will be the same, but their vision of it will have changed.

To me, this is the meaning of sannyas. It is an individual decision and choice. If such a sannyas can be spread all over the earth, then sannyas can be prevented from disappearing. Otherwise it will be very difficult for it to survive. The more emphatically communism will spread, the more the system of sannyas will be destroyed.

Today in China, wherever there used to be a statue of Buddha, they have been destroyed and replaced by a picture of Mao. The slogans seen on the school walls in China are strange. In one school it says, "A child who doesn't read Mao's little red book for one day loses his appetite, and a child who does not read it for two days cannot sleep. If he doesn't read it for three days he becomes sick, and not reading it for four days causes his life to become completely dark." There is nothing in Mao's book which any child in the world should read but this is what is being taught to the children.

A visitor in China was passing near a monastery situated on a mountain. He asked his guide, "Do monks live in that monastery?"

The guide said, "Excuse me, but you appear to be a very old-fashioned person. That is the office of the Communist Party. No monks live there anymore. They used to, but those days of exploitation are over. Now in China there is no place for those exploiters; now it is the Communist Party office."

Mao will be seated in place of Buddha, Communist Party offices will exist where monasteries used to be. There is nothing wrong in Communist Party offices, there is nothing wrong in a picture of Mao – but the world will lose a lot if they are put in places of meditation. Can Mao's height be compared to the height of Buddha? On one side is the bliss of Buddha's life, the compassion and love of Buddha's life, his heights, the nirvana that has descended on his consciousness, and each and every immortal word he says. Do you want to compare that with Mao? There is no comparison at all, there is no connection between them at all.

But this is what is happening, and it will happen all over the world. It is happening in Kolkata, it is happening in Mumbai. On the walls in Kolkata there are writings which say, "Chairman Mao is our chairman too." The distance between Kolkata and Mumbai is not so great, and I don't see much difference in the hands that are writing these things in Kolkata and the hands which could write them in Mumbai.

The flower of religiousness will disappear from the world if we want to stick to the old concept of sannyas. If we want to preserve the flower of religiousness, then it is necessary to give birth to a new concept of sannyas.

Question 2

Osho,

Beings like Mahavira reached enlightenment on their own, through constant seeking and searching rather than following anyone. This sounds very reasonable, and yet didn't Mahavira create an organization by creating a four-fold commune of men and women – sadhus, *sadhvis, shravakas*, and *shravikas*? Did not this commune become a direct following? What could Mahavira's intention have been? In the same way, isn't an organization of men and women sannyasins also being created near you? Please enlighten us briefly.

Words have their own journey. A word which had a particular meaning two thousand five hundred years ago may not have the same meaning today, and this creates a lot of misunderstanding. A tremendous change has taken place between what Mahavira called a commune and what we call a commune today. Mahavira did not name any organization or institution a commune. He called an assembly of similar-minded individuals a commune, people experiencing a similar kind of music. Mahavira was referring to a friendship of people, fellow travelers on a similar journey feeling a harmony.

To Mahavira, a commune did not mean an organization. An organization is always created against something or somebody, in opposition to something or somebody. An organization is created for protection against somebody or to attack them.

Mahavira had neither to protect himself against anybody nor to attack them. So a commune did not mean the same thing to Mahavira as it does to you. As far as you are concerned, you make an organization in the first place to protect yourselves or to attack. A Mohammedan says, "Get organized because Islam is in danger." A Hindu says, "Get organized because the Hindu religion is in danger." India says, "Get organized because China is going to attack." Pakistan says, "Get organized because India is an enemy in our very neighborhood." Mahavira had no one to attack or to protect himself from.

To Mahavira, a commune has a very different meaning. To Mahavira, a commune means a communion, a meeting place of like-minded individuals, fellow seekers, fellow travelers. There is no organization in it, there are none of the outer arrangements of an organization. It is just like music lovers in a village who sit together in the evening to play music. Someone plays the tabla, someone plays the harmonium; it is not an organization, it is a meeting, a coming together of like-minded people with similar interests. A few people in a village practice meditation. They sit down together in a room and surrender themselves at the feet of existence. There is no organization at all. It is simply a meeting, a coming together, not against somebody, not in favor of anybody.

For Mahavira, the meaning of commune is communion; a meeting circle for people who are on the same search, the same journey. Such a commune can be useful, not in the sense of an organization but in the sense of a merger, a unification. It can be useful, very useful, because in this world our life is always connected with everything all around us. If you are the only music lover in your village, and if someday ten musicians come and sit together in that village and sing and play music, everyone is all the more enriched; you become happier, more blissful.

I have heard that if a sitar is played in an empty room and there is another sitar lying in a corner, an expert sitar player can make the strings of the other sitar vibrate. Only one sitar is played, but its vibrations touch the strings of the idle one and make it vibrate. If ten people come together and practice meditation, and if one of them goes deeply into meditation, his awakened vibrations will arouse the dormant vibrations in the others. Therefore, a group meditation has its own usefulness, a group practice of devotion has its own usefulness, a community prayerfulness has its own usefulness. A group activity becomes very useful and meaningful for the people whose minds will be changed without effort.

The sanghas, the communes that Mahavira talks about, are meeting places of like-minded seekers. There, there is no place to be for or against someone; in that meeting, there is no other reason besides love.

And I believe that people who have love in their hearts should gather – after all, people with loving hearts do gather for bad things, so can't they gather for good? Thieves gather together, but it is difficult for good people to come together. Bad people gather together, but it seems difficult for good people to gather together. But a community of bad people is either for or against someone. A community of good people is not for or against someone; they simply meet for the joy of meeting.

It is not surprising that if only bad people come together, they become more powerful. There should be ways for good people to come together too. If the bad people of the village congregate and create a bad perception – if they collect in hotels, in clubs all around, if they pollute and cast a shadow on the village – and if there is no place for the good to meet from where they can create the perception of truth, of love, then this is harmful for the society.

Earlier, people met in temples or mosques. Earlier, temples or mosques were where such people met – and from there, pure vibrations were created and the call of the journey toward the ultimate truth. Even today we ring the bells in the temple, but no one hears them. Earlier they were a call to godliness, they were a source of remembrance, and sometimes they were a wakeup call. It was a reminder that there is some other search too. Even today, a call to prayer is being given in the mosques, but this only disturbs people's early morning sleep and nothing else. The person who gives the call is a professional; it is just a job for him to give the call to prayer in the morning. He too thinks, "Today the morning seems to have come early!" Today everything has become absurd.

What Mahavira was wishing for about such meeting is meaningful; it is not a commune in today's sense. In the language of the bad people, *commune* has one meaning; in the language of the good, it has a totally different meaning. If one understands this much there will be no problem. All that is best is produced by the greatest people like Mahavira, and it is unfortunate that people could not save it. They tried to save it in its purest form but things change. There is a reason for this. Mahavira lived for eighty years. What he contributed has fallen into the hands of others, who are not Mahaviras, who have no relationship at all with him, and who do not know at all of that peak of consciousness which was Mahavira's. Then people do what they want to do with what he left behind.

I have heard that Moses had a flute, and he used to go to a mountain sometimes to play it. Hearing it, the shepherds passing by on the path stopped to listen. The deer in the forest stopped moving, the birds became silent and gathered around him. After Moses' death, shepherds who had heard the music of that divine flute kept it under a tree and began to worship it. It was a bamboo flute.

After just one or two generations had elapsed, people began to say, "What is there in a simple bamboo flute? There should be something more to it for us to worship it." They gave it a covering of gold so that people could worship it.

After another generation or two people said, "What is there in this simple golden flute?" So they bought diamonds and jewels and encrusted the flute with them. But now no sound could be produced by it.

After some time an expert musician was passing by, and he said to someone, "I have heard that Moses' flute is being worshipped somewhere here. I would like to see it." When he went, the flute was not there. It was wrapped in a thick covering of gold, diamonds, and jewels. He blew into it from both ends. There was not even a hole in it for the sound to come out.

Mahavira's flute has also been distorted like that, Buddha's flute has been changed in the same way, and we have done the same to that of Jesus. The people who have taken possession of them have made them ugly. The responsibility for this ugliness is not Mahavira's, or Buddha's, or Krishna's. This ugliness is entirely due to us – it is our responsibility.

So if an individual like Mahavira was born today, he himself would have to speak against Mahavira. In order to destroy the image of Mahavira that we have created, he would have to speak against Mahavira – just as, if some expert musician came again, he would have to speak against the flute because it was not Moses' flute. If Jesus came again, he would have to speak against himself; he would not be able to recognize himself because of the distortion of his image that we have made. He would doubt even his own image, and whether he had come to this earth before.

Everything is distorted when it is handled by man, but there is no way out of it. We need to tell the lovers who gathered around Moses not to worship that flute but to learn to play it. It does not matter if they can't play like Moses but one thing will be certain – the flute will not get covered with gold and jewels. Then they can at least claim that it is not flute worship but real music coming out of it. This music can be produced only when the flute is hollow. If it is filled with gold, no music can come out of it.

If we do not worship Mahavira and Buddha, rather what has happened in the lives of Mahavira and Buddha, the heights that have been revealed in their lives, the Everest peaks that have touched their lives – if we too go in search of these small hills – then perhaps this distortion will not happen. But we are busy performing pujas and rituals, and they cause distortions. We not only destroy what we worship, but we cover it up with our own images and ideas and weave our own stories around it. Only then can we worship, otherwise not. The original slowly turns to ashes and loses all its individuality. But what can be done? This has kept on happening until today – perhaps it will continue to happen. This is unfortunate and should not be so! This is all very unfortunate; we helplessly continue our long-established habits.

Almost everybody in the world has Moses' flute, and no tune is coming out of it. Buddha used to tell people: "Don't worship me." Mahavira says: "You yourself are God." In saying these words he is emphasizing his teaching: "Don't worship me, worship yourself. You don't need to worship anyone else." Mahavira says: "Be independent, drop all dependency. Who are you depending upon? *You* are the one you are seeking." But we seek shelter in Mahavira. We say, "You showed us the way of nondependence, it was so good of you. At least now let us come to your feet." Buddha says: "Do not worship." We say, "We will not worship anyone, but you have spoken about such heights, at least allow us to worship you!" So we continue to worship Buddha.

This is the cause of all the fundamental mistakes of mankind. Until now, man has succeeded, and Buddha and Mahavira have been defeated. No one knows whether this will change in the future or not, but efforts to change it should continue. The efforts must continue, so that in future Mahavira and Buddha are not defeated; any individual who brings a message of godliness should fight against those past errors of mankind. It cannot be certain that people will believe them because nothing can be certain, but the efforts should continue.

Finally, no matter how much gold or how many jewels cover Moses' flute today, no matter how many errors mankind has committed up to this point, we can discover that flute hidden within.

If we remove all that has been attributed to Mahavira by his followers, remove all the coverings, if we cast away all the clothes that have been put on Buddha by his followers, we will see the real truth there even today. Those outer coverings of Mahavira and Buddha two thousand five hundred years ago have no value today.

You need to search for Buddha and Mahavira within yourself. And remember: "As long as I do not reach my inner Mahavira, I cannot recognize any Mahavira outside. As long as I do not reach the Krishna within me, no outer Krishna will have any meaning for me. As long as the Buddha is not awakened in me, no word of Buddha's can be a word of my language." If you can discover your own self, then you have found them all.

Question 3

Osho,

You have said that to steal masks, to make an effort to become like others, to become a disciple or follower, are all subtle forms of theft. Then, receiving inspiration from others, learning meditation, visiting awakened ones, are all these thefts too? If so, what is the right form of education?

You may go to those who know, but don't accept what they say they know. Search for it yourself. Do not make a belief out of what they know; turn it into an inquiry. Don't become a blind believer, open your eyes about it, make your own search. Inspiration does not mean to blindly accept the other person, inspiration means to accept the challenge that the other person presents.

If you approach Mahavira and are inspired by him, it does not mean that you should start trying to be like Mahavira. Inspiration from Mahavira means that if this knowing could arise in Mahavira, why could it not arise in you also? This is the challenge.

The English word *inspiration* is very important. It is necessary to pay attention to the *in*, in it. We always get inspiration from others, so the word is misunderstood. *Inspiration* means inner impulse. The other can be instrumental in this, but the other cannot become a support. The other can be a challenge; he cannot become a fixed rule. A lit lamp can become a source of information for an unlit lamp, which can also burn because it has a wick and it has oil. But if this burning lamp does not become a source of inspiration for the unlit lamp and simply becomes an object of worship and following, then even if the unlit lamp sits with its head bowed down at the feet of the burning lamp forever, nothing will come of it.

Inspiration means a challenge. Wherever inspiration is received, it should be a challenge for the seeker: "Why is this not happening within me? Why should what happened for one individual in this world not also happen within me? All the means are available in me. This heart is there, which could become Meera's songs. This intellect is there; it could become wisdom. This body is there, in which many others have attained godliness. These eyes are there, with which the unseen as well as the seen can be perceived. These ears are there, which can hear not only the outer but also the inner music that Kabir has heard. If Kabir could hear this inner music, why can't I?"

The meaning of *inspiration* is challenge. To find inspiration means to go in all directions, to search in all directions, to see those who have reached the highest peaks, those who have reached the depths, and to look beneath your own feet to see where you are standing. You too can reach those heights and those depths. That's all there is to the meaning of the word *inspiration*. If you put any additional meaning into it, it is no longer inspiration; it becomes following, copying. Then you will become a blind follower, not someone with eyes. It is absolutely essential not to become a blind follower. Such a person cannot search for godliness; he will always be groping about, following somebody and wandering here and there.

How can you find truth by following someone? Truth is within me, let it impact you. The impact can come from Mahavira, or

Buddha, or Krishna, or Christ – let it fall on you. Accept the challenge from wherever you find it and thank the person who gave you this challenge. But don't just learn what you have seen, discover what is possible within you.

Understand the difference between the two. Don't learn from others what has happened to them. Understand that whatever has taken place in them has the same potential to happen in you: "That seed is also in me; that is possible within me too."

Put a seed next to a big tree, and the seed is not in a position to know that such a big tree is lying hidden within it. But if the seed saw that tree and asked it, "Have you always been such a big tree?" the tree would reply, "I was a seed once, exactly like you. I also asked the same question. All the trees replied, 'We were as sweet and as small as you are now. All this greatness was hidden within. It has only manifested itself now.'"

Now the seed has been challenged and it will break open. But it cannot be exactly like the tree next to it. It will only be what it can be. It is possible that another kind of tree lies hidden in that seed. If you remember this much, then inspiration is not harmful, then it becomes helpful and fruitful. Then inspiration is not an enemy, it is a friend. Inspiration only appears to be coming from the outside but in fact, it comes from within. That is inspiration. It is an internal hit. It is a hit coming from something outside that arouses something asleep within you. Then for the first time you come to know that you too can find truth.

This remembrance is called inspiration. In this sense, you will have to learn, you should go on learning. But learning and believing are quite separate things. A seeker is one who desires to learn, who will not believe. He will search and search, and will continue not to believe until he has achieved. When the search begins, it will not be in search of belief but of knowing.

The meaning of learning, the meaning of *learning*, is not faith or blind belief; it means to find out. Learning means there is curiosity. It is a journey; it is the beginning, not the end. But after learning something, we stop. We say we have learned from the Gita, but what happens through learning from the Gita? You can learn the Gita, but you cannot be a Krishna by learning it. Even if you memorize the whole Gita, nothing will happen. One thing is quite certain, that Krishna did not memorize it, and if he had been asked to repeat it, he would have made many mistakes.

The Gita is a spontaneous flow, it is not something to remember. It is a stream which has sprung forth from Krishna. And what are you doing? You are turning it around. After reading Krishna's Gita, you should be filled with the desire for the day when your own Gita appears in your heart and pours out: "When will that day come when my own soul also becomes the Gita, when it becomes the celestial song?" You should only be filled with this remembering. Leave Krishna alone, leave his Gita alone, and start to search for your own spring.

One thing is certain: "If it can spring forth from Krishna, why should it not sprout in me? Existence is not biased in favor of anybody. If Krishna could produce a divine Gita, I can also produce one. If it arose from the music of his soul, if a celestial song arose, then it can also arise from the music of my soul."

But what about us? We are doing something quite different. We think that to learn the Gita is to memorize it. But the meaning of learning the Gita is simply this: now we have received a challenge. We will not be at ease until a Gita breaks forth from within us. There will be no rest until every word of our speech becomes the very word of existence itself.

You can learn it, cram it in; it is easy to memorize the Gita. To commit the Gita to memory is child's work, and the less intelligent a person, the easier and quicker it is for him to memorize it.

We need to know what right learning is. It is something other than simple memorizing. We need to understand the very experience through which Krishna has known. We don't want to learn what came out of Krishna's mouth. We don't need to learn what Krishna was wearing. What we need to understand is that our seeds can also sprout just as the seed within Krishna sprouted, blossomed, and became a tree. We need that same aspiration, that same longing to break open the seed. What we need from Krishna is the madness, the persistence, the firm determination to break open that seed. It can be learned from Buddha and Christ also. It can be learned in thousands of ways from all that is around us. And whoever is eager to know will be reminded even by the flowers blooming on a tree, by the stars shining in the sky, by the streams pouring from the earth, by all and everything.

I have heard…

Once a Sufi saint was passing through a town. It was evening and a child was going to a temple with a lamp. The saint stopped him and asked, "How did the light come to this lamp? Have you lit the lamp?"

The child replied "I lit it, but I don't know where the light came from." Then the child blew out the light and said, "It has disappeared in front of you. Now tell me, where has the light gone? It has disappeared before your very eyes, hasn't it? Only then will I be able to say where it came from; it had appeared in front of me."

The saint fell at the feet of the child and said he would not ask any wrong question from that day on, because it was foolishness to ask a question which he could not answer. He further asked the child to forgive him and declared that even he did not know where the light had gone.

Then he said, "Forget about the lamp; you did well in reminding me. I do not even know where the light burning within my own being comes from. I do not know where it will disappear when it is extinguished. Let me first know my own lamp, my own self, and then I can wonder about this worldly lamp." He learned something from this incident.

There was an old woman living in a Zen monastery. She told the master, "Realization has not happened yet. Teach me something more, something new." She had learned all the main principles, had learned the scriptures, but fulfillment had not come. So she urged the master to teach her more and more.

The master said, "You are not learning what is being taught all around you." Later, she was sitting under a tree and a dry leaf fell from the tree. This was enough for her, she began to dance and shout out what she had learned in the monastery.

The people asked, "Which scripture did you learn from? Please teach us; others are ready to learn."

She replied, "I did not learn from any scripture, I saw a dry leaf falling from a tree and my longing was fulfilled."

But the people said, "Oh mad woman, we have also seen many dry leaves falling from trees. How did that affect you?"

She said, "No sooner did a dry leaf fall from the tree than something within me also fell away and I understood that, if not today, then tomorrow I shall also fall just like this dry leaf. Then why should I be so pleased with myself, so proud, when I have to fall like a dry leaf? I saw the dry leaf dancing in the air, pushed to the east and to the west; the wind was pushing it around. It began to drift on the road. Not today, but on the day I call tomorrow, I will be reduced to ashes, and I will be pushed here and there by the currents of the wind. I will roam about like that dry leaf. From today the 'I' is not there. I have learned all of this from the dry leaf."

The meaning of this story is to keep our eyes open and to accept challenges. Let the challenges come. They come from all sides. A father gets them from his son, a son can get them from his father. They can come from a stranger walking on the road. They can come from a neighbor, they can come from anybody. We just need a mind eager to learn and to know the true meaning of learning.

But we have not understood the meaning of learning. We understand learning as memorizing. Our learning is intellectual, learning words, learning principles, memorizing. When someone is truly learning, he learns from every small aspect of his life, he learns with every little hair on his body, with every breath, with each throbbing of his heart. When our whole being is ready to learn, even a very small challenge thrills us, and our dormant life energy is aroused.

We have to prepare ourselves for this state. Those who are busy learning in a worthless manner have no time left, no interest left, and no place left in their minds. Everything is full. If you stand before God someday and ask him why you could not learn to know him, he will not say that you did not come to know him because you did not learn enough. He will say, "You learned so much that there was no place left for you to know me."

We have learned much, but what is worth learning has been left out. We have not learned to recognize a challenge. Religion is a challenge. If you learn to recognize a challenge, you will get it from anywhere. There are no royal roads for it; there are no hard and fast ways for it. The essence of life could break forth from anywhere. Life can take hold of you from anywhere. Keep the doors of your mind open. Keep on learning. Walking on the road, sleeping, getting up and sitting down, keep on accepting challenges. You may receive a deep hit someday, and the harp strings of your heart will begin to vibrate.

One more, last question:

Question 4

Osho,
You have said that an uncivilized man is able to change faces only with effort, whereas a civilized, educated man changes them easily. So the ability to change faces easily is a gift of civilization. In this regard, what subtle differences do you make between reaction and response? What are the keys for being free from reaction and attaining the ability to respond? Please explain briefly.

Generally we react, we retaliate. If someone insults us, we want to take revenge. We do not want to abuse, but something causes us to abuse and then we are slaves of someone else. If I wanted to make you angry, only a slight push is needed to arouse you. Anything which can be aroused in us by others is a sign of slavery – reaction is slavery. Someone praises us and we are tremendously pleased. Someone criticizes us and we feel dejected and lost. Someone says, "You are very beautiful" and we immediately become very beautiful. And someone says, "You are not at all beautiful," then we immediately become ugly. By ourselves we are nothing, just public opinion; we are what others think of us. We save newspaper cuttings to remember what people say about us. Why don't we stick them on our clothes? It could be considered a matter of great honor. All the time we are simply reacting. We do what others force us to do. We are not individuals.

We only begin to become individuals when we begin to respond. Response involves feeling. There is a great difference between response and reaction. For example, someone insults you; there will always be an urge in you to return the insult. But if you *respond*, it will be different.

A person insults you, and if you pity him you say to yourself, "Poor guy! I don't know what causes him to behave this way." This is a response. You have not reacted to his insults. You have continued to act according to your own views. Whatever arises in you is not a mechanical result of his insults, it is a conscious response. There is a great difference between these two actions.

When we press an electric switch, the fan begins to turn. The fan does not think whether to turn or not. When the switch is pressed it starts working; the switch is pressed again, it stops working. Likewise when you are insulted – the button is pushed – you become angry. You are praised – the button is pushed – the anger vanishes. So think about it: are you an individual or a machine? Your behavior is mechanical, your reaction is mechanical. Response is a sign of consciousness; it is a very great thing.

When Jesus was being crucified, he prayed to God in the last moments of his life. He asked God to forgive the people because they did not know what they were doing. This is response. This is a conscious reply. If someone is being crucified, he would not generally show this type of reaction. His reaction would be to abuse the executioners, to curse them, to curse them to destruction. He would pray, "Oh God, these people are crucifying your dear son. Burn them, throw them all in hell." This would be reaction; it is mechanical.

Jesus said, "Forgive them, for they know not what they are doing." This is response.

Anyone who wishes to enter the world of sadhana, of spiritual practice toward self-fulfillment, who wishes to travel the path of sannyas, should be constantly aware of his actions, and whether he is reacting or responding.

You are walking on a road and someone pushes you… Stop for a moment. What is the hurry to react? Stop for a moment and see whether the answer you were about to give was mechanical, or a conscious response. Then you will find yourself in difficulty. You will not be able to give a mechanical answer. Perhaps you will laugh and go on your way; you may not answer. But that will also be your answer. But we do not even give this much of a chance to ourselves. On one side, a button is pushed, on the other side there is a reaction. Or you get a push, and anger is the result. Somebody praises you, and immediately you get a swollen head.

There is an interesting joke about Bertrand Russell. It is said that the words, "Oh God," came out of his mouth at the time of his death. A priest was standing near his bed. He was very surprised. He had been nervous about going there because Bertrand Russell did not believe in God; so it was not possible to ask him to pray or confess.

He was standing there anxiously, but when he heard the words, "Oh God," from Russell's mouth at the time of death, he became a little bolder, and asked him, "Do you believe in God?"

Then Bertrand Russell opened his eyes and asked the priest who he was. He replied that he was a priest, and was afraid to ask him to repent or confess as he knew he did not believe in God.

Russell then told him, "It is not proper to ask a guest who has come to my house to go away so I shall repent." Russell said, "Oh God, if there is a God, please forgive my soul, if there is something like my soul."

Then the priest said, "What are you talking about?"

Russell replied, "I cannot do anything without thinking about it. I do not know if God exists or not, I do not know if there is a soul or not. At the most I can use *if* in my statement: if God is there, please forgive this Bertrand Russell, if Bertrand Russell is there."

He was not showing any reaction, even toward death. He was responding to his own death. He was not afraid, even at the moment of his death.

I have a friend who is an old thinker and a learned man. He always attends Krishnamurti's lectures. Once he told me, "All the mantras like Ram, om and such have disappeared from my mind."

I asked him, "Are you sure about this?"

He replied, "They have completely disappeared. There is no place left in my mind for all these things. I neither sing devotional songs nor repeat God's name – he has no name, so there cannot be any songs about him. I listen to Krishnamurti's lectures and have understood his views completely."

I thought, this is very good, but when he asserts so forcefully that he understands Krishnamurti completely, there must be some doubt within him. Again I said, "It is good that you have understood Krishnamurti's arguments."

After a couple of days he had a heart attack. His son sent me word that he was very anxious and that I should go and see him. I went there. His eyes were closed and he was repeating, "Ram, Ram."

I shook him and asked, "What are you doing?"

He opened his eyes and said, "I don't know. When I felt death was approaching, my mind said, 'Let go of Krishnamurti,' and then it was out of my control. Then 'Ram' began to come out of my mouth. I uttered the word. It was coming out by itself. It was simply happening."

The words "Ram, Ram" were coming out due to anxiety. This is called reaction. This man believes in God but he is reacting. Bertrand Russell does not believe in God and yet he is responding.

I believe Bertrand Russell will reach godliness someday. This other man will never arrive. This statement, "If there is a soul, if there is a God, he should pardon me," is a great statement, full of consciousness, a very conscious statement indeed. A person who uses *if* even in relation to the soul, who uses *if* even in relation to God at the time of his death, is giving a positive indication of himself as a man of consciousness. He is not anxious, he is not afraid of death. Whatever his consciousness is indicating, he is completely in tune with it. This is response. This is response; it is conscious. A mechanical response is not conscious, it is dead.

If you remember this difference between the two, you will be able to save yourself from reaction and grow toward response. And consciousness is produced, created, in your life when you begin to respond consciously. Full of consciousness, someday you will attain godliness.

I am grateful that you listened to me with such love and silence. Now to end, I bow down to the godliness that dwells in you all. Please accept my *pranam*, my offering of respect.

11

A New Energy Is Born, a New Life

Question 1

Osho,
What mental states determine the upward or downward movement of sex energy? Please shed some light on this.

Life can be viewed in two ways at all levels. Life has two aspects – one is material and the other is spiritual, so it is necessary to examine sex from both perspectives. One aspect of sex is biological, which is linked to the body and its cells. The other is of energy, of the soul, which is linked to the mind by consciousness. So it is necessary to comprehend these two aspects first. The first is biological energy, which is related to the cells which constitute the human body. These cells are part of the body.

This biological portion, which we call semen, the sex cells, can be seen with the naked eye. But there is another aspect behind it that is related to consciousness, to energy. I call this sex energy or soul energy, or it can be called whatever name we want to give it.

It is like a magnet. In a magnet there is a piece of iron which is seen by us and there is also a magnetic field on all its sides which is not seen. But if we place pieces of iron around it, the magnetic power draws them toward it. There is a field in which that power works. This iron will remain as iron even if it loses its magnetic power. There will be no difference in the weight of that piece of iron, there will not even be any difference in its constitution. There will be no difference in its form but it will have one fundamental difference – there will be no magnetic power in it, its power of attraction will have gone. I tell you this as an illustration.

The soul is a field, a magnetic field. The body is seen, but for the being, only the effects are seen, just as only the effects of the magnet are seen. This earth is visible, it is constantly pulling us, but the gravitational energy itself is not seen. If this pull of the earth leaves us, then we cannot be here even for one moment. The greatest difficulty for space travelers comes when their spaceship leaves the magnetic field of the earth and enters space, where there is no gravitation. Then they can wander here and there in their spaceship like currents of wind. If their belts are removed from their chairs, then just like gas-filled balloons touch the ceiling in a house, they will start touching the ceiling of the spaceship. The earth pulls us, but we do not know about it because it is not something which can be seen.

What is seen is the earth; what is not seen is its gravity. What is seen is the body; what is not seen is its energy. What is seen is the body; what is not seen is consciousness or the soul. In the same way, it is necessary to understand the two aspects of sex energy. What is seen are the biological cells, and what is not seen is their sex energy. If this fact is not understood correctly, it will be difficult to understand the deeper aspects.

Great experiments have been carried out on sex energy in this country. There is a very long history dating from prehistoric times. We have statues at Harappa and Mohenjo Daro, which are now in Pakistan, which tell us about highly developed systems of meditation. The statues of Harappa are nearly seven thousand years old. In this long history of seven thousand years, many rare experiments were conducted on sex energy, but we have not understood them correctly. We run into difficulties because we take sex energy to be biological energy.

The yogis of this country have said that sex energy can rise upward. But scientists say that when the body of a yogi is dissected, the semen cells are in the same place as in an ordinary man. Sex is not seen to be rising; it does not travel upward, it cannot. But we are not able to understand the rising of the sex energy: it is not a question of semen but of the invisible energy which is linked with it which can travel upward. When someone is engaged in sexual intercourse, the semen leaves his body and along with it, his sex energy leaves his body. His sex energy vanishes into space. And the semen travels on to give birth to a new life.

Two events take place at the time of sexual intercourse – one is biological and the other is psychic. The event taking place on the biological level, which the biologists are studying, is the ejaculation of the semen. The semen travels in search of the female egg to give birth to a new life. There is also another event, which meditation investigates: the energy of consciousness is released at the time of sexual intercourse. It simply vanishes into space, but there are ways and methods to bring this energy of consciousness upward. In no way should this be confused with the biological aspect of sex. The semen cannot move upward. Semen has no means to reach the *sahasrar*, the highest center, the highest levels of existence. What rises is the energy, the magnetic force. When this magnetic force goes downward, the semen becomes active.

A child is born with all its sexual inheritance. A female child is born with all the sex cells which she will use in her life. Thereafter no new cells are born. A one-day old girl has up to three million very minute eggs. Out of these, about two hundred at the most will become alive and reach the womb. From among them, twenty at the most will become active and can be fertilized. Until the age of thirteen or fourteen they remain dormant. Then, when the brain is fully developed, it releases the sex hormones and activates the sexual functions.

On the other hand when a woman reaches the age of forty or fifty, the biological function of sex is finished for her. But the energy from her mind still continues to descend. A woman of seventy can have sexual desire but now her sex has no biological significance.

Even in a man of ninety, sexual energy can descend from his mind to his body. Even though his body is not fit from the biological point of view, his mind can still harass him with thoughts of sexual pleasure.

I am saying this so that we can understand that until thirteen or fourteen years of age, as long as the information is not received from the mind – and now even the biologists are accepting, they too are accepting that until the body receives an order from the mind – until then, the sexual organ does not become active.

Hence, if we cut out some parts of the brain, then a person's sexual life will finish forever. Alternately, if some part of the brain is injected with hormones making it ready to give orders to the body, then even a seven year old boy or a five year old girl's sexual organ can be activated. If we were to inject an old man with semen, then he would be able to impregnate even at eighty years of age. If we were to put an egg into the ovary of a ninety year old woman, then too it could be fertilized – because the sexual energy is still flowing; only its bodily part has become nonfunctioning.

Sex energy is infinite. Mahavira has named it infinite energy. In fact, Mahavira got his name from this. Mahavira got his name from this. He called it infinite vitality – not in the sense of biological energy or semen. Infinite vitality means sex energy that continually descends from the mind to the body. The energy that descends from the mind to the body does not come from the mind. It comes from the soul to the mind and from the mind to the body. It will descend from the soul to the mind and then descend from the mind to the body. These are its stages, without which it cannot descend. If the mind is disconnected from body and soul in the middle, the connection will be broken. This sexual energy, the power which I call sex energy, then is the same as in the yogic and tantric texts, which describe mystical formulas for the attainment of supernatural powers – it is not biological sex energy.

This sex energy can rise upward. If it were to move upward even in an old man, his life would become as innocent and simple as that of a small child. That innocence would shine in his eyes again.

The innocence and simplicity which are found in a child would return to his personality, perhaps even more so. The simplicity of a child is full of danger because it is going to disappear. Behind a child's simplicity there is a live volcano ready to erupt, and it will erupt soon. But if the sex energy of an old man comes back, his life will be even fuller of innocence than that of a child. This is saintliness, this innocence is saintliness. This upward rise of sexual energy is the journey to saintliness.

Sexual energy is directed by the mind, and is firmly controlled by the mind. It does not flow downward without instruction from the mind. If the mind can control the flow of this sexual energy, it can also control sexual desire accordingly. If it is allowed to flow more, it will increase and vice versa.

During the last twenty years in America, the age of puberty for boys and girls has gone down by two years. Whereas earlier girls were sexually mature by the age of thirteen, now they mature at eleven. This is because the American mind has exerted so much pressure from so many directions to send signals to the sex center. It is the most natural course of events in these circumstances. It may go down from eleven to nine years, even down to seven or five.

All around, we fill the atmosphere with sexuality; all around, there is nothing else to attract besides sex. Everything has become a sex symbol. Sex is being exploited to sell anything from cars to cigarettes, with pictures of half-naked women. All this has a terrible effect on the mind; it starts giving out instructions to the body two years early. This is premature and the results are bound to be dangerous.

Quite the reverse has happened in India. We were successful in keeping young boys and girls totally untouched by the world of sexuality until the age of twenty-five. But the whole framework was just the opposite, the whole system was different. Measures and arrangements were in place so that the mind should not issue commands in that direction. Certain exercises were used, various body postures were used, and different meditations, thought processes, and methods of contemplation were used, to create resolve and willpower to prevent the mind from issuing commands to the sex center.

If someone could prevent his sex energy from moving downward until the age of twenty-five, he would experience so much bliss that in the future, upon becoming sexually active, he would be able to make a comparison. He would realize that there is a fundamental difference between the bliss he experienced before and after entering the world of sexuality. His mind would continually want to return to the old experience. So someone who lived a celibate life up to the age of twenty-five would be drawn toward sannyas by the age of fifty because he had the opportunity to compare.

Talking about the joys of celibacy makes no sense to anybody today because they know nothing about the bliss of celibacy. People have experienced only one kind of joy, that which they get from sex. Hence to talk about celibacy seems absolutely worthless to them. Being without desire is not a part of their experience. This is unfortunate because once the energy has started to flow downward, it becomes difficult to make it rise upward. Tracks are created. If you spill a glass of water on the floor, the water will run off leaving a track behind it. In the heat that water will evaporate; no water will be left on the floor but a dry track will remain. If you throw water onto the floor again there is a ninety-nine percent chance that the water will flow along that dried-up track.

It is natural to follow the path of least resistance. There is a desire to flow in the direction of the least amount of resistance. When an immature mind enters the world of sex, the life energy is eager to flow downward, according to the law of least resistance. There is pain and uneasiness in the mind as long as the sexual energy is not released. When it is released, the mind is relaxed. It feels as if it has become light and has been freed from a burden. But once the upward path is traveled, we experience this freedom all the time. It is necessary to understand three things in relation to how the mind can methodically divert the sex energy upward.

The first thing to understand is that anything which can go down can also go up. It is a scientific principle that anything which has the possibility to go down will also have the possibility to go up, whether we know it or not. If we travel down a road, we can also travel up it. The road is the same – just the direction is changed.

You have come here from your home on one road and you will take the same road to go home. Then, your back was toward your home, now your face will be toward your home. There is no door that allows you outside that does not let you in. Life expands in two dimensions. So, if energy can go downward, it is also able to rise upward. This first principle has to be understood very clearly in your mind because the mind wants to do only that which is possible. The mind drops any search for the impossible. It needs to clearly understand that this is possible: it *is* possible.

If water flows from a mountain, it usually flows down the mountain, it does not flow up to the top. For thousands of years we did not know how to take it to the top. But anything that can come down can also go up and now it can also be sent to the top of the mountain. It can be lifted by methods that counter the law that makes it flow downward.

Sex energy moves downward, it is natural. It comes from nature. If anyone wants to move it upward, it will not be easy or natural. This cannot be done naturally; it can only be achieved by a firm resolve, through will. It can be achieved through man's efforts, by his keen desire, his longing, and his hard work. He will have to work hard in this case, because he will have to swim against the natural current.

If you want to float down the river toward the sea you don't have to swim at all. You only have to float, keeping your arms and legs still. The river itself will take you to the sea. But if you want to go to the source of the river, to the place of its origin, you will have to swim, to work hard because there will be a fight against the natural flow of the river.

Those who want to rise, to lead a higher life, should understand the next point. They will need a firm resolve; the way will be full of conflicts. One can move upward, and the joys of the journey are beyond words. Because if by flowing downward one finds happiness – although momentarily, but one finds it – then what one can achieve by moving upward is beyond imagination.

What the sexual energy brings by flowing downward is called happiness and what the same energy brings by rising upward is bliss. Whatever the sexual energy brings by moving downward is momentary because that phenomenon is temporary. The phenomenon of losing has to be momentary, whereas the phenomenon of gathering can be eternal. By moving downward you lose; so the phenomenon of losing is temporary. It seems that the moment of losing is the only moment there is. But higher up, you accumulate; higher up, reservoirs are created. This reservoir can be infinite. It goes on increasing every day.

As soon as you achieve pleasure, it starts decreasing. When you find bliss, it keeps on increasing. With pleasure, as it begins to decrease, unhappiness begins to rise. So behind all pleasure stands the shadow of unhappiness. But with bliss, there is an ever brighter world of bliss beyond bliss, with no shadow of unhappiness following behind. The bliss accumulates because it grows by the day, becomes deeper, with the potential to create an infinite reserve.

I also mentioned resolve and conflict. It will be useful here to understand what resolve means and how that energy can rise upward with determination. I shall give two or three illustrations through which you can understand it fully.

The Mohammedans observe fasting; the Jainas, the Hindus, and the Christians also observe fasts. Yesterday a friend was asking me the meaning of observing a fast. What happens by staying hungry? Nothing ever happens by staying hungry. Nothing *can* happen by staying hungry. The people who started these practices were not fools. I am not saying this to the people who are practicing it because most of them must be fools, since they know nothing about what they are doing. But the people who started these practices were not fools. The need for food is the greatest of all needs in a person's life, it is the most important requirement for survival.

A man can give up love, or a mother can kill her own child to get food. During the Bengal famine, many mothers sold their children. A husband can kill his wife, can sell her, and a wife can get rid of her husband. When death threatens, the need to save oneself, the instinct for survival becomes very powerful. Other things can be replaced, but not one's life. A woman can find a second husband, another son can be born, but you cannot replace yourself. So food is the greatest need for survival.

If a man fasts, he will think of food twenty-four hours a day. Every cell in his body will demand food. Twenty-four hours it will demand food. Awake or in his dreams, he will be longing for food. A place inside is empty; a biological gap is created within. The body demands food and he is busy praying to God. The body is crying loudly for food, and he is praying loudly to God. In a short time, in two or three days' time, the body's keen desire for food will be converted into a thirst for God.

The demand of the body is for food, and if the body does not yield to it and goes on insisting that it is God, not food that is required, then within four to six days the body will begin to cry loudly for God instead of food. A metamorphosis has taken place. Energy which was demanding food is now demanding God. Thus the strong resolve for food is now turned toward God.

This is a great metamorphosis. Determination leads to a transformation of energies. When the mind demands sex, when it demands the other, the opposite, a woman, a man… When the mind wants to flow toward the other, you will have to transform this energy. You will have to adopt the opposite process, so that the longing of the mind becomes a longing for liberation.

Two or three things need to be kept in mind. As soon as the mind desires sexual pleasure, the body begins to make preparations for it. A demand for the other is triggered at the sex center, the *muladhar*, and the sex center becomes other-oriented.

Tantra says that if the sex center turns inward in this moment – it has been called the sex mudra – then within moments you will find that the body has stopped demanding sex. But because the demand has arisen anyway – the energy has arisen, and now the body's demand has dropped – this same energy can be taken upward. The moment we think of sex, the attention of our mind begins flowing toward the sex organs. The moment the sex organs are physically contracted inward, as in the sex mudra, all outlets for sexual energy are closed.

When the energy has already been awakened, your eyes should be closed. Then the eyes should begin to look at the head from within, just as you see a ceiling from within a room. With constant practice, within a month you will experience that something has started to rise from below. Some call it kundalini, some give it another name.

Pay attention to two points here. One is the *muladhar* and the other is the upper center, *sahasrar*. The *sahasrar* is our highest center and the *muladhar* is our lowest center. The *muladhar* is contracted inward, and the energy created in it tries to find a way out. Now direct the mind to the higher level because that path is open. The energy of the body starts to flow in the direction that the mind is showing. This is a process of transformation. If you experiment with this, celibacy can be achieved without suppression.

This is not suppression, it is sublimation. Suppression means that the upward path is not open and you are guarding the door at the lower level, keeping it in check. Then the result will be a troubled madness, perversion. If the path is there for the energy to flow, there will be no suppression, only sublimation. The energy from below will begin to flow upward.

This is something practical that I have told you about: do the experiment and grasp its significance. This is not theoretical, nor is it intellectual or scientific. It is experienced by millions of people, and it is an easy experiment. And as the flowers of joy and bliss begin to blossom in the higher regions of your brain, sex will begin to disappear from your life. It will disappear slowly and a new energy will be born, a new vigor, a new splendor, a new light, and a new life.

It has nothing to do with physiology. If you dissect the body, the rising energy will not be seen; it is like a magnetic field. Even if you cut into the bones, no clue will be found anywhere. It is not at a physical level, like pain; it is psychic. It takes place in the mind and at the level of the body, but it does happen. With the downward movement of that energy, semen will be expressed. If it does not flow downward, semen will also cease flowing.

It will certainly preserve the body, but this experiment is not meant for the preservation of the body; the body is limited by age and it will pass away. It will not affect the aging process in any way. The experience is a psychic event. The individual begins to expand, to spread, to be enormous, in proportion to the psychic energy he has.

The day when not a single particle of psychic energy flows downward, such a person can declare, "I am *brahman*." The statement "I am *brahman*," is not a logical conclusion, it is an existential conclusion. It is an individual experience. When you are connected with the vastness of existence, you feel you are not an individual but existence itself. But this experience only happens through the preservation of that enormous energy. And this preservation is impossible if the sex energy does not flow upward.

Question 2

Osho,

You have said that by living in the present, moment to moment, sex energy starts being accumulated and rises upward; but by thinking of the past and future, it starts dissipating and moving downward. What are the different processes that happen in these two situations? Please explain the science of this.

Life is here and now, in each moment, but man's mind is thinking of the past and of the future. When the mind is thinking of sex, it is thinking of those sexual experiences which have already happened in the past, or is imagining those which may or will happen, or which are longed for. When the mind is occupied like this, lost in the past and future, the semen is not affected but the psychic energy I talked about is destroyed. Semen will certainly be destroyed in lovemaking, but psychic energy is destroyed even while thinking, so just thinking of sex or imagining it directs the energy downward. By simply thinking about the sexual pleasures of past and future, not a particle of energy will be lost by the body, but it is enough to destroy the psychic energy. The mental, psychic energy is bound to be destroyed – and this is real energy.

In sexual intercourse only a few of the body's cells are lost, but in this cerebral sex, enormous mental energy is lost. One day the body will die, it is not worth thinking about, but the important question is of this mental energy, which remains with you into your next birth. That is why I said that whoever lives from moment to moment, not thinking of the sexual pleasures of the past or the future, whoever really lives from moment to moment preserves this mental energy.

One more interesting thing to remember: if you worry less about the past and the future, only concern yourself with what is right in front of you, plunge yourself deep into it and live it, there will be less tension in your life. The less the tension, the less will be the need for sex. The more the tension, the more is the need for sex because then sex begins to work as a relief. It functions to dilute the tensions. So a person is as sexual as he is anxious. The more anxious and worried a society, the more sexual it becomes – as is the case today in Europe and America. The more anxious you are, the more full of sexuality your whole life becomes. The more carefree you are, the less you need sex, because so much tension does not accumulate that you have to lighten it by throwing energy out of your body.

Worrying too much about the past and the future creates tension. Living in the present makes one free of tension. Be a person who, when he digs a hole in the garden, just digs a hole; when he eats, he is engrossed in eating; when he sleeps, he just sleeps; when he's in the office, he is only in the office; when he is at home, he is at home. Whoever he meets, he only meets, whoever he leaves, he leaves.

There is so little burden on the mind of someone who lives without carrying too much past and present that every day his need for sex is reduced. I say this for two reasons: one, by thinking about sex our mental sex energy is dissipated. Secondly, tension accumulates when we are occupied with the past and future – and when tension accumulates, our body inevitably has to lower its energy. Because the relaxation that we feel when our energy is low gives a feeling of rest, we think that this relaxation is rest. When we lie down completely exhausted, we think we are resting. If one is tired and totally exhausted then one feels like sleeping, as now there is nothing to worry about. Energy is needed even to worry. But worrying is an energy that becomes a whirlpool and has started causing us pain. Now that energy will have to be thrown out; we are continuously throwing it out. And we know of only one way in which energy can be thrown out – we have no idea of how the energy can rise upward. There is an established way for energy to move downward.

So, someone who does not worry does not stay lost in memories of the past, does not stay lost in future imagination, but lives here and now in the present. This does not mean that if you want to catch a train tomorrow you will not buy a ticket today. To buy a ticket for tomorrow is a job that needs to be done today. But to travel today in tomorrow's train is dangerous! And sitting today in tomorrow's train, imagining all the difficulties that will come and everything that is going to happen – getting lost in this thinking – is dangerous.

No, sex itself is not as bad as thinking about sex. Sex can be easy and natural but thinking about it too often is unnatural, it is a perversion. A man keeps thinking, thinking, and thinking; he is making plans, twenty four hours a day he is thinking about it. After examining the experience of thousands of people, psychoanalysts tell us that man is too interested in mental sex, and he does not derive any pleasure from actual sexual activity. The sex that is going on in the mind seems more interesting and colorful. If sex is perverted in the mind like this, confusion will be created within.

Thinking about sex is not the function of the mind. Gurdjieff used to say that someone who uses the mind to do the work of the sex center destroys his intelligence. It is bound to be so because the functions of the two are so different. It is as if you try to eat food with your ear; your ear will certainly be damaged, and the food will also not reach the stomach. There will be a double catastrophe.

There is a center for everything in our body. The sex center is not in the mind, it is at the *muladhar*, the lowest energy center. Let the sex center do its work, and the mind, the consciousness, its own; otherwise the mind will become obsessed with sex. That is why man already seems obsessed. He looks at nude photographs but the *muladhar* has no connection with them – it has no eyes. He looks at nude photographs and thinks about them in his mind. He plans and imagines, and creates colorful images. All these together create confusion in his centers. His mind starts doing the work of the *muladhar*, but the *muladhar* has no connection with such work and remains unfulfilled. His intelligence will be spoiled, and his mind will become confused and insane.

Ninety percent of the people in lunatic asylums are there because their minds are attempting to perform the functions of their sex center. If we look into it, we will find that ninety percent of the people outside lunatic asylums are also mad, and all due to sexual perversion. If we look at their poems, their photographs, their novels, their films, we will find that they are all polluted with sex. This is nothing but madness.

If animals could know about us, they would laugh at the human condition. And if they read our poems, even the poems of Kalidas, they would be very puzzled and wonder – what is the need for all this, what do these poems mean? If they could see our paintings, even if they are by Picasso, they would fail to understand their purpose and meaning. What is the need of so many paintings showing women's breasts? What is the purpose? Man has certainly gone mad. He has gone mad because his intellect is doing the work of the sex center. Then there is no time left for the intellect to do the work which it should be doing.

The intellect could be moving toward godliness, but it is doing the work of the sex center. Consciousness could be living at the highest level, and it is wandering around with sex images.

Hence I say, do not think of the past and do not think of the future. Do not think about sex at all. Live in the present, and allow sex to come, if only for a moment – do not be afraid of it. But remember also what I told you about the transformation of sex; then that energy will begin its upward movement. Nothing is more blessed in life than that upward journey.

Question 3

Osho,

You said that in any action which is total, no energy is lost. What do you mean by total action? What does it mean to be total in sexual intercourse, and what is the meaning of energy not being lost in it?

When a deed is total, when an action is total, energy does not diminish. In any action that it is complete, energy does not diminish. When I said that, I meant that action is not total when we are split, divided, and in conflict.

When I am split within, my action is partial – not total. For example, you meet me and I embrace you. If in the moment of embracing, one part of my mind says, "Why are you doing this? This is not proper, don't do it," and at the same time, another part says, "I want to do this, it feels very good," then I am split between the two parts. I am embracing you with one half, and I am rejecting you with the other half. I am doing two opposing actions at the same time and in so doing, my mental energy is diminished. But if I were to embrace somebody with all my heart, with no trace of regret, there would be no reason for my energy to diminish. On the contrary, this total embrace would fill me with more energy, would fill me with extra bliss.

Energy is diminished in conflict. Inner conflict, inner duality causes a loss of energy. However worthy the work you are doing may be, if there is conflict within, your energy is bound to diminish because you are fighting with yourself inside. It is like building a house, in which I lay a brick with one hand and remove it with the other. My energy will be lost, and the building will never be constructed.

All of us are split into self-contradictory parts like this. Whatever we do is confronted with opposition. If we love someone, we hate him also. If we make friends with someone, we make an enemy of him also. If we flatter someone, we also manage to show disrespect at the same time. We are constantly two-faced, so everyone becomes slowly bankrupt of his inner energy as it diminishes. Everyone dies fighting against himself.

If we look into the truth of this, we will understand. When we start any work, if we are fully engrossed in it we always come out more fresh and energetic. On the other hand, if we do it half-heartedly, we will end up tired and shattered from the same work. Whoever can do his work wholeheartedly never gets tired, like a painter totally engrossed in his painting, in creating his picture. He returns from his work completely refreshed and satisfied. But if this same painter is employed on a fixed salary to produce paintings, he goes home completely tired because his mind has not been totally there in the job. No sooner does a part of our mind oppose us than our energy begins to diminish.

What I mean by total action does not only apply to a particular type of work, it applies to everything you do. Be total even in routine activities like eating and bathing. While taking a bath, just be with the act of bathing in that moment, your mind thinking of nothing else. If you are totally involved in the bathing, not only your body but also your soul will take a bath. After the bath you will realize that you have gained something. But it is possible that when you are taking a bath, your legs are running on the road, and your mind is in the office. Then there is no bliss and joy in your bathing. It will be split, a divided activity. You will simply throw water on your body and run to the next activity. Completing a task in this way, you waste your energy – and this is happening every moment, twenty-four hours a day.

You are lying on your bed, but you haven't slept. You can rest only if the act of sleeping is total. You are simply lying and dreaming, lying and thinking, lying and changing sides. Thousands of thoughts enter your head; you are thinking of what you did today and what you will do tomorrow. In this condition you will get up completely tired, exhausted in the morning. Even sleep will not give you rest because you are not total in that sleep. Hence sleep is disturbed, sleep is decreasing.

One of the most puzzling problems of the future world will be about sleep. It decreases by the day. It is going to decrease – even disappear, because you can sleep only if you sleep totally. But we are split personalities twenty-four hours a day; how can we be united and total in sleep when we are split in everything else? Night and day are a pair, they are linked. At night in sleep we will be in the same condition as we are during the day. And tomorrow will be an extension of today. Then our life becomes completely shattered. We cannot live a normal life.

A friend was brought to me recently. The people who brought him told me that he had already tried to commit suicide five times. I said, "This is amazing, it seems he has not tried hard enough." It is difficult to believe that someone could still be alive after trying to commit suicide five times. If someone lives totally, what is the need to die, to commit suicide? This man already tried to die five times. I told him, "You should be ashamed of yourself, now don't try it again. Five times is quite enough."

But what does that mean, to attempt suicide five times and fail? It means that one part was trying to save himself while he was trying to die. Otherwise who else could stop him from ending his life? When honesty is not there even in dying, how can it be there in living? When there is no honesty even in dying, there cannot be any honesty in living. His life will be one of total dishonesty. So I told him he should be ashamed of himself; he should have died at the very first attempt. And he was brought to me after he had tried for the fifth time. I told him not to try anymore; he would be judged severely.

He was very surprised as he had thought that I would persuade him not to commit suicide. He said, "What kind of man are you? Everyone I was taken to persuaded me that suicide was a very bad thing to do."

I said, "I do not call it bad, I say to do anything halfheartedly or incompletely is bad. If you want to do something, do it totally."

He went on staring at me for some time, then said, "I don't want to commit suicide, I want to live but on my conditions. If they are not accepted, I will commit suicide." So he wants to live but on his own conditions. If he lives, he lives as if dead, and when he dies, he will die a miserable death, all the while wishing to live. Whoever cannot live fully cannot die fully. He will be a shattered person.

We all belong to this category. There is not much difference in any of us; we are doing the same thing. We say we love someone – but we do not love them because in the morning we think of divorce. Then again we ask for forgiveness and in the afternoon we regret it. We say sorry in the evening and think of divorce in the morning.

I was staying at a house. The husband and wife kept their divorce application ready, only it was not signed. I saw it with my own eyes. The husband told me many times that the situation would become so bad that he would think of putting his signature to it. He was fully prepared for that. I told him, "There is no harm if you sign it, but to keep the application ready is very dangerous. Is there any meaning in calling that woman your wife when you are prepared for divorce? This has no meaning at all. She is still your wife." He said that the application had been ready for the last seven years. There was nothing new about it.

This conflict of living half-heartedly, I call a discharge of energy. It causes a wastage of energy. In this way we never achieve anything. I will tell you a small story to explain my point.

I have heard…

There was a very famous swordsman, a samurai, in Japan. There was no one to compare with him in swordsmanship, and his fame reached many faraway countries. One day he learned that his watchman had fallen in love with his wife. He arrested both of them.

He was the chief samurai and he told the watchman, "My mind tells me to cut your throat, but you have also made love to my wife, so it would be proper for us to fight a duel with swords. Whoever survives will get my wife."

The watchman said, "Why do you want to play this game? You can cut my throat even without a duel. My throat will be cut anyway because I don't know how to handle a sword, and there is hardly another man in this world who is as good a swordsman as you. Why do you unnecessarily mock and make fun of me by giving me the chance to fight you with a sword?"

But the samurai said, "It would spoil my good name. It would be said that I cut your throat without giving you an opportunity to challenge me, so take your sword and come to the field." The watchman had no choice; the poor fellow took a sword and proceeded nervously to the field.

The whole town was gathered there; the news had spread. They knew the watchman would be killed because it was difficult to ward off even one stroke of the samurai, since he was such an expert swordsman. But the situation was reversed: when the watchman started to fight with the sword, the samurai began to lose courage because the man was handling his sword in such an awkward manner. He did not know how to handle it. It was difficult to fight him; he just waved his sword around with such unbelievable totality because it was a question of life and death for him.

It was just play for the samurai. He expected to cut the watchman's throat in no time. But for the watchman it was a question of life and death. The watchman became one with the sword. The samurai knelt before him and begged for mercy. He asked him how he managed to handle the sword so well. But it was very difficult to stop the watchman; he cut down a nearby tree with his sword, he had become so integrated using that sword. The samurai turned aside and knelt but the energy which had been aroused in the watchman did not subside until he had cut down that tree. Only with great difficulty could he be stopped.

Then, when he was asked what had happened to him, where he got so much energy, the watchman replied, "When death was certain, when there was no escape from it, I could be total in handling the sword." For the first time in his life he became integrated. He saw death right before him and that it was his last chance to do whatever he could. He had no thought for the past or for the future, for the samurai or for his beloved. Gradually he even forgot how and where his hand ended and the sword began. He did not even hear the noise of the people when they were shouting.

He was total in his action. The samurai said, "Today I learned that the greatest skill is in total action. I had acquired great skills but I was not total because handling a sword was an art for me. I used to think of myself as a separate entity in my swordplay, and I was continually careful not to get hurt."

The watchman said, "For me there was not even the possibility of survival. The only purpose was that you should feel that I used a sword, that you didn't kill someone who couldn't even use a sword. That would have brought a stain on your name. So I thought I would be total in the few moments that I had left."

This is what I mean by total action. Krishna has said that totality is the skill in every action – this swordsman, a complete novice, immediately became an expert. Why? – because he had achieved the heights of a yogi with his total use of energy. When someone is totally at one with himself, this happens: he becomes integrated. Then there is no division within. Making love, he only makes love. When he is angry, he is totally angry; when an enemy is before him, he thinks of him only as an enemy. When he is totally involved in any work, he does not lose energy. And it is very interesting to note that when anyone is totally engrossed in any activity, gradually it becomes impossible for him to be angry. His anger burns up completely, it is completely burned away. Then it is difficult for hatred to remain inside him, because hatred turns into poison. It covers his entire body, every fiber of his being with poisonous blisters. Then it becomes difficult to be an enemy, because enmity seems to be suicidal, it seems like piercing oneself with a sword.

We can only be angry as long as we act partially. We can be inimical toward others only as long as our acts are not total. Only when our acts are total can the flower of love bloom in our life, only then can prayer become the longing of our being. When every act in our life is total, then godliness is the only reality for us. Only when oneness arises within is nonduality seen outside. As long as there are two inside, there are two outside also. It's not even correct to say two, there are many inside us.

I have heard a story…

Jesus was passing through a town. It was night, and there was a man in the cemetery beating his chest and his body with stones, bleeding. Jesus approached him and asked, "Why are you doing that?"

The man replied, "I am only doing what the whole world is doing." Again he began to hurt himself, beating his head till it bled.

Jesus asked, "What is your name, madman?"

The man replied, "My names are legion. I don't have one name, I have thousands of names."

Jesus used to tell this story often: "A man told me, 'I have a thousand names because I am a thousand people. I am not one person.'"

There are thousands of people within us too. We too have a thousand names. Someone is trying to protect himself, another wants to hit someone, a third wants to make love, a fourth wants to murder, another wants to live, another is making his tombstone, and another is entering a temple. Someone inside is saying that everything is a lie, untrue, that there is no God; another is ringing the bell of the temple, while another is laughing: "What you are doing is madness! Nothing will be achieved by ringing that bell." Someone is fingering his prayer beads, while inside he is running his business. That madman was right when he said, "My names are many, I have a thousand names. What name shall I give you? I am not one person; I am a thousand different people."

Having a thousand people inside destroys us, it dissipates our energy. If those one thousand people were to become one integrated being, our energy would be preserved. So whatever you do, do it totally, with all your heart. And when the task is over, something in you will begin to accumulate, to be integrated.

Gurdjieff used to say that totality is crystallization. When a person does any activity totally, many things in him become crystallized. That crystallization, that integration gives birth to individuality. It is the birth of the real man. I am explaining this so that you will experiment with it, understand it and examine it, so that it can be clearly fixed in your mind.

Ask one last question:

Question 4

Osho,

Please shed some light on the chemistry of diet, *ahar*, in relation to the accumulation and upward movement of sex energy.

The word *ahar* has a very deep connotation, deeper in meaning than *diet*. Let us first understand the word *ahar*, then we can talk a little more about it.

Whatever we take in from the outside is food. If we look at a beautiful flower with our eyes, the act of seeing is taking in food, nourishment. Our eyes are feasting on beauty. When we listen, we are feasting on music; our ears consume the sounds. When our hand touches someone's body it is taking in the nourishment of sensation. Any smell becomes food when it touches the nose; then the nose is taking in its food. In the same way our whole body is taking in food; every cell is breathing, every cell is feeling. Our whole body is a mechanism for food. All our organs are doing the work of taking the outer world inside. But we have a mistaken view that only the food we eat is *ahar*.

This whole concept of food must be understood for the sublimation of sexual energy – because the food you eat may help in bringing your sex energy upward instead of pushing it down. Or your eyes may have seen scenes, or your ears may have heard sounds, or your body may have touched objects which may push your sex energy downward.

So it is important to examine food from all angles, to see the meaning of food from every point of view. We take in food with our eyes, our nose, our mouth, with the touch of even the minutest hair on our bodies. We are eating twenty-four hours a day. Many things from outside are entering us, and whatever has entered will have an effect. Naturally what we are accumulating in our bodies has an effect. If you drink wine your behavior will change, your whole personality will be in a swoon. You will behave in a drunken way. Whatever you eat will certainly have an effect, and will go on affecting you.

A famous Indian musician, Pandit Omkar Nath, went to Italy, where he was invited to a dinner with Mussolini who was then in power. While they were having their dinner, Mussolini asked Omkar Nath if it was true that when Krishna played his flute, people went almost mad and flocked around him. He found it hard to believe that even deer came out to listen to the music, and the peacocks danced.

Pandit Omkar Nath replied, "I am not Krishna so I cannot play the flute, but I know a little about the elements of music. I will demonstrate this to you with an experiment." Mussolini agreed, but there were no musical instruments in the dining hall, only spoons and forks. Omkar Nath took a spoon and fork and began to play on the china dishes.

Mussolini has written in his autobiography that within a few moments he became unconscious: "My head began to droop, and it fell onto the table many times. His playing became so intense that my head began to rise and fall to the rhythm. It began to bleed and I cried out for the music to stop. I was unable to stop my head from making these rhythmic movements on the table. Then he stopped playing. There were drops of blood on my head and the whole head was bruised."

Mussolini declared that he had no idea that music could produce such an effect on him – he could not stop his head movements. He said in his autobiography, "My body was out of my control; I could not control my head and I felt I would die right there and then. The greater the effort on my part, the harder my head slammed on the table."

Omkar Nath said, "This is nothing. It is not proper for me to give any opinion about Krishna but if this is possible, that is also possible."

Islam banned music, not because music essentially pushes the sex energy downward, but because ninety-nine percent of the kind of music that was prevalent brought the sex energy downward. Hardly one percent of the music saved in this world can carry sex energy upward. Even that one percent is being lost, and there seems to be no way to save it.

The dancing of the Sufi saints carries sex energy upward; it transports the spectators into meditation. Gurdjieff organized a group of Sufis – the dervishes, proficient in sacred dances – and traveled all over Europe and America with the troupe, asking people to simply watch the dances and not to do anything. It was a band of thirty people. They would dance before a crowd which would move into meditation just watching the movements. The movements would enter their hearts, and corresponding movements would be produced within their bodies. Whatever was witnessed on the outside produced corresponding movements within them, and they began to move within. The rhythm, the pace, and the sound that the dancers created, slowly, slowly became the rhythm, pace, and sound of the spectators. A certain dance began within them, and a transformation of their energy took place.

What we see with the eyes, hear with the ears, taste with the mouth and smell with the nose are all interrelated.

The bells we now hang in temples have no special meaning, but some special bells can be of use. The Tibetans have a special kind of bell; some of you might have seen it. It is not like a hanging bell, it is like a bowl. A short round stick is turned round and round inside it, and struck to produce a sound. It is a kind of bowl which is struck with a short round stick. After the stroke is made with the stick on the bell, a particular sound is produced, a humming sound is heard: *om mani padme hum*. The whole Tibetan mantra emanates from it and continues to resonate in the temple. There is a meaning behind it.

This mantra goes inside the body, activating the energy centers, and the energy of those centers begins to rise upward. The word *om* and its humming sound are meant to take energy upward. Not only *om*; the *amin* of the Mohammedans and the *amen* of the Christians are all forms of *om*.

The English words *omniscient*, *omnipresent*, and *omnipotence* are derived from *om*. *Omniscient* refers to someone who has seen om, the vast ultimate reality. *Omnipresent* refers to the presence which permeates this reality. *Omnipotent* refers to the very power of this presence. Only then is one connected with the source energy of existence itself. The sound comprises *a*, *u*, and *m*; it has three fundamental sounds in it. If these sounds are systematically hummed and repeated, they seem to bring the energy upward.

There are opposing sounds which make the energy go down. If you watch someone dancing the twist, you will find that within a short time a twisting begins inside you; energy begins to spin inside. All these modern dancing styles and the music of today's world are exploiting the sex instinct of man.

So this question about *ahar*, or food, is very important. The food we take in will definitely have an effect; there is no escaping it because our whole biology is psychochemical. Those chemicals are working all the time and they will be affected by what we eat, by what we drink.

There are certain types of food which make man more sexual. There is a special kind of jelly in honeycomb. You may know that there is only one queen bee in a bee colony, and she alone lays eggs. The others are female bees but only work as laborers. Favre, who studied these bees extensively, was surprised to find that there is nothing like sex in the lives of thousands of bees. After all, they are females and they have fully formed sex organs, and yet there is no sex in them. The amazing result is that only the queen bee eats the jelly which is collected by the bees. All the rest get it for only three days after their birth; after that they don't get any. The whole mystery is in that jelly.

Many crazy people have experimented with it for rejuvenation: "If tablets are made out of it and given out, perhaps an old man will become young." Creams have been prepared from that jelly and thousands of women apply the cream to their faces to make themselves beautiful. The jelly contains unique compounds, and it enhances sexuality to an extraordinary degree. It is difficult to estimate the sexual capacity of the queen bee. So much sexual energy is produced in her by that jelly that she gives birth to two thousand eggs every day.

We now know that the discovery of hormones has clearly proved that if female hormones are injected into a man, his body will be transformed in a few days. And if male hormones are injected into a female body, her female body will be transformed into a male body in a few days. Some women start to grow mustaches between about forty-five and fifty years of age. This is because the female hormones diminish and the male hormones lying dormant in the body become active, so a mustache begins to grow. After fifty, a woman's voice begins to sound like a man's because the ratio between the male and female hormones is disturbed. Female hormones decrease and male hormones increase, causing a change in the voice.

All these are chemical phenomena, many of which depend on the kind of food we take in. If the food we eat contains intoxicating ingredients or ingredients that cause unawareness, they will cause the body energy and the sex energy to flow downward. Stimulants in the food will cause the sex energy to flow downward. And if there are soothing ingredients in our food, they will calm the mind and help the energy to move upward. This is a very important subject, so we should understand its principles.

We should always avoid food which contains intoxicating ingredients, or whatever causes unconsciousness or drunkenness, or makes our body and mind heavy. The food we take in should be the kind which cannot make our body heavy or excited, produce drunkenness or unconsciousness, or make us lazy or sleepy. Such food is useful for a seeker, and eases the way for his upward journey. If his food is of the opposite kind, a seeker's upward journey can become difficult. A seeker can continue his upward journey when eating the wrong food, but there will be unnecessary hardships on the way.

When I talk about food, one point should be borne in mind: a seeker who wishes to move his sexual energy upward will avoid reading, watching, or listening to anything which is exciting or intoxicating. He will avoid music which is exciting and use music which is soothing and meaningful. He will not watch things which stimulate him.

Your movies are generally thrilling, exciting; they make every tiny hair on your body stand up. You are eating the wrong food. Detective stories, full of murders and blood are all exciting. If you watch the audience at a movie you will notice everybody tensing in their chairs, they almost stop breathing when they see some exciting scene on the screen. And when the excitement is over, they again relax into their seats. The more exciting the movie is, the more we help the sex energy to flow downward.

But you go on staring at everything on the way without even bothering to realize that it is not necessary or right to look at everything. It is not necessary to look at or read everything on the path. Each moment you should choose. Take in only that which will lift the level of your life. And if you want to take your life downward, then do it deliberately. Then take in only that which leads you downward.

But we wander here and there like blind people. We raise one hand and lower the other. In the morning we go to church and in the evening visit a theater. We ring the church bell in the morning and then go to a nightclub to watch dancing. Thus we divide our lives with our own hands; we stretch our lives at both ends. As a result we reach nowhere.

There should be a firm commitment in your life. If you wish to lower yourself, do it, touch the bottom and come back. But even then, there should be some order, some effort. Then give up talking about the upward journey, don't look toward the church even by mistake, and don't turn your steps toward a temple. Have nothing to do with the Gita, save yourself from the sadhus, forget that they are in this world. Forget about Buddha, Mahavira, and Krishna because they are not the right sort of people. They will be hurdles in your way. If you want to go to hell, catch the train there and stick to it vigorously.

But man is very strange; he keeps one leg on the train to hell and the other on the train to heaven – and he reaches nowhere. His whole life becomes a drudgery, a burden for him. He drags himself from one place to another, he is a bullock cart yoked at both ends, pulling in opposite directions. Sometimes one bullock pulls toward heaven, and then he regrets that he missed hell and pulls a little in that direction. Then he moves a little toward hell and again repents because he might miss heaven. In this way, his whole life is wasted and he reaches nowhere. Finally the cart breaks down and the bullocks die. Then again a new birth, a new world, a new life, and he starts the same course in life with his old habits.

So decide first where you want to go, what you want to be, what you want to achieve, what your aim is, what your direction is, what your decision is. And then start acting accordingly. Change everything in your life according to that decision. Change your eyes, your ears, your mouth, hands, and everything else.

Then make the connections which lead you to godliness. Listen to that which thrills your heart and raises it upward. Eat that which lifts your life to a higher level and makes you light. Only look at that which becomes a guide, a lamp for your eyes, to dispel darkness from your path. Then everything will change.

We use certain kinds of fragrances in the temples. Mohammedan mystics have chosen certain fragrances, in India some Hindu sannyasins have also chosen certain fragrances and there is some basis, some reason for this. It is because often a person deep in meditation is filled with a sandalwood-like fragrance. So in the temples sandalwood was used: perhaps this may enhance and remind him of his inner fragrance. When a person enters a certain state of meditation, he is filled with a fragrance similar to that of frankincense. Hence Mohammedan mystics have chosen frankincense so that the fragrance awakens the sleeping fragrance inside someone by stimulating it. All this is by intention, not without a reason. There is a reason behind it all.

There is something I want to say and then I will end my talk. Yesterday a friend asked why I chose orange clothes for sannyas. There is a reason for it. As the mind becomes more silent, the light within the heart begins to expand, and that is an orange color. The orange clothes continue to stimulate the inner color, so this is the reason for the clothes. Getting up, putting on the clothes, sitting, sleeping, a sannyasin sees the color, so the dormant color within him may be stimulated and he may experience a new sunrise in his meditation. It is like the spreading of reddishness as soon as the sun rises.

The whole eastern sky becomes reddish even before the sunrise. Birds begin to sing, the cool morning breeze blows all around. The same happens in meditation at a certain fortunate moment. As that color is seen within, this color was selected for the outer life of sannyasins.

Other colors which are also seen within have been selected too. The Mohammedan mystics selected green because it too is seen within. The Buddhists selected yellow, which is also seen within. At one time the Theosophical Society searched for a shade of indigo that Colonel Alcott saw while he was meditating. So, to find that color, he sent out agents to various markets of the world because he wanted it for the seekers to use. Many shades of indigo were available but Alcott rejected them all. At last, after two or three years of searching they found one color from a market in Italy which was approved by Alcott.

When looking at the color that Alcott saw, vibrations can be awakened within another's heart too. Orange is the color of the sunrise, and that color spreads within when our inner life is awakened. On the upward journey we have to select even the right color, the right sound, smell, taste, and touch. We are all confused because we make unrestricted and incoherent selections. It is like boarding a broken boat; our life is dissipated and we reach nowhere.

Enough for today: there will be more tomorrow.

12

The Seed Transforms into a Tree

Question 1

Osho,
What is the contribution of Tantra to the transformation of sexual energy into meditation and enlightenment? Please give us an outline of how this works.

Tantra is a philosophy of nonduality. It accepts life in its totality – even the evil, the bad or the dark. Tantra accepts them, not with a view that the dark should remain the dark, or the bad should remain the bad, or the evil should remain the evil, but because there is a possibility of transforming the bad into the good. Darkness can be changed into light. What we call matter is nothing but godliness in its basic form. Tantra is nondual; it is the acceptance of oneness. Evil is also a form of that oneness. The bad is also a form of that oneness. Tantra does not condemn anything.

G. N. M. Tyrrell has written a book, *Grades of Significance*, which means the stages of greatness. According to Tantra, all the different qualities that are found in life are equally important. Even the first step into a temple is a part of the final step: if the first step is removed, there is no way of reaching the last step of the temple. The ugly roots hidden in the ground are the source of life for the flowers blooming toward the sky. If those ugly roots hidden in darkness are cut, there is no possibility for flowers to bloom. The unshapely stones buried in the foundations of the temple support the golden dome at the top. If they are removed, that golden dome will fall down.

Tantra accepts life in its totality, and it is necessary to understand this first – because Tantra has developed the science of transforming sex energy based on this principle. According to Tantra, sexual energy is the earthly, material form of the same energy as the divine. Sexual energy is the first step toward godliness. It doesn't mean that Tantra wants us to be immersed in sex. It means that we have to start our upward journey from where we stand. If the place where we are standing is not linked with the place we want to reach, there is no meaning in the journey.

Man is standing in sexual energy, he is there all the time. We are born out of sex; nature has made us that way. Any journey will have to start from the sex center. And we can begin our journey from this center in two ways.

The first is to fight against the very position in which we stand. It is the way which is generally tried, and it can never be accomplished. We become enemies of ourselves, divided into two parts. One part, the one which we condemn, is ourselves as we are. The other part, which we admire, is what we want to become but are not at the moment. We divide ourselves into two parts: that which we are and that which we want to become. It has to be understood that anyone who divides himself in this way is rejecting what he is and he is accepting in himself what he is not. His whole life will be an absurd conflict, rejecting who he is, believing in what he is not. Such a person can only become confused and agitated. Tantra says this inner conflict is our situation in life.

If someone wants to attain brahmacharya, celibacy, he cannot do it by fighting against sex. Tantra declares that we cannot reach anywhere by fighting against ourselves. What will we fight? With whom will we fight? We are one whole, undivided entity. To fight means to divide ourselves into two parts. We become schizophrenic. We will be torn apart; a split personality will be created and many parts will lie scattered within us.

Tantra proclaims that even sex is to be transformed; the powerful energy of sex is to be transformed into celibacy. That same sexual energy which flows toward others is to be taken inward. That same power of sex which desires the company of the other is to be transformed into a longing to reach the depths of the inner being. That same energy which seeks a lower form of happiness is to be turned toward the vastness of the whole, toward endless, eternal bliss, toward liberation. I call this tantric point of view, nonduality.

A dualistic nature is always in conflict, fighting with itself, body against soul, God against nature, sex against meditation. In such a state, the truth can never be seen. The tantric view is that this fight is meaningless. What is really required is transformation. This is in total agreement with the fundamental principles of the last three hundred years of modern science, that state that energy cannot be destroyed. Even a tiny particle of sand cannot be destroyed by the greatest energy. We can only transform what is hidden in every particle of it – give it another form, or shape, or life – but whatever energy it has cannot be destroyed. Science says nothing in this world can be destroyed.

Look at it this way: nothing is ever created. Nothing is destroyed nor is anything created, only forms change. It is like a seed that transforms into a tree. The seed seems to disappear, but this is because of our faulty vision. The seed is never destroyed, only its hidden energy is transformed and grows into a tree. The tree dies after some time, but leaves behind thousands of seeds with the same potential energy. Energy only changes form, it is never destroyed. Neither anything is created in this world, nor is anything destroyed.

So, those who think in terms of creation and destruction think in nonscientific terms. Sex cannot be destroyed, but in one sense sex can disappear completely, just like the seed disappears. Today, where is the seed which was there yesterday? Now it is transformed into a tree. If you go looking for the seed you will not find it anywhere. Where can it go? – the seed has disappeared. But this will be wrong linguistically. The seed is not destroyed; it is transformed, because now there is a tree where there was a seed.

So celibacy does not mean the destruction of sex; now celibacy is present where yesterday there was sexuality. Where the energy of sex was flowing outward yesterday, today the same energy is transformed into celibacy and is flowing inward. The energy which had an outward momentum until yesterday has an inward direction today. The energy which was running from the center to the circumference is now running from the circumference to the center. But it is the same energy, it is not destroyed. Tantra proclaimed this before modern science could understand it.

Tantra says never commit the folly of trying to destroy energy, otherwise you yourself will be shattered, wasted, and you will not succeed in destroying the energy. So those who fight against sex cannot become celibate; they pervert themselves instead. One who is at war with his sex will become inimical toward it – and most of us have become inimical toward sex.

Actually, we don't know how to remain separate from friendship and enmity, how to stand between the two. Either we make friends like mad, or we make enemies like mad. But madness always remains. We are never able to look at the issue from a detached, neutral point of view.

Tantra says its first principle is to look at sex from a detached point of view. Do not consider sex as either friend or foe; don't consider it as something to be indulged in or renounced. Consider sex as pure energy: that is the truth of it. To be for or against are our viewpoints, they are not the reality; they are our interpretations. The reality is that this energy, this vast energy – which goes on flowing and expanding outward, which goes on demanding the other, demanding the opposite – is simply energy. See it as such; this is the first principle of Tantra. No sooner do you look at it as energy than your whole perspective changes – because then you are neither eager to enjoy it nor anxious to renounce it.

Someone who is anxious to renounce is a defeated, exhausted, bored pleasure-seeker. Whoever talks of renunciation is really a pleasure-lover. But how long can someone merely bored with pleasure maintain his renunciation? One who is fed up with pleasure will also be fed up with renunciation. How can you save yourself through renunciation if you are fed up with pleasure? Renunciation is the other side of that same pleasure, the other side of the coin. If you are fed up with one side, you will certainly be fed up with the other. It is essential to understand this point clearly because that is absolutely necessary in order to understand the transformation of sex energy.

Every activity has two sides to it, and sexual activity also has two sides to it. For example, if you are hungry, you are so eager to eat that you may risk everything to get food. When you have eaten, you completely forget about food. And if you have eaten more than necessary, you have to vomit that food you were so eager to get. A sort of disgust, a loathing, arises in you for the very food for which you were prepared to risk everything.

Every instinct of the mind is also like the two sides of thirst, the state of being thirsty and the state when the thirst is quenched. Similarly when sexual desire demands satisfaction, you become confused and chase it like a lunatic. Then sex takes you to a climax, where energy is simply spent, and you come back and sink into a deep pit of despair. And in that pit of despair you start thinking against it.

It is hard to find someone who loves sex but does not also think of renouncing it afterward. The idea of renunciation arises in the background of sex: renunciation comes from the repentance which follows sexual enjoyment. Renouncing comes from the misery caused by the wastage of energy. All sex-seekers, after satisfying their urge, experience feelings of dejection, despair, and hatred – and then renunciation.

When the husband turns his back on his wife and goes to sleep, that act of turning his back is very significant. The wife understands the implication of it. She always weeps behind his back because she sees that this man was mad for her a moment ago, and now the same man has turned his back. He is now so dejected, so exhausted and frustrated that it seems he will never indulge in sex again. In about twenty-four to forty-eight hours, according to his strength and age, he will be seized with desire again, his mind will be ready for sexual pleasure again and he will forget his past repentance completely. And then again repentance, and in that moment of repentance, he forgets everything that he had wished for his whole life: all the hopes for sexual enjoyment, dreams, desire for pleasure.

Renunciation and pleasure are two sides of one coin. Everyone is moving back and forth on the pendulum of renunciation and pleasure in twenty-four hours. Some people cling to one of them: some people stick only to pleasure and spend their time in brothels. Others cling to the other side of the coin, to repentance, and take refuge in monasteries, in ashrams. But both of them are holding on to only one side of the coin, while the other side is hidden behind it. So someone who has escaped into an ashram or a monastery will feel sex rising in his mind every day. The desire will continue to come from the other side; it was supposed to have been renounced but in fact is only suppressed. Both sides of the coin can be dropped together, but it is never possible to give up only one side entirely. At the most we can reduce one side and increase the other. Both sides of the coin remain within reach.

One who renounces always feels the attraction of pleasure and so always speaks against it, criticizes it. He is not trying to convince you, he is trying to console himself. The ascetics have really criticized and condemned pleasure, sexual pleasure. They must feel the attraction in their minds; otherwise there would be no reason for this criticism, there would be no point in this type of criticism. If they had sincerely given up pleasure they would not find any interest in condemning it. If you read the scriptures of the renouncers, you will be surprised. Just the way the pleasure-seekers are praising, in a similar way the renouncers are condemning!

Why does a pleasure-seeker glorify pleasure? He praises it in order to cover up his sorrow and regret. He is trying to persuade himself that his regret has no meaning. He believes it to be a moment of weakness – the attraction was there, it was heaven. He cherishes the pleasure to wash away his regrets. And he is praising it in a way that is not true. Praising is never authentic.

In contrast to this, the ascetic denounces pleasure. He tries to deny the memories of enjoying a moment of sexual pleasure. He says to himself, "This is all false, it is absolute hell." He has memories of heaven and calls it hell, and tries to destroy the memories. But both are trying to suppress; the pleasure-seeker suppresses renunciation and the ascetic suppresses pleasure. Both are repressive minds. This is important to bear in mind. Generally we refer to an ascetic as a man who suppresses himself, but we don't say the same about the pleasure-seeker. This is a mistaken view. The ascetic practices suppression of pleasure and the pleasure-seeker suppresses his regrets, his denunciations. Both are suppressed.

Tantra teaches us not to suppress but to watch, to know, to recognize. Save yourself from the duality of both. This duality is false. Neither praise nor condemn because if you praise now, sooner or later you are bound to condemn yourself. This cycle of admiration followed by condemnation, and condemnation followed by admiration, goes on and on just as day is followed by night, and night is followed by day. Tantra says to understand the meaninglessness of it and see that the energy is neutral. The whole energy is neutral. It is neither good nor bad. It is worth neither renunciation nor enjoyment. If you can save yourself from this duality and see your life energy, what will happen?

According to Tantra, when you look at life energy just as energy without any judgment, without any evaluation, it stops moving at once. It moves neither forward nor backward. It neither goes outward nor goes inward. Only we cause it to move. By praising it, we push it outward; and by condemning it, we take it inward.

You have seen the pendulum of a clock moving back and forth. But you may not have thought of the principle that while going toward the left, the pendulum accumulates the energy to go to the right, and when it is moving toward the right, it is accumulating energy to go to the left. This is how it moves back and forth. When you are praising and favoring your sex energy, at the same time you are also preparing yourself to condemn it; and when you are condemning it, you are preparing yourself to praise it. This idea of reverse effect will not be understood immediately. It is called the law of reverse effect – opposing forces are collecting in the mind.

A Jewish mystic, Hasid, had written a book. It was revolutionary, so orthodox Jews were very much against it. Hasid gave the book to one of his devotees and asked him to give it as a gift to the most religious man among the Jews.

The disciple was very confused. He said, "I don't know how he will react."

Hasid told him not to react to what the religious man said or did, but just to observe him and see how the man behaved, and then come back and tell him what happened. So, he should make sure not to react to the man's behavior; otherwise he would not bring back the correct information: "Just witness how he behaves. Don't do anything. If he swears, don't reply to his swearing. If he gets angry, don't try to make him understand." The disciple should be just a witness so that he could bring back the correct information.

The devotee went there as a witness. It was evening and the rabbi was sitting in his garden with his wife. The disciple gave him the book and said, "The mystic Hasid has sent this gift for you."

On hearing that name, the rabbi took the book and angrily threw it away, ordering him to keep it away from his house: "Such irreligious books are not even allowed to enter this house!" For a moment the devotee felt something should be done, something should be said, but he had been told to watch the man's behavior, not to react; not to be a participant, just to observe as a witness. He just stood there.

Then the rabbi's wife said, "Why be angry? There are thousands of books on the shelves; keep this one there too and if you want to throw it away, do it later. There is no need to hurt this man's feelings so much."

The disciple wanted to thank the rabbi's wife, but again he remembered he was sent there merely as a witness. It was not proper for him to do anything. He went on watching. After some time he asked to leave.

Both the rabbi and his wife said, "You have said nothing at all."

He replied, "I am sent here merely as a witness. I have to report what has happened here. I have been told not to be a participant. But before I go away I would certainly like to tell you that this is the first occasion in my life in which I have acted as a mere witness, and this is also the first occasion in my life when I am laughing at my whole life. Alas! I wish I had been such a witness throughout my life." Then he went back.

Hasid asked him what had taken place at the rabbi's house and he described what he had seen.

Then Hasid asked, "Did you not react in any way?"

"No," said the disciple.

Then Hasid asked, "What do you think about this now? What would have happened if you had reacted at that time?"

He said, "If I had reacted, I would have considered him an enemy and his wife a friend. But behaving as a witness, I can now see a possibility of the rabbi becoming a friend – if not today, then in the future – but I have no hope of his wife becoming a friend."

Hasid asked the reason.

The devotee said, "The rabbi threw away the book so angrily and violently that he will have to read it because he will repent, if not now, then in the very near future. But with a very cool mind his wife said, 'Keep it in the library; there are thousands of other books, this one can also be there.' There is no chance she will read it. So I can say that his wife is certainly our enemy. The rabbi can become a friend."

Hasid laughed and said, "You have understood the principle of the pendulum of the clock."

Life collects opposite reactions. A pleasure-seeker vows every day to renounce and a renouncer indulges in the longing for pleasure. Tantra says both are futile, futilities. They are two sides of the coin. Tantra says energy is just energy. Do not see it as indulgence; do not see it as renunciation. Do not see energy as something with which to *do*. According to Tantra we have to understand sex energy by witnessing it. When someone becomes a witness, energy goes neither outward nor inward; it stops, it becomes still. No sooner does it become still than transformation takes place.

I will tell you about another very interesting principle. Nothing remains still in this world, nothing can remain motionless. Everything in this world will either move outward or inward, forward or backward, nothing can remain still. If energy becomes still, goes neither in nor out, then for a moment it might appear that the outward flow of energy has stopped. But remain a witness, and within moments you will find that the energy has started to flow inward. Energy is a living thing; it cannot be stopped, it has to go somewhere. If it does not flow downward, it will flow upward.

Tantra says you have to make great effort to move it outward, but to take it withinward you have to be effortless. You have to make great effort to move it outward because moving it outward is unnatural, but no effort is needed to take it inward. There is only one way to take it withinward, and that is to give up the efforts that move it outward. But both the pleasure-seeker and the one who renounces pleasure go on fighting against it on the outside. One tries to pull the energy inward and as much as he does that, the energy tries to push itself outward. And for the other, as muchas he tries to push the energy outward, it pushes itself inward. Just as a ball thrown to the wall bounces back, similarly these conflicts with energy lead to absurdities.

Tantra says: Stop! Be a witness, observe but don't make judgments, don't give interpretations, don't take sides. No praise, no condemnation. Be at a standstill, just watch for once. And as soon as you are at a standstill for a single moment, you will immediately know that the next moment the energy has started to flow inward.

To flow outward means to flow downward. And to flow inward means to flow upward. On the inner journey the words *withinward* and *upward* are synonymous. Similarly, the words *outward* and *downward* are synonymous. As soon as energy moves inward, an inner intercourse begins, which is a unique event in the wondrous art of Tantra. There is one kind of sexual intercourse or *sambhog* that happens between two people. It is a sexual relating that one creates with someone of the opposite sex: man with woman, or woman with man. But when the inward journey begins, a relating is created with one's own inner centers.

When the *muladhar* chakra, the center of sex energy, relates with the *muladhar* chakra of a person of the opposite sex, sexual intercourse takes place. The two people are also two energy centers, and out of their interaction lovemaking happens, which brings momentary pleasure. But when the energy from the sex center within begins to flow toward the next highest center, two energy centers again meet. It is a meeting of inner centers. This is the beginning of Tantra, the beginning of inner intercourse. There are seven such energy centers, and each time the energy arrives at a higher center, an ever deeper bliss is experienced, with its climax in an explosion of bliss at the seventh, the highest center. Then the energy is one with the ultimate. This meeting and merging of the energy within at the inner centers is called inner intercourse.

Tantra calls this "the great bliss" because it is not right to call it just bliss. What is called bliss is what we experience in meeting and merging with the other, even though we can never really meet the other. The meeting is not even complete before the separation sets in. Even before the meeting can take place, it begins to wither; the energies begin to fall apart. So in fact, only the desire to meet the other arises, the phenomenon itself never really happens.

But in the inner meeting, there is no question of falling apart. The merging goes on becoming deeper and deeper, and as one reaches the deeper and deeper centers, the great bliss springs forth and begins to flow. This great bliss is a transformation of the sex energy.

So it is necessary to be a witness. An unidentified attitude is necessary. There should be neither friendship nor animosity, neither attachment nor aversion toward sex – just a natural attitude. And secondly, at this natural moment, this moment of stopping, this moment of being still, patience is needed, a deep waiting. Why? – because our sexual experience is momentary. It may be a thousandth part of a second – and before even that moment is complete, our mind swings back to the opposite, which is against it. So at the moment your mind comes to a standstill, it has a tendency to return to its old habits. So, great patience is needed. When the energy begins to flow toward the inner centers, one needs to have patience. One will experience great bliss, but do not return to the old habit: the initial experience of bliss is like sexual pleasure and the mind would like to return back to its old patterns. You will not realize, and you will find that you have returned to the old patterns because our minds work mechanically. All the mind's habits are mechanical. It lives according to its own habits. It keeps doing things according to its habits. This is natural too, since the mind does not know anything other than habits. This is its only knowledge, and so it will repeat its habits. So, the first and most important thing to be remembered in the discipline of Tantra is that the experience of the first moment at the first energy center will be like sex, and then the mind will want to go back immediately.

Don't be in a hurry. Patience and waiting, a patient waiting, is required. It will be difficult; sometimes the mind will manage to fall back to old patterns, but stay patient and just go on watching. Each single moment will appear very long, stretched out endlessly. When the great bliss descends over us, the mind is perplexed and wants to go back to the old pattern because our minds are only used to that momentary pleasure. This is the moment of great discipline. Stop, and go on diving deeper and deeper. The anxiety can be so much that this experience of great bliss can appear like death.

In fact, sexual intercourse does have a deep connection with death. In each sexual act, man dies to some extent; in every sexual act his life energy dissipates. If we examine the lives of certain animals, we will be amazed. Certain animals die after just one sexual act. The dead body of the male has to be removed from the female. They do not return from sex alive. Just one sexual act and they are dead. There are other animals whose sex, when understood, will surprise us even more. There is not much difference between animal and human sexual behavior. The only difference is that of the time gap.

A female African spider devours its mate while making love. By the time the lovemaking is over, half of his body has been eaten up. But although other spiders see this, it doesn't stop them from having sex themselves. No, they go on having sex. They think in the same way as man: "This happens to the other, and it will not happen to me; I am the exception." This is everyone's way of thinking. There is not much difference between the spider's logic and the logic of man. The logic is the same; everyone thinks, "I am an exception."

If someone dies on the roadside, the event doesn't trigger the thought in you that you will also die. No, the thought that comes is, "Poor fellow!" The thought doesn't come that the person who is thinking this is also a poor fellow, and that the news of this man's death is the news of your death too.

If we observe all the sexual behaviors in the animal world, we will be amazed. In many cases, sex and death are simultaneous. Where they do not happen simultaneously, even then each sexual act brings death closer and closer. The connection is deep. Hence, the remorse that follows lovemaking is in fact also the remorse of having died a little. Someone has died a little; he is not the same as he was before the lovemaking. Something has been lost, destroyed, disintegrated, and there is repentance. Some life energy has been dissipated.

Hence, when for the first time the energy reaches the inner energy centers or even the very first energy center, a sense of fear as if you are dying may arise. That is when you have to have courage: "Okay, even death is welcome. I accept." Just as you have always been accepting of sex and thus welcoming death, in this first moment of inner intercourse you also have to agree to die. And whoever accepts death in this moment instantly discovers that he has entered the dimension of deathlessness.

In the outer world, each sexual act leads to death; in the inner world each sexual act leads to deathlessness. Each outer sexual act is an act of death. Each inner sexual act is a taste of deathlessness. It is what Kabir sings: "Oh seekers, the nectar of deathlessness is showering from the inner sky onto the palate." – when life energy ascends in the inner centers, then the taste of deathlessness showers. Deathlessness is not something material that will shower. Is death a material thing which showers? No, death is an event, and in the same way, deathlessness is an event, it is an inner event.

Let me tell you its other aspect too. Through sexual union with another person we give birth to a child, but the sexual union of one's own inner energy centers becomes a new birth to oneself. Inside, a new person is born. Every day a new person is born. We call someone who has taken a second birth, *dwija* – twice-born – but in reality, *dwija* is the title of the new person who has just been born.

One birth is from the parents; it is a birth given by others. There is another birth that is given by oneself to oneself. It is the birth of Tantra; it is the state of twice-born. One who has attained a new birth by bringing the life energy to the inner centers is described as *dwija* – twice born. All outer births are followed by death; all inner births are followed by deathlessness.

If this process of Tantra is understood properly, it is not at all difficult to take sex energy toward celibacy. But it is difficult to fully comprehend this tantric vision because the feeling of enmity toward sex is seated deep within all of us. But the negative attitude that has been instilled in us toward sex does not cause us to become enemies of sex; together with the negative attitude comes a deeper attraction. On one hand we continue to condemn sex, on the other hand we continue to indulge in it. The same pendulum keeps swinging from left to right and from right to left.

Anyone who wishes to raise his sex energy upward should know that this energy is the energy of existence itself, so both condemnation and indulgence are meaningless. To know it is meaningful, to live it is meaningful. One has to live neither in indulgence nor in renunciation of it.

The more, the deeper, sex energy moves inward, the more energetic it becomes. The more it rises upward, the more it goes on becoming part of one's being and fills up all one's inner emptiness. Then you can say, "I am fulfilled. Now there is no inner space that is empty."

Question 2

Osho,
Just now you have said that in sexual intercourse both woman and man lose energy. But it is generally believed that woman receives nourishment from the semen. Please clarify this.

Generally, beliefs are just that. For example, it was a common belief that the sun rises and the earth is flat. Common beliefs are often wrong because *common* indicates something seen superficially, into which we have not penetrated in depth. The sun appears to be rising but we know very well that the sun neither rises nor does it set. But we will never get rid of words like *sunrise* and *sunset.* These words will go on. The earth appears flat, it is not seen to be round anywhere. For millennia people used to believe that it is flat. Today, when we have to accept it as round, it creates difficulty: the common mind finds it difficult to believe it to be round when it appears to be flat.

So, common beliefs are often wrong because they are based on two factors: first, we accept something as it appears on the surface; secondly, we believe what we want to believe. Generally we don't want to accept the truth – rather, what we call the truth is what we want to believe in. Man is less of a rational being and more of a rationalizing being. It is not that he thinks with great intelligence; the truth is, he gives the mask of intelligence to whatever he thinks. It is easier.

We want to indulge in sex so we bring in all sorts of rationalizations: the woman will be nourished, the man will be nourished; it is healthy, it is medically beneficial... We attribute all these things to it. And if we want to denounce sex, we will attribute opposing views to it.

Mankind has passed through all kinds of states here on earth. If you look at what they said in medical books from medieval Europe, today's doctors do not say the same things at all. Those doctors said that sex is a dangerous activity – because the attitude of medieval man was against sex. Today's doctor says it is not dangerous at all, it is very good. The reason is that modern man wants it to be good. It will be no surprise if the situation changes again tomorrow. Fashions in thinking processes also change.

Thousands of times throughout history man has revived ideas he had previously abandoned or become tired of. Then he swings to the opposite idea – but then he gets fed up with that too, and falls back on the old ideas. Every day, man revives the past truths, and then gets fed up with those too.

The interesting thing is that even intelligent people of all ages support the ideas of the common folk. To accept the beliefs of the common man as though they are facts is essential for them to maintain their status as intelligent. There are rarely people in the world who are crazy enough to oppose the beliefs of the common man – although it is such people who are the source of what little truth is discovered in this world. But generally we accept what the common man believes. The common man's beliefs are there to console the mind.

So when I say that both man and woman lose energy in sex, then two things need to be understood in order to grasp this. First, they both lose that energy that I was talking about yesterday – sex energy, not biological or psychic energy. This will not be difficult for you to understand; this can even be tested medically. During intercourse, breathing is faster, just as when someone climbs the staircase and is puffing; the blood pressure increases, they start sweating, and are exhausted at the end of it. If after an hour he is told to again have sexual intercourse, then he will know whether he has gained or lost energy. You will have to wait for twenty-four or forty-eight hours. There is a tale of a man – one does not know how far it is true. There is a story of a man that seems to be a rare event: he was able to have intercourse twelve times in one night! But this type of story is generally like the story of Ali Baba and the forty thieves. It is not possible.

If a man were gaining energy, then he should have increased energy to do it again the second time. But the sperm count is reduced by half the second time, and the third time it will be even less, and so on. By the fourth time he will feel as if he has grown old; no energy is left in him.

There is some misunderstanding about the woman because she is passive in sex. She also loses energy but she is not aggressive, so naturally she loses less energy. In aggression one loses more energy. The man takes the initiative, he is aggressive. The woman is not aggressive, but only tolerates the aggression – it should be said she only defends. Women lose less energy than men and that is why female prostitution could arise. It is very difficult to have male prostitutes because women are able sell something they have, but the men… Only now in some Western countries do *purush veshya*, male prostitutes exist. But they are very expensive because they can sell themselves only once a night. I am not calling them Vaishya, the Hindu caste – so that no one gets annoyed! So I am calling them male prostitutes. A woman is passive, but she too loses energy.

Secondly, the loss of energy is not so obvious in a woman because she does not reach orgasm often. In fact, the peaks in men and women are different. Woman's sexual energy rises very slowly; in fact, it often happens that the man is already finished before the woman is even close to orgasm. Then she loses nothing. So the pace of man and woman in lovemaking is not equal.

That is why the woman often loses nothing. A man loses energy and is finished with sex in no time. But a woman may get deluded that she lost energy. If she can also reach an orgasm, if she can also discharge the energy, then energy *will* be lost. The energy is bound to be lost. In fact, the pleasure arises out of losing energy. This is also why women are not as interested in sex as men are. According to the statistics of a survey conducted by Alfred Kinsey over a period of ten years, seventy percent of women never experience orgasm in sexual intercourse. Children are born, but rarely do women experience a discharge of sexual energy. Hence, women very soon become disinterested in sex. That doesn't happen to men; their interest returns every day.

So when I said that both lose energy, it is so. But that does not mean that someone can become strong by suppressing this energy forcibly. If energy is suppressed forcibly, it is also lost in the act of suppression. Sometimes more energy is lost in suppressing than it would have been in living it. That suppressed energy will find a release sooner or later. It will flow out in dreams and be wasted. Suppressed energy perverts and creates even more difficulties.

Hence I am not in favor of suppressing. The whole purpose of the doctors and physiologists who say that sex is natural, healthy, is so that a man does not try this madness of suppression. If he suppresses he will become a pervert and more troubles will be created. No, by suppressing, energy is not saved; by suppressing, the energy moves in wrong and unnatural ways which prove to be even more dangerous.

I am not advocating suppression. I am only telling you that there are other ways of channeling this energy. If you can see it that way even once, you will realize how much energy you have wasted.

We do not have any experience of positive gain, so how can we measure the waste without that positive gain as a comparison? As long as we have not known the dimension of gain, how can we compare? How can we measure? What is the scale?

I was staying in a house… The friend in whose house I was staying was very worried and he could no longer sleep. So I asked, "What is the matter?"

He said, "I have suffered great losses, some five- or six-lakh rupee losses."

I asked his wife, "So much loss and so much worry!"

She said, "To tell you the truth I do not understand that it is a loss. Actually he was hoping to earn ten lakh rupees and he earned only four. So he is saying he made a loss of six lakh rupees. I see it as a profit of four lakh rupees. But he feels it is a loss of five or six lakh rupees. Now, who will make him understand?"

Actually you will not know that you have suffered any losses until you have a way to compare it with gain. How will you compare? What will be the calculation, the measure? You have suffered only losses in your life. You have nothing to weigh it against. Comparison can begin only when your sex energy moves upward; to measure the loss, there has to be something on the other side of the scale. All experiences in life are relative. You can fully comprehend what I am saying only when some gain enters your life. How else can you realize what you have been losing? You have suffered only losses, and you consider a slightly smaller loss to be a gain. You can only make comparisons between two losses.

When your energy rises for the first time in your life, you will realize all the harm that has been done, not only in this lifetime but in all your endless past lives. But you cannot have this experience until you know the opposite side.

When I say that both people lose energy, I am saying it with the idea that there could have been a gain of ten lakh rupees. But they don't know anything about that. And if they think there is a profit even in four lakh rupees, it is a different matter. But in fact it is a loss of six lakhs! The loss may be of six lakhs, ten lakhs or millions, this one finds out only when the door of profit opens for comparison.

Experiment a little with this. Let the energy rise upward, then you will be able to say what has happened. In life, everything is relative. When I say that both lose energy, if both of them think about it after sexual intercourse, they will realize it. After some time the energy will fill up again. The body is a machine: you use up the energy and then the body produces energy and fills up again. If the body does not replace the lost energy every day, then you will know that energy has been lost. It is as if it is raining and you remove water from a pothole and again the pothole fills up. You will say, "Who says that the water has been taken out? The pothole is full!"

A small experiment was performed at the University of California in the US. Thirty young men were starved for thirty days. After three days, their interest in sex began to fade. The psychologists noticed that magazines showing photographs of naked women were left untouched.

After seven days, the photographs were placed in front of them but they did not look at them. After ten days, when psychologists wanted to discuss sex with them and told them dirty jokes, they were just not interested. After fifteen days they lost all interest in sex. After thirty days, all sorts of sexual stimulants were given to them – showing them pornographic films, naked photos, posters were put in front of them – but they just sat there as if they had no concern with all those things. What happened? In fact, the body was not supplying any energy; no replacement of energy was taking place at all. The potholes remained empty. There was now no interest left in the mind. It was only after three days of eating food again, when their potholes started filling up, that they showed interest in sex. The magazines were once again being looked at. After seven days of proper food, they started telling dirty jokes again. Once again, most of their talk was about women. After fifteen days of food, they were the same young men again. And if the psychologists were to say to them that they had become great renouncers, that they had been filled with great indifference, they would say that it was nothing, they were just hungry!

So in this world, if there are renouncers sitting hungry, do not be mistaken: the body is just not replacing the energy. The energy which has been used up has not been refilled. When your body does not replace energy, you will step away from the body. Normally your body replaces your sexual energy within twenty-four hours. Because of this you feel that nothing is wasted in sex. The interesting thing is that for all those twenty-four hours, eating, doing business, laboring, effort, education, everything – all this – is taking place just to produce semen. And after all this, what has to be done with this semen? That semen has to be thrown out and again the same cycle continues. Why are you doing all this? Just to produce semen!

If you ask the biologist, he will say the whole function of a man seems to be: work, earn food, eat, digest, make blood, make semen, throw out the semen, and get busy again in the same cycle. But these are all biological functions of life.

Is this whole life only for this function? If a person understands clearly that this is his only function, a revolution will happen in his life. Then you will start thinking, "What is being done through me? What am I doing? Is this my only function? Is this the only thing to be done? If this is life, then this life is worth nothing at all! Then life is nothing at all.

No, in life there are more doors that are as yet unknown and unfamiliar. But we are trapped in a vicious circle and, being trapped in it, we are destroyed. If energy can be saved from this vicious circle then we can knock at a new door. But this vicious circle is moving so fast, and we don't get the opportunity even for a single moment to stop and think what we are we doing throughout our lives.

The energy is lost, but you can only realize it when something in the positive dimension of this energy is attained. Before this, you cannot know.

Question 3

Osho,

Some days ago you said that there is subtle violence in sex. So is there violence even in the sex out of which people like Mahavira, Krishna, Christ, and Buddha were born? If not, then what is the reason for it? Is it possible to engage in sex which is completely devoid of violence?

It is impossible to have sexual intercourse without violence even if Mahavira, or Buddha, or Krishna is born out of it. It may be less violent, that is a different matter. There will certainly be violence; no birth is possible without violence. Therefore, longing for birth is also violence. The longing for birth is also violence. Even in Mahavira's birth there will be violence. If Mahavira was desirous even to a small extent in his previous birth, he will be born. Mahavira is also accused of that violence: his parents are certainly guilty of violence and Mahavira shares in that violence because he was eager to take birth. Parents only create a situation. This situation...

A Western scientist has announced that we will soon produce babies in a test tube. So it can be possible for life to be born in this way, it *will* become possible. There is no difficulty in this. Mahavira's parents only create a situation where the soul of Mahavira can enter. Mahavira's parents are being violent, which seems all right, but Mahavira too is committing some violence. The desire to be born is also violence. Buddha has said that the desire to live is violence: there is violence in the lust for life too: "I should live, I should be born." So Mahavira has also been violent. So, when this violence on the part of Mahavira is over, he cannot be born again. He cannot be born again.

There is an interesting story about Mahavira. It applies to all the Jaina tirthankaras. The Jaina tradition says that to belong to a tirthankara clan or family is also a bondage. The law of karma, or action, also applies to a tirthankara. It is the last bondage; it is a gold chain, but a chain all the same. A tirthankara also takes birth because of some final, deep desire. He takes birth because he is eager to give others what he knows. This is also a desire for a new life; this is a tirthankara's bondage.

The birth, the desire to become such a teacher is also violence. Whoever desires birth, whether Mahavira or Krishna, will have to pass through this violence. And when this violence is over, all the births of men like Mahavira will be finished, will be void. Then there is no way to come back; the last desire to return is finished. The desire to teach someone is also finished. Hence I do not say there is no violence, there *is* violence. Yes, there is violence in my birth, in your birth, and in Mahavira's; it will be so.

That violence will be in proportion to the intensity of the desire to be born. Mahavira's desire must have been small because after this he was not born again. It was his last birth. Birth cannot take place without this violence. It is necessary to understand that birth is violence, life is violence, death is violence. We cannot live without violence.

It does not make any difference whether you eat meat or are vegetarian. There is life in vegetables, so you commit violence by eating them. You will certainly drink water and there is life in water too. You have to breathe and there is life in breath also. I utter one word, my lips open and shut once, but thousands of bacteria die in that single act. Violence will be there. During the night, Mahavira slept only on one side. He would not turn because if he turned a few times in the night, some insects could be crushed underneath and die. But even if he slept on one side, some insect may still be crushed underneath his body and die. That much violence is bound to happen. It is another matter that Mahavira committed less violence, but he was certainly not completely out of violence. There will be violence in walking, stepping forward, breathing, standing, and sitting.

So our whole life stands on violence, our whole life is swimming in this ocean of violence. We are the fish in that ocean of violence –although the proportion may be more or less. The lower it is, the better, but as long as we live, total nonviolence is not possible. The attempt to achieve total nonviolence is worthwhile, but total nonviolence is not possible as long as you are alive; some level of violence will remain, a little remains. Even when I breathe the last breath, a little violence remains. If I go on decreasing violence throughout my life, if I go on diminishing my desire for violence, if I go on taking less and less interest in violence, then when I reach the point of my last breath, that will be my last act of violence. And when that happens there will be no new beginning of a first breath again. Then the matter ends for me.

Buddha talked of two kinds of nirvana. He said: "When I achieved supreme knowing under the bodhi tree, it was nirvana – but soon it will be *mahanirvana*. That will take place with my last breath." There was a gap of forty years between the attainment of supreme knowing and the final breath. In the case of Mahavira, it was a gap of almost forty-two years.

There was violence before these forty-two years, and there was violence after his enlightenment also, but a change in attitude had occurred. The violence that happened before was unknowingly, now it is knowingly. The violence that happened before was unconscious and afterward he was aware of it, so it was minimal. Mahavira does not commit violence of his own accord. Only that violence is committed which is absolutely necessary to live. Even then he tries to commit as little as possible.

He sleeps on one side. He takes food but he can survive on one meal a day – he only takes food once. Then he takes food once every two days. He does not eat meat, only vegetables. He prefers ripe vegetables and ripe fruit to green ones because to pick green vegetables and fruit would be to inflict pain on them. Ripe things fall by themselves but there are innumerable lives in them also. They will certainly be killed.

Whatever violence is committed by Mahavira after attaining enlightenment is committed through sheer helplessness. He has no interest in it happening, it is just helplessness. With that final breath the helplessness will go. There will be supreme liberation after that last breath. Then the journey will be entirely different. Then there will be life without the body. It will be the life of pure atman, pure soul. Only pure atman is totally nonviolent.

All things in the world are impure; the impurity can be more or less. There is nothing absolute in this world, nothing complete. Even in what we call the most perfect, there remains at least some imperfection. In this world even Rama, however great he may be, has some of Ravana left in him. In this world, however evil Ravana may be, there will always be some of Rama within him. Actually, the very presence of some Rama within Ravana shows the possibility of his evolution. And the presence of some Ravana within Rama indicates the possibility of his rebirth. The presence of some Ravana inside Rama is the very basis of his life. And inside Ravana that little bit of Rama is the only option for the journey of his growth. It is bound to be so.

There will be a sinner within the greatest of saints and there will be a saint within the greatest sinner. But the real saint knows this sinner inside and accepts him as a necessary evil. He knows this to be inevitable, a part of life. If any saint proclaims to be perfect in this world, he is somewhat mistaken. He is refusing to look at some part of his nature, some part of himself. It cannot be rejected, it will remain. It is impossible not to be a sinner if we live alongside sinners in this world. It is impossible.

This life is a sharing. It is possible that you may be rich and I am poor, but my poverty and your richness are connected. You may have millions of rupees and I may have a single penny, but still I have a single penny. Actually it must be said, I am only a little rich and you are a little poor. In this life everything is relative.

In the life of Mahavira, Buddha, Krishna there is violence, there is violence even in their birth. But that violence is because of utter helplessness, the last barrier. The day it drops, that day another birth becomes impossible.

Question 4

Osho,

There is another question in this connection. Can people like Buddha, Mahavira, and Christ impregnate a woman even after their enlightenment? And why don't they move into sex so that they can give birth to higher souls? Is conception a possibility that happens only between two unenlightened, ignorant people?

Ordinarily the act of procreation happens between two ignorant people. It is worth understanding that people like Buddha and Mahavira will not be willing to be instrumental in conception. There are two reasons for this: first, they cannot be prepared or willing to send someone on the journey of birth and death. They cannot be the cause of that. In fact, people like Buddha and Mahavira are eager to send us all to that place of no return, from where there is no rebirth.

They are the individuals who are eager to free us from birth and death. We desire to bring someone into the world, while they wish to free us from this earth. Mahavira and Buddha also want us to be born into that place known as moksha. They want to send us where there is neither body, nor misery, nor anguish. They are in a hurry to give us a new life but they are not eager to give us a body. I will tell you about an event in the life of Buddha which will explain this point to you.

Buddha returned home after a period of twelve years. He had escaped when his son Rahul was only one day old. He was now twelve. Naturally the mother was angry with Buddha and had said many things against him to Rahul. So she had prepared her son well to quarrel with Buddha in case he came to the palace. When Buddha came, she told her son to ask this beggar – his father – what legacy he had left for his son. She further asked Rahul to say, "You gave birth to a son, now give him provisions for his journey through life."

It was a cruel joke. It was deeply ironic. But Yashodhara can be forgiven because Buddha had left without telling her; her anger was quite natural. No one could possibly think what happened then could happen: Buddha asked Ananda, "Where is my begging bowl? Give it to Rahul and initiate him into sannyas."

Hearing this, Yashodhara began to weep. She said, "Why are you doing this?"

Buddha replied, "As a legacy to my son, I can give him that supreme treasure which I have achieved. I wish to give my son the ultimate bliss that I have found."

Rahul was initiated into sannyas. A young boy of twelve became a sannyasin. Others also said to Buddha, "Don't do this!"

Buddha's father said to him, "You left home and now you are removing him too. He is the only star in our eyes. Who will be the master of this kingdom?"

Buddha replied, "I have brought with me the knowing of another, greater kingdom. This kingdom is very small, and it would be unfair to leave that kingdom for this small one. I have come with the knowing of that great kingdom and I will make him the great monarch, the imperial monarch of that great kingdom."

Being very unhappy, the father asked Buddha to initiate him also. Buddha said, "What can be more auspicious than this?" He initiated his father also.

Then Yashodhara began to cry aloud, "Why do you leave me alone here? Initiate me also."

Buddha said, "What better omen can there be than this?" Thus the whole family was initiated.

An individual like Buddha gives birth to someone in some other kingdom of life. So people like Buddha and Mahavira, after becoming enlightened, will not be willing to bring a soul into the prison of a body. There is a prison in each of us. People living in prison have no idea of the world outside, of flowers, of the sun, of the moon and stars, of the open sky, and of birds flying in the sky. They have always been in the prison: they are born there.

Then a day comes when the prisoner, having climbed the wall, looks at the open sky, the moon and stars, the sun, and the birds singing. His wife tells him, "Look, other people are producing children, won't you do the same?"

The man will reply, "I don't want to give birth to a child in this prison. I don't want my child to live in a prison. If I want to give birth to a child, I shall produce him and give him birth into the journey toward the open sky. But who in the jail will understand this? The prisoners will say to me, 'Have you gone mad? Come back home, come home to our jail, to our cells.'"

No matter how much he may try to persuade the prisoners that the moon, the sun, and the flowers will all be there in the open, it will all be in vain. They will understand nothing as they haven't seen the sun, the moon, or the flowers. They have seen nothing but darkness and chains. Just as we are asking now, they will also ask if anyone, having once sat on the walls, can return and give birth to children. Only those who have never climbed the walls can give birth to children.

This question is exactly like that. We don't know anything about that world, about the great life which people like Buddha and Mahavira see. We are imprisoned in this small body, and throughout life we wander and toil for this prison. We consider this a great life, an important life, and think of giving birth to other souls and bringing the good souls here. And meanwhile Buddha and Mahavira are busy figuring out how to liberate even evil individuals and send them away from here. And we are trying to bring good souls here.

There is a fundamental difference between our vision and their vision, between our dimension and their dimension, so we don't understand them. An individual who has attained the highest knowing cannot give birth to others. He cannot do so because he cannot take the responsibility of throwing someone into prison. He can give birth; he can give birth to someone into another, infinite world, into a life of liberation, into ultimate freedom. But that birth is not the birth of a physical body, it is the birth of a soul.

It is a birth that cannot be seen. It is the birth of the unseen; not of the known, but of the unknown. Mahavira and Buddha have given rise to many such births. Mahavira had fifty thousand sannyasins around him. Is Mahavira anything less than a father to them? Certainly he is much more! Buddha had thousands of sannyasins. Is Buddha anything less than a father to them? In fact, he was much more than a father. What have their fathers given them in comparison to what he has given them? But only they can know what they received. We have our own problems, we know nothing, and that's why we have so many doubts and questions. So it will be good if we try to understand those questions fully.

I am grateful that you listened to me with such love and silence. Now to end, I bow down to the godliness that dwells in you all. Please accept my *pranam*, my offering of respect.

13

The Inner Journey Begins

Question 1

Osho,
What obstacles can confront a seeker passing through the discipline of waking up to the unconscious, the collective unconscious, and the cosmic unconscious? What precautions can the seeker adopt to avoid them? Please throw light on this.

Someone wants to go to the depths of the ocean, but ties himself with chains to the shore. He wants to go deep into the depths of the ocean and also wants to know what difficulties, what hurdles he will have to face. We have to tell him that his first hurdle will be to stop clinging to the chains on the shore. The second one will be to learn to swim to save himself, instead of going directly into the depths of the ocean. The third hurdle will be the experience of those depths, which is like death itself. As he goes down he will start losing himself – and, at the final depth, only depth remains. If he has even a little attachment to saving himself, it is impossible for him to go into his depths.

The world is all around us, and we have tied ourselves to many things in it. This tight hold is the greatest hurdle on our way to the depths of the self. Hence it is essential to understand a few keys. Buddha used to tell his bhikkus, his sannyasins, that life is a great deception, and whoever understands the meaning of this statement loses his grip on life. So try to understand this first key: life is a deception. Things are not what they appear to be, and whatever we hope for is never fulfilled. We try to find happiness and we get unhappiness. We try to find life and get death. We want fame, and nothing remains in our hands but infamy. We strive for riches but our inner poverty goes on increasing. We desire success and our whole life is a long story of failures. We start out to be victorious and return defeated.

It is essential to understand the deceptiveness of our entire life. If a seeker who wants to go within realizes that life is a great deception, then life's hold on him will be loosened; it will disappear. His hand on the chain fastened at the shore will let go immediately. We know this but we do not want to see it, we ignore it. We want to persuade ourselves that life does not deceive us. In this way we hope to deceive ourselves.

Life is only an opportunity; to some it becomes an instrument for awakening, and to others it becomes an excuse to go to sleep. It is like mistaking a rope for a snake in the darkness while walking on the road. I don't want to see the rope as a snake, but I see it as a snake. The rope is merely an excuse – I imagine a snake in it and run away, sweating and fearful. In fact, the snake is not in the rope but it is in me. It is not right to say that the rope deceived me; it is my projection on the rope which deceived me. If I go close to examine it, I see the rope clearly, and my fear vanishes immediately. The drops of sweat will dry. The heartbeat will start to steady; the blood pressure will return to normal. And I will sit next to the rope, the very rope from which I ran away, and laugh.

In our lives, the situation is the opposite. Rather than understanding the rope to be a snake, we consider a snake to be a rope! So, if tomorrow we come to know that what we are clinging to very tightly is a snake, we will not take even a moment to drop it. So it is important to look at life accurately, as it is.

When a child is born, it cries, and we are all happy and celebrate the birth with music. It is said that in this world, only once was there an exception: when the child Zoroaster was born, he laughed. Until then, no child had laughed at the time of his birth. Ever since, people have asked why Zoroaster laughed when he was born. The question has not yet been answered, but I think Zoroaster must have laughed at the people around him who were happy and singing. Every birth is sure to be followed by death. So the people who were happy at the birth were holding tightly onto a snake, thinking it to be a piece of rope, and Zoroaster must have laughed at them. He must have laughed at those people who look at life superficially and do not go deeply into its meaning.

We also take life only at its face value because we cannot see the soul. In spite of the reality that life shows us, we close our eyes to it. Life wants to be visible but we refuse to see it.

An old person, a friend of mine, lost his son. He was crying and very sad. When I went to his house he asked how it could happen that he had lost his young son. I replied, "It is better to ask how it happened that you, a man eighty years old, have not died yet." Here, the death of the young is not a surprise: death is nothing to wonder about. You can wonder about everything else, but death is the only certain thing in the world.

Yet death surprises us. In this life, everything is uncertain except for death. Everything is happening, everything can happen, everything changes but only death is there, as steady as the polar star. But we take it as a great surprise. When we hear that someone has died, it seems to us that a surprising event has occurred, that something unexpected has happened. People say, "That death is so unexpected. It should not be, but it is!" But the truth is that death is the only certainty; everything else is a possibility. There is nowhere that we can go and ask, "Why did death not happen?" – even if death did not happen once, the whole world would be surprised! But we are denying this certainty. In life, we have denied all truths.

Life is insecure. The whole scheme of life is insecurity. There is insecurity throughout, yet we go on feeling fully secure. We live as though everything is fine. But this is just like when someone meets you in the morning and asks you how you are. And you answer, "Everything is okay." Nothing is ever okay. If anything *is* okay, it is suspicious. It is doubtful whether anything at all is okay but man's mind continues to deceive itself. He continues to say everything is all right when nothing is all right, when the ground under his feet becomes more slippery every day. When nothing but death seems to be approaching, man says everything is okay.

Buddha used to advise his sannyasins to go to the cremation ground to see what life is. But when we go to a cremation ground, we waste our time talking about the death of someone who has passed away. We come back talking about his death, how unexpected it was and so on. We never stop to think that each death is an advance warning of our own. If we can see life in all its true colors, our grip on life, our infatuation with it decreases automatically.

We have purposely kept the cremation grounds at the edge of towns so that we won't have to see them. We beautify them to hide death among the flowers. We construct our whole life as a great deception. Therefore I tell you that whoever desires to go into the unconscious, to touch those depths within, will have to loosen his grip on the outside world. That grip will only loosen when we are able to see what is.

So the first thing to remember is that things are not what they appear to be in this world. Have you kept accounts for all the times you desired happiness, and accounts of your achievements? We do not do that kind of arithmetic. Every evening we check our accounts to see how much we earned and how much we lost during the day. But there is never an evening in which we check the accounts of what we have gained and how much we have lost in our lives. When you go to bed, for five minutes, contemplate how much happiness you have gained. How much of the happiness that yesterday you thought you would gain today, have you got? And the miseries that yesterday we had not even thought would come, how many of those have suddenly arrived as guests in our home today?

If we contemplate this every evening for a few days, we will find it very difficult to entertain hopes of happiness for the future. And when it becomes absolutely impossible for us to hope for happiness, then our inner journey begins. As long as we hope to find happiness from the world outside, the inner journey can never begin. If happiness is outside, a man cannot enter his depths. When no happiness remains outside, there is no possibility other than to go into the depths. So the first thing to remember is: that which we see and know as life is a deception. That which we think to be life is a deception. But this deception must break down and when it does, there is nothing left to do.

Does it really break down at the last moment, when nothing remains to be done? Generally it happens that we continue to repeat those old desires, to make hopes for the future stronger inside, to continue to hope for future happiness. So death becomes the cause of a new birth, and the same old circle which was completed by death begins again.

When a seeker approached Mahavira or Buddha, they did a remarkable, unique experiment: they would ask him to remember his past lives. Mahavira called this remembering *jati smaran* – self remembering. He would ask the seeker to first enter a meditation to know his past lives. The new seekers would say, "Past lives have no meaning for us, we want to be calm, free of cares and anxieties; we want to know the soul, we want to be liberated." Mahavira would reply: "You cannot expect all that and you cannot know the soul without first seeing your past lives."

The first thing to do was to see their past lives. They could not understand what would happen by looking into their past births, but Mahavira would take them through that process. The process took one year, two years but in deep meditation they could reach that state of remembering. Mahavira would ask them what they saw. When he heard their replies Mahavira would ask them, "Is this what you want in this life also?" The man would reply, "I have attained wealth many times and yet gained nothing. I have loved many times but yet my hands remain empty. I have reached the thrones of fame in other lives, but besides death nothing has been achieved." When he heard this Mahavira would ask, "Do you still desire for fame in this life?"

We forget our past lives, so we go on repeating what we did yesterday. Man is so absurd that even if he remembers his past life, it is not certain that he will change. You remember you were angry yesterday, and you also remember what you got from it. But you get angry again today and you will be angry tomorrow as well; that is more likely to happen.

You desired happiness yesterday, and what did you get? You remember it well, and yet you wish for it again today, and tomorrow also. You have desired it every day and unhappiness has come instead. It seems that man has endless capacity to deceive himself.

Every day you are pierced by thorns and never receive flowers – but the search for flowers goes on. Looking at us, it seems that we do not think at all. Perhaps we are afraid of thinking: if we think, we may stop running after happiness like children run after butterflies. Perhaps we are afraid that if we pause, we will see the futility and stop running. Perhaps you are afraid to see life in its true colors, so that you won't have to change. But if you want to consciously enter the world of spiritual practice, devotion, and awareness, you should first remember this key twenty-four hours a day. As soon as you get up in the morning, remember that you woke up yesterday and the day before yesterday, that fifty years of waking up have passed – and also remember that the same desires as yesterday are taking hold of you today.

Don't do anything, simply remember. Don't swear not to do what you did yesterday. Swearing means you did not realize your mistakes of yesterday. You did not benefit from them, so you had to swear. Remember your yesterday well, and completely. Don't say, "I will not do it again." Don't say, "I will not be angry." Say only this much, "Yesterday too I was angry." Remember only that you repented yesterday and the day before yesterday.

Don't make any decision about it today, just remember. It will be impossible to be angry if the memory of yesterday shadows you. To run after happiness will seem like madness. The hope that anything can be obtained from someone else will decrease. Day by day your hold on life will loosen, and your fist will open. Your entry into the inner world begins as soon as your grip on life loosens. So always keep this first key in mind, that life is a deception.

The second key to remember is that the body is sure to die. This body is death: it is death embodied. Norman Brown has written a book called *Love's Body*. I think someone should write a book entitled *Death's Body*. This body is moving toward death. This body is simply a preparation for death. Nothing but death is to be gained out of this body. When we consider the world a deception, our grip on the outside world will be loosened. We also have such a tight grip on our body that it seems to be everything to us.

Anyone who thinks the body is everything cannot go within. They are clutching that chain on the shore of the body very tightly. They will have to give it up and let the boat loose. Just remember: this body will die. You don't know anything of who you are, so don't think, "This body will die and I am immortal." Don't entertain the desire to be immortal, know only that when the body dies you are nowhere. If someone says, "I am immortal, the soul is immortal, only the body dies," they cannot go within. These are superficial words you picked up. You have heard these words from the Gita and the Upanishads. They are words from the Koran and the Bible, they are not yours. They will not help you to go within.

Those words will stop you at the intellectual level, a barrier which has to be broken to go inward. I will discuss this point together with the third key. It is enough to remember that the body will die. And please don't link this second key with the immortality of the soul – because you don't know anything about it. You can know it but when you know it, it will not be necessary to repeat it. At present, know only that the body is going to die. This is not very difficult to grasp. "The soul is immortal" – you will doubt this. Doubts will arise about whether the soul is immortal or not. So unless you come to know the soul is immortal, you do not attain a sure-footed state, you don't attain that trust. Unless you know it, if you just keep insisting that the soul is immortal, it will make no difference. Inside you know that you are going to die.

The body is perishable, this is certainly true; it is the experience of the entire human race, it is a proven truth of all life. It is not necessary to believe in somebody to accept it. This body is dying. This body was a child, it has grown up, it is getting old, it is on the path toward death. Every step it takes leads toward death. After birth, it is doing nothing but dying. It is on the path of death. What we know as a body's life is in fact living in a gradual death process. People are wrong when they say somebody died at the age of seventy. Dying is a process which is completed in seventy years; nobody dies suddenly at that moment. He goes on dying – the process of death is ongoing – but we only see the final part.

The process of dying goes on from the moment of birth. Just as water is changed into vapor at one hundred degrees – but the change starts from the first degree, the second degree… Gradually it gets ready to become vapor; it is slowly heated. And at ninety-nine degrees it is completely ready and then it jumps to vapor at one hundred degrees: in the same way, we make preparations to die our whole life. What we call life is only the commencement of death. It will be easy to loosen your grip on the body if you develop and deepen this remembrance.

Remember who you think you are, and then when you look in the mirror, remember death is standing there, not you. But you can see your face; you are not able to see the face of death. But in this land on which you are sitting, there is not a grain of sand that has not given someone the illusion of being their face: wherever you are sitting, at least ten people have their graves there. On this earth, there is not a single inch where the ashes of at least ten different people cannot be found. And I am only talking about human beings;

it is not even possible to estimate about the birds, insects, and plants. They too have lived.

Wherever you are right now, you have no idea how many people have lived there in the illusion, "I am," have thought that they are the reflection they are seeing in the mirror. Today they too are just ashes. Between you and them there is only a gap of time. It is only a matter of time: you are standing in the same queue in which they were standing, but they were in front. In a short time, the queue will reach where you are. And the queue is moving all the time. Whenever someone dies, the queue moves forward. But you move forward with great enthusiasm, thinking that some space has been made, that you have the opportunity to move forward. It is not that the place is vacant; it is only that death has moved one step closer to you – or you have moved one step closer to death.

When you get up in the morning, look at your body thoughtfully and know that it is going to perish. When you go to bed at night, look at it thoughtfully again and know that it is going to die. Taking a bath or eating your food, look at the body thoughtfully and remember that it will die. Repeat this several times during your daily activities, like turning prayer beads. If this remembrance enters your inner self, your attachment to the body will be broken in no time. Your identity with the body, with the "I," is shattered as soon as this is realized. It must be shattered, it must be wiped out; the identification must be broken. This is the chain which is tying the body.

Now the third key: we can never learn truth by what we call the mind, the intellect, or the thought process. Truth has never been known that way. It creates only appealing untruths. Man has produced thousands of philosophies; he has established innumerable principles in the holy books. No one knows how many systems have been formulated to show what life is. But philosophies have failed, they could not find the right answer.

Bertrand Russell has noted in his autobiography that when he went to university to study philosophy as a young man, he expected to get answers and solutions to at least the essential problems of life.

Philosophy looks for answers to the doubts and questions which arise in a person's life. After his experience of ninety years, Russell wrote that he was old enough to say that from his study of philosophy, he only got new questions but he did not get any answers. Due to his foolishness, every answer which he considered true became the source of new questions; he got nothing more than that.

Philosophy was defeated by reasoning, by intellect, so no new book on philosophy is being written nowadays. Now the students and experts in philosophy in all the universities of the world do not establish new principles. Now they are only trying to prove that the old philosophies were wrong. So a vacuum is created. Philosophy has no solutions, no answers. The religions, the scriptures, have given answers but they are just memorized, not understood. Our intellect tries to be satisfied with them but it has never been satisfied. As long as true knowing is not gained, there will be no contentment in our life.

Belief cannot provide contentment, and our minds are full of belief. Someone is a Christian, someone is a Hindu, someone is a Mohammedan, someone is a Jaina, and someone is a Buddhist. These are all characteristics of people who live in the mind. Truth is not found in the mind, and it cannot be found there because truth existed when there was no intellect, and it will continue to be there even when the intellect is not.

The mind cannot be compared to the truth. Man's brain is like a small computer. Now computers better than the brain are being manufactured, but no computer can claim that it can provide the truth. A computer can only provide the information for which it has been programmed. The intellect is also no more than a computer, it is a natural computer. The intellect repeats what it has accumulated. When I ask you, "Is there a God?" the reply which you give is not your reply, it is the reply given simply by your intellect, echoing what it has accumulated.

If you are born into a Jaina family, you will say, "What God? There is no God. The soul is everything." If you are born into a

Hindu family, you will reply, "Yes, there is a God." And if you are born into a communist family, you will say, "There is no God, it is all just a story." All these are computerized answers; they are accumulated by the intellect and repeated. The intellect only reproduces, it doesn't know anything. It has never known anything – neither religion, nor philosophy, nor science.

As for science… It looks as if science has acquired much knowledge. This is a great illusion because what Newton knew was disproved by Einstein. And what Einstein knew is being disproved by the next generation. No scientist in this world can die with the satisfaction that what he knew was the truth. He can only say that his untruth was more appealing than the previous one. The future generation may disprove it. The approximate truth – this is how so-called great statements are made.

Are there approximate truths anywhere in the world? Something should be either true or untrue. When a thing is approximately true, it means it is untrue. What would it mean if I said, "I approximately love you"? It would mean nothing. On the contrary it would be better if I told you that I hated you because it would be the truth. The phrase "approximate love" has no meaning. Either there is love or there is not. Things do not happen approximately in this world.

Science declares approximate truths, but every such truth becomes questionable every day. Over a hundred years ago, science declared quite confidently that matter existed. But it has been known for the last hundred years that matter doesn't exist. Before that, science said that the existence of matter was a fact, a truth, and that God was not a truth.

Today the scientist says, "We don't know; there may be a God, we have not been able to disprove it." It is now established that matter does not exist. Now they say there is only energy. It is difficult to say how long they will continue to say that. All the principles of man are found wanting. Truth is vast. Truth is always found to be vast – and unattainable.

So it is important for a seeker to always remember the third key, which is not to confuse truth with the beliefs of his mind. The mind does not know truth, it knows only notions of truth, principles of truth; it only knows words as truths. The mind contains the word *God*, but it has no experience of God at all. It is crowded with words, it deceives us with words, and the deception is very deep. Deceptions about the world outside are destroyed quickly. Deceptions about the body do not take much time to destroy, but to destroy the deceptions of the mind takes a long time. Therefore a seeker should always remember that what the mind says is his imagination. It is not the truth, it is his mind's work.

The mind does not know the truth, and it cannot know it. If this third key is remembered, the mind will become empty of principles. By and by, it will gradually become free from all scriptures, free from philosophy, religion, and all "isms."

If these three keys are realized, an individual will immediately jump into his unconscious mind. He will go deep within himself. His attachments will be broken, and transformation will begin as soon as he enters the unconscious mind. He will come in contact with the deeper face of life for the first time. He will experience life from within for the first time.

The unconscious is the first stage. Three things are to be borne in mind about the unconscious. It has its own body, which is composed of impressions of the actions of all past lives. It is one's own body of the unconscious. In modern times psychologists like Jung, Freud, and Adler talk about the unconscious but they do not have the seeker's experience of it.

The unconscious has been used as a principle to understand the conscious. But those who have known the unconscious as a seeker say that the unconscious body is made up of impressions of actions. These actions of innumerable past births have their own body. When he enters the unconscious, an individual will have to remember that this subtle body of actions is not who he is. It will also perish: "This present body of mine is made up of tangible substances, and it dies in every life cycle. The body of actions in the unconscious dies only once, at the time of liberation, but it also has to die."

We have to remember the same keys about the inner body of the unconscious that we have kept in mind for the outer body. Both have the same ideas, thoughts, imaginations, and desires. The unconscious body is made up of past births, and the unconscious mind is the storehouse of memories of past births. Everything lies hidden within it.

There is one wonderful law about the mind: it never forgets anything which it has heard even once. You might say it does not seem to be so. You forget many things but that only appears so. You cannot forget. Everything can be remembered. It is only in a disorganized condition.

Someone tells you that he had your name on the tip of his tongue but could not remember it. What this man is saying is a very interesting thing. What is the meaning of these two contradictory claims? "If you have it on the tip of your tongue, please say it." In fact, the person remembers two things. He remembers that he had it on the tip of his tongue – he knew it – but for the present he cannot get at it. After some time he goes to the garden, digs a hole, does some other work or smokes a cigarette or reads a newspaper or switches on the radio; it suddenly bubbles up and he exclaims, "Yes! Now I remember the name."

In exactly the same way, when you enter the unconscious, all the memories of your previous lives come to the surface. But this is also the mind. When you remember that this is also the mind and that you will not be able to reach to the truth through this mind, then the second jump happens. The second jump is into the collective unconscious.

The first jump was into your own individual unconscious. The day this jump from the unconscious happens, you enter the collective unconscious. When you jump into the collective unconscious from the individual unconscious, then, for instance, you can see another person passing in front of you, and you know that he is going to murder someone. That day, hardly does a person come in front of you, and you know what he wants to ask. That day, you can see someone passing by and you immediately know that his death is very close. When you know all this, that day you enter the collective unconscious. At that depth you will be connected to the whole, you will be connected to the unconscious of everyone.

It is an immense experience. It is a very deep experience because the whole universe starts to appear as one from within you. All living beings in the universe appear as one with you, all life seems to be your own. But you have to take a jump from here also; this is also not the ultimate state. This state has its own body, too. In this state, the whole body of actions of everyone becomes your own body; in this state you experience yourself almost as God. That's how many people in this state start declaring, "I am God," the way Meher Baba declared, "I am God, I am the incarnation of God."

One who has entered the collective unconscious cannot deceive you. He feels he is God because everything from everyone's unconscious starts to appear as his own. We feel that someone is crazy when he calls himself God. Deep down it is crazy; in fact, this too is not the ultimate state. In this state, everyone's unconscious and the actions of everyone's unconscious appear to be one's own.

That's why Meher Baba could say, after Gandhi's death: "I have absorbed Gandhi in myself." When Nehru died he said the same thing. People might think that he is a clever imposter, some kind of deceiver. From the level we are living, it seems to be a deception. In fact, there is deception in it, but not cheating: the deception is happening to Meher Baba himself – he is not deceiving you. But it does appear like this when the collective unconscious, when everyone's mind, starts to appear like your own. When anybody dies, it seems as though the person has been absorbed in you. Everyone's body, everybody's karmic body, has become your body and the thoughts in everyone's mind have become your thinking.

But even in this stage, the "I" is present. That's why Meher Baba could say: "I am the incarnation of God." But as long as the "I" is present, the ultimate truth has not been attained.

If we can remember at this point as well that this god-like body is still a body, and this god-like mind, this divine mind, is still a mind… If we can remember these keys, then another jump happens and we enter the cosmic unconscious. In that state of cosmic unconscious one can say, "I am *brahman*, the ultimate."

One then experiences the moon and stars revolving within him, the sun rising within him, as Swami Ramateertha used to say. If you tell that to a psychologist, he will call this man neurotic or psychotic, that he is not in his right mind. The moon and stars are always in the outer world, how can they be within?

There is truth in what the psychologist says. He is right as far as his understanding goes but he hasn't had the experience of people like Ramateertha. A person like Ramateertha has expanded to become the cosmic body. The endless boundaries of the universe are now his boundaries, so he will experience all the revolutions of the cosmic bodies within himself. He will experience the moon and stars revolving inside him. Such an individual can say, "I see the world being created and destroyed, I see the moon and stars forming and dying." The memories of such a person arise from the cosmos itself.

People who have talked about the birth of the universe – when the world was created, when the earth was created, when the moon and the stars were created – are mostly those who have experienced the cosmic unconscious. There can be mistakes in the chronological dates, because at that moment it was very difficult to keep track of dates; the experiences of these individuals are authentic, but not ultimate. If an individual even in this cosmic unconscious can remember those keys, he will know that his body is also the body of that vast universe. Whether the body is small – just six feet tall – or is expanded for endless miles, there is no difference.

Then it makes no difference if the thoughts are mine or of the ultimate, *brahman*. There is only a difference in degrees. If that can be remembered at this stage, then there is the fourth jump to take and the individual enters *mahanirvana*. The mind is completely wiped out there, the "I" disappears. Here even an individual like

Buddha does not even say, "I am *brahman*, I am God," he does not even say, "I am the soul."

Buddha found it very difficult to explain this – because he says there is no soul, there is no God, there is no *brahman*. Then the question is what remains now? Only the void remains, which has no limits, in which there are no currents of thought, no center and no ego. Only the void remains; it can be said that nothing is saved, nothing remains. Losing everything is the ultimate achievement. It is supreme, it is final. And beyond it? There is no way beyond it because there is no beyond. The jump from the cosmic unconscious is into the void, into the supreme, into truth, into *mahanirvana*, into moksha. You can call it whatever you like. In fact, all names are worthless. All languages are useless; obstacles arise because of them. The first obstacles come from us ourselves, so I have discussed them in detail.

So there are three main difficulties: the hope of happiness in the outside world, the hope of deathlessness in the world of body, and the hope for truth in the world of mind. These difficulties, these obstacles return at every stage but you do not have to be very concerned about them. If you go beyond these three obstacles, existence will give you three new ones. If you cross them, there will be new hurdles at a deeper stage. The obstacles will be the same, only their form at each stage will go on changing. They will pursue you until the end. When no hurdles remain, when you experience that nothing remains, then and only then will you know that you have known the ultimate: known that for which the sages of the Upanishads were thirsty, about which Krishna speaks in the Gita; for which Jesus was ready to hang on the crucifix; for which Buddha and Mahavira knock at the doors of each and every person, from village to village. But to know it, one has to erase oneself completely, totally. One has to erase oneself as a body, as a soul, as God and even as the ultimate reality.

I will end this topic by quoting Jesus. Jesus said: "Blessed are those who are bold enough to erase themselves because they alone can reach God. Those who are busy saving themselves are unfortunate because those who save themselves will lose everything."

These are the three keys. Begin from where you are, and the further journey will go on unfolding on its own. Just continue to use these three keys as long as anything remains. And when nothing remains, not even you, and the keys also disappear, no space will remain for making any proclamations, and no space will remain even for statements like Meher Baba's "I am God," or Ramateertha's, "Moons and stars orbit within me."

No space will remain even to proclaim: "I am the ultimate reality." Who will proclaim it? And who will be there to make proclamations for? When all words cease, all speech drops, and all personality is gone, what then remains is the ultimate. That alone is the search of all religiousness, the thirst of all beings, the longing of all souls. That alone is deathlessness.

As long as there is form, there is death. Where there is formlessness, there is deathlessness, there is bliss. As long as the other exists, there is sorrow and suffering. Only when the other no longer exists is bliss possible, only then is there peace. As long as "I" am, there is unrest. Only when "I" am not, is there peace. Only then is there *sat-chit-anand*, truth-consciousness-bliss. Not in talking, but in experiencing; not in saying, but in knowing; not in telling, but in being. It is not that *sat-chit-anand* is known; one *becomes* it.

Question 2

Osho,

In the practice of awareness, please explain to us the similarities and dissimilarities between witnessing, awareness, and acceptance.

In spiritual practice it will be useful to understand these three words – *witnessing*, *awareness*, and *total acceptance*. Witnessing is the first step, to pass through life as a witness. It means I will live as an observer, a seer, a witness throughout my life. If you abuse me, I will not feel abused. You are abusing the "I." If you hurt me with a stone, I will not feel that you threw the stone and *I* was hurt, but that you threw the stone and this person was hurt.

I will always stand at the third corner of the triangle. I will not continuously divide myself in two, I will always jump to the third corner. If my house catches fire, I will not feel that *my* house is on fire, but that *his* house is burning and I am looking at it. Spiritual practice begins with this witness, separating life into three parts.

Normally we separate life into two parts: I am here and you are there. You are the abuser, I am the receiver; that's all. There are only two parts, the third is not there. In becoming a witness, we add a third person. In all circumstances, I should always be the third person and not the second person. As this third angle becomes clearer, it seems right to laugh at the other two angles – the abuser and the abused.

When Ramateertha was in New York, some people threw stones at him, others abused him. Returning to his room he told his friends, "Ramateertha was caught up in big trouble today, people began to abuse him and some people threw stones at him. It was great fun."

The friends said, "What are you talking about? You yourself were abused."

Ramateertha replied, "How can they abuse me? I myself do not know my name, how can they know it? They were abusing Ramateertha."

His friends asked, "Aren't you Ramateertha then?"

Ramateertha replied, "If I were Ramateertha, I would have come back very upset and unhappy. I was standing and watching some people throwing abuse, and poor Ramateertha taking it. As I said to myself today, 'Ramateertha got caught up in great difficulty.'"

To be a witness is the first step for a seeker, to manifest this third person. It is easy. *Witness* is the easiest of all these three words. Try to be always aware of the witness. When you are eating your food, see that the food is being eaten. The person who you have known as "I" until now is eating. Wait at a corner of the table and watch. You are not eating, but the food is being eaten. Somebody is eating and you are watching it.

As this witness manifests itself, your interest in life becomes less and less because a witness cannot be harassed. The witness just cannot be harassed, only a doer can be harassed. When you think "I am eating my food," you can be made unhappy. When you say "I am making love," you can be disturbed. But when you say that someone is making love and another is being loved, and you are the third person witnessing it, then you cannot be disturbed. You are not anxious or worried.

If you remember to act as a witness five to ten times a day, you will stop dreaming at night. Only those who remain as doers throughout the day dream – they are the same at night. How can the habit of being the doer the whole day be given up during the night? If someone runs a shop during the day, he does the same thing at night. If I am quarreling in court the whole day, I will stand up in court at night also. Someone who takes an exam in the university during the day also takes an exam in the night. Whoever remains a doer during the day becomes a doer at night too. And, one who is a witness during the day also becomes a witness at night.

Now this is a very interesting thing: if you become a witness during the day, your shop will not stop functioning. But the shop within you will be closed. Since the shop in your dreams is not a real shop, it is only an idea, when you become a witness it disappears. The shop outside will go on working, but the shop in your dreams will disappear. There is no possibility of cares and worries when you become a witness.

Worries and anxieties increase whenever the idea "I am the doer" becomes prevalent. America today is the most worried country because the notion "I am doing" is the strongest there. Whatever is being done, the "I" is always standing behind it. In the past, in the ancient world, there were not too many anxieties and worries. The reason is not because people were traveling in bullock carts rather than airplanes. It is altogether different.

Why were there fewer worries in the past? The witness, the third angle of the triangle, was known in the ancient world along with the doer, and people always tried to develop this idea. They saw that things were happening but also that "I am not doing them." They would say this in many ways. Sometimes they would say that God was doing something. This is one way of saying "I am not the doer." Sometimes they would say that fate was doing them. Sometimes, they would just say "It is written." This is also a way of saying "I am not the doer."

We are crazy; we misunderstood their ways so completely that the reasons for saying what they did are completely forgotten – but we still cling vehemently to the words they used. We still believe in fate, even today. We run to a palmist or an astrologer for a reading, to find ways and means to change our fate by performing a sacrifice, some worship, and so on. Even today we say, "Whatever happens is God's doing," but this is only talk. There is no place for this in our beings. There is no place left for this anywhere, just mere words remain in our hands: all these words are just different ways of saying it. Those words were simply used to denote the real concept behind them – that the witness was present in the third corner, that there was no doer.

So Krishna can tell Arjuna to fight: "Why do you worry and think that you are fighting? I am the one who is fighting." And

Krishna further tells him: "Kill them. Why do you worry and think you are killing them? Those who you think you're going to kill have already been killed."

Arjuna doesn't understand this statement of Krishna because he considers himself the doer. He says, "How can I kill my loved ones, they are part of me. No, I cannot kill them." His worries are those of a doer.

If you want to understand the essence of the Gita, it is contained in two phrases: Arjuna is deluded in thinking of himself as the doer, and Krishna goes on persuading him all the time to be a witness. There is nothing more to understand in the Gita. Krishna goes on repeating: "You are simply an observer, a seer, and not a doer. All this has already happened." This is just a way of telling him that he is not the doer: "Forget it completely. This delusion alone will defeat you and will throw you into self-deception. This delusion is keeping you worried, keeping you obsessed."

To be a witness is the first step of the seeker. It is not the easiest of things, but compared to the higher steps, it is certainly easy. From the point of view of what we are doing, it seems difficult, but if you practice a little, it is not. Swimming in a river, see how others swim. Walking on the road, watch how others walk. This is not difficult. Sometimes you will get a flash of the witness. And as soon as you get that glimpse of the third angle, all of a sudden you will see that the whole world has changed. Everything will have changed, things will now have a different color. The whole world exists in the way we see it. When our vision changes, the world changes.

The second step is awareness. It goes deeper than being a witness. In the act of witnessing, we take two people, you and me, and in that act stand apart from them as a third person. In witnessing, we divide the world into three parts; we make a triangle. It is three parts: in witnessing, there are three. In awareness, no such division is made. In awareness we do not say that we are aware about something. We say that we live in awareness. While walking, we are aware that we are walking; we are doing it consciously.

What generally happens is that all our actions are executed out of habit. When you are eating food, you do not really know that you are eating. When you turn toward your home, you do it automatically, like a machine. You pat your son's head and ask, "Are you okay?" but you don't realize at all what you are doing. You had said the same thing yesterday and the day before. You have become like a gramophone record. You smile when you see your wife; it is a recorded smile and you smile out of sheer habit. It is only a defense measure, performed unconsciously, since you don't know what she will do! And the answer that your wife is giving is not given consciously. All this has become part of the habit. So if you observe in the right way you will notice that you do not meet each other at all, you only go on repeating the same old routines like a record. You can only meet when you relate to each other in full consciousness.

I had a professor who, whenever I asked him about a book, "Did you read it?" would say, "Yes I have read it, it is a good book."

But from his talks it never seemed to me that he could have read those books. One day I went and gave a false title of a book to him. Neither was there an author of that name, nor was such a book ever written.

I went and asked him, "Have you read the book of such and such an author?"

He said, "Yes, it is a very good book, really a good book." He said what he always did.

I kept looking in his eyes. I sat quietly for some time.

Then he asked, "What are you doing?"

He became restless. He asked, "Why are you quiet? Did I say anything wrong? It could be a matter of each person's taste, you may not have liked it."

Even then I remained quiet and kept looking in his eyes, and his anxiety increased further. He said, "What are you suggesting? There can be only two possibilities: it is possible that you may not have liked it, but why are you silent?"

I said, "I am not silent for this reason, I am silent so that perhaps even now you may remember."

He said, "What do you mean? I remember it very clearly!"

And then he remembered; his facial expression changed. Even then I remained silent.

He said, "Forgive me, I have caught this bad habit and now I must admit it. I have decided many times that I must stop saying this. But I don't know what happens: by the time I realize that it has happened again, I have already said it. I don't know what sort of weakness this is that I am unable to say that I haven't read this book. No, I have not read this book. But surely I have seen it in the library."

I said to him, "You are going back on your words. This book does not exist! So you cannot have seen it in the library."

Such is the mind of man – unconscious. He knows nothing of what he is saying, what he is doing, where he is going. In the state of full consciousness you are always totally aware of every action you do. You are always aware of what is being done. It may be eating, talking, anything. In witnessing, the third point manifests itself, and as a witness you will find awareness easy – because to be a witness, you have to be aware. But with awareness you are not separate; whatever is happening, is happening in the light of the awareness burning within. Just raising your foot, you do it consciously. You utter every word in a state of full consciousness. If you say yes, you mean to say yes; you have said it consciously. And if you say no, you mean to say no; you have spoken with awareness.

In this state of awareness, everything that is meaningless in life ceases because nobody can do anything worthless and meaningless while being aware. The web of meaningless things in life, which we spin like spiders and often get ourselves caught in, is broken immediately. If we tell a lie, to maintain that lie throughout life, we go on telling other lies. We forget the original lie; the net goes on spreading and step by step we thoughtlessly move into it. We walk on paths where we did not want to walk. We make connections which we did not want to make. We do things we never wanted to do. Then our whole life becomes madness.

Awareness means to be totally aware of what you are doing at the time of doing it. Experiment with that and you will see it, and you will experience such peace as you have never known before.

The third step, suchness, is even more difficult. One can cultivate awareness only if one includes suchness. Suchness means things are as they are. Suchness means total acceptance. Suchness means there is no complaint whatever. Suchness means what is, simply *is* – and I accept it. In witnessing, I am a watcher of whatever is happening; it is possible I may not accept it. In awareness, I am awake. Whatever should not be, will slowly drop away, and only what should be will survive. In suchness, I accept all that is. Suffering, death, meeting with the loved one, separation from the loved one, I totally accept whatever is. There is no complaint, no denial whatever from any corner of my being.

Suchness is ultimate religiousness. A religious person is not one who says "I believe," who says "I have faith, I have trust." A religious person is one who does not complain, who says, "Whatever is, is right. I have no opposition to it anywhere in me, not in any corner of me. I accept it." His every breath is one of acceptance. That total acceptance is his every single heartbeat. Whatever is, however this world is...

Even an atheist does not believe this. Voltaire has written somewhere: "Oh God, we might accept you some day but we cannot accept your world." There are some who accept the world but are not able to accept God. We all accept happiness, but who would accept unhappiness? And as long as it is not accepted, unhappiness will remain. Perhaps this is the importance of unhappiness in the evolution of spiritual life. Whatever comes in the scheme of life has to be accepted. Total acceptance brings showers of bliss. Anybody can accept flowers, but the real question is to accept thorns. Everybody accepts life, embraces it; the question is to accept death.

Tathata means total acceptance, we do not even remove a small piece of anything; everything is accepted in toto. Such acceptance can take place when one is totally aware, and that is only possible after becoming a witness. When such acceptance is fixed in someone's heart, a dance of endless bliss begins in his being. The music of the flute of the void, and the dance with no movement enter his life. The veena that has no strings starts playing in his life. The fragrance which has no flower begins to pervade his life. But total acceptance is a very difficult thing to achieve. The feeling of total acceptance is very difficult: nothing is more arduous than this. It means whatever is…

A monk was passing under a tree. A man hit him with a stick, but in his nervousness his stick fell and he ran away. The monk took the stick, went to a nearby shop, and told the shopkeeper to keep the stick and to return it to that poor man if he came back in search of it.

The shopkeeper said, "What a kind man you are! He hit you with that stick."

The monk replied, "Once when I was passing under a tree, a branch of the tree fell on me, and I accepted it. That man must at least be better than that tree."

For example, if you are sailing in a boat on a river and an empty boat comes from the side and bumps against your boat, you say nothing. You accept it and sail on. But if a man was sitting in that boat, there would be a quarrel. You would forgive the boat, but you would not forgive the man. You would forgive the boat because you accepted it – there was no other way for you, other than to accept it. You would not forgive the man because it was difficult to accept him.

When both situations – whether the boat is empty or a man is aboard – are one and the same to you, this is total acceptance. Even if there is the slightest difference in your attitude, you have missed. If somebody throws flowers at you and another person throws stones at you, if you accept both situations and make no distinction between the two, then there is total acceptance. Then you have no desire for anything other than what is happening in this world. You are content with this whole, huge, endless universe where waves are moving in the ocean, tempests are rising, flowers are blooming on the trees, stars are moving in the sky, someone is throwing abuse, and someone is singing songs. You accept the whole as it is; this is suchness, the third step for the seeker.

To reach a state of full awareness, you must begin with witnessing and end with total acceptance. Begin by standing at the third corner, then awaken, be aware, and then attain acceptance. First separate yourself as an observer from the doer, then bring awareness to your actions, and then acceptance to the whole. Following these three steps, awareness slowly becomes stronger and deeper. One cannot even say what will happen the day there is total awareness, a conscious mind!

I remembered something about total acceptance that I will tell you:

A Zen mystic has written a small song. He has written: "The swans fly in the sky, they do not have any desire for their reflections to be made in the silent lake below."

But the reflection *is* made. When the swans fly over that blue lake below, the lake does not have any desire to catch the reflection of the swans, but the reflections are made.

Then the swans fly away and so do the reflections. Neither the swans know that their reflections were caught in the lake, nor does the lake know that the reflections of the swans had disturbed its silence.

Suchness, tathata, means a state of being where, whatever happens, he agrees with it: he does not want to make it in any way different, he has no complaints.

Buddha is called Tathagata; he liked this name very much. Whenever he passed through a village he would say that Tathagata is passing: it means "one who has achieved the attitude of total acceptance." Thus come, thus gone, just as the swans fly over a lake, cast their shadows and are gone – neither the swans nor the lake know of their reflections. There is no desire to do anything other than what is happening. Whatever happened, happened; no account is kept, there is no hope for success or failure, no frustration is entertained and no victory is contemplated. One who came like a swan, a reflection was made on the water, and disappeared.

In Japan, the Zen mystics say that Buddha never happened. Only great mystics can make such great jokes! Rinzai, a Zen master, would say, "Buddha never happened – why are you telling such stories!" He would pray to Buddha every day, he would stand with folded hands in front of the statue and say, "*Buddham sharanam gachchhami*, I go to the feet of the awakened one."

His disciples caught hold of him and said, "You are fooling us! You tell us that Buddha never existed and you stand in front of the statue saying *Buddham sharanam gachchhami*."

And Rinzai said, "That is why I say so! Even if he had existed a little, I would not have said to go to his feet. He was not, he did not exist."

He was like a line drawn on the water; it is just drawn and disappears. Or one could say – perhaps the line drawn on water may be an exaggeration, the description of the swans seems right – the reflection was made and disappeared.

He says, "He was not, that is why I have made his statue, in the hope that one day I too may reach that state where being or not being become one and the same. Where I am or I am not are the same. Where life and death take on the same meaning; where existence and nonexistence are the same, synonymous."

Rinzai said, "So I say, *Buddham sharanam gachchhami*. This means I come to your feet, one who has no feet. I come to your refuge, you, who is not. I would like to be like you, one who never was. You are not."

Tathata is individuality, it is emptiness, it is the void. It should be said that it is a living void within. It is a void surrounded by bones, flesh, and tissues. He who becomes like this void is a tathata. He reaches the fourth stage. To be a tathata is to jump from the collective unconsciousness into the cosmic unconsciousness.

In the stage of witnessing, we move from the outer world and enter the unconscious. In awareness, we move beyond the unconscious, and enter the collective unconscious. In that stage we have to practice acceptance; then we enter the cosmic unconscious. After the cosmic unconscious is reached, there is no spiritual practice. In tathata there is no sadhana, no spiritual practice: it becomes your very quality. In this stage, everything in life goes on by itself, effortlessly – just as breathing happens by itself, we do not make it happen; just like the heart beats by itself, we do not have to make it beat. No effort is needed to maintain it, no more effort to go within. What we were within is lost. Tathata is the ultimate attainment. It means to descend into the temple of the infinite abyss.

Religiousness is the door. Meditation is the process of approaching that door. Suchness is the presiding deity in the temple.

One last question:

Question 3

Osho,

You have said that an unaware person doesn't do anything – things just happen to him without his wishing or choosing them. Please explain the difference between someone who is asleep and an awakened person.

Gurdjieff says that an awakened person becomes crystallized. What does that mean?

Is it not that the ego of an awakened person disappears rather than becoming crystallized?

An unawakened, sleeping, person is not a doer. Things are happening to him, and he thinks he is doing them. The awakened person also is not a doer, but he knows it. This is the only difference. An unawakened person thinks he is a doer; although he does not do anything, everything happens. Even an awakened person does not do anything, everything happens, but an awakened person *knows* that everything happens: "I am not a doer." There is no difference in their actions but there is a difference in their knowing, their attitude, in their awareness of their actions. The one who is awakened walks, the unawakened also walks. An individual full of awareness walks with the knowing "I am not," and a person without awareness walks full of ego, full of arrogance. This is the difference.

You have also asked, "Gurdjieff says an awakened person becomes crystallized." The crystallization of a person who is awakened happens when individuality arises in him. Jung says the same thing as Gurdjieff; that when a person is awake within, his individuality becomes stronger. So it is natural to raise the question of whether the individuation of a person who is awakened becomes stronger or dies. Is it transformed into ego or does it go away? This is merely a difference in language, nothing more. I call it the birth of the void, emptiness. Gurdjieff calls it crystallization. Actually the real individual is born for the first time by becoming empty, because in that process he attains vastness. By becoming the void, by losing individuality, one becomes a real individual for the first time.

But it is difficult to understand. It is one of the paradoxes of religion that we fail to comprehend. When a drop of water falls into the ocean, you can say the drop is lost: Where is it now? You can also say that the drop has become the ocean. You can say the drop is lost, is nonexistent, has become a void. Or you can say it has become the ocean. It was nothing before but now for the first time it has become the ocean. These are negative and positive ways of speaking.

Gurdjieff and Jung call this individuation, crystallization. The person has become an individual for the first time, just as the drop has become the ocean. Mahavira calls it the atman, the soul; it means the same. Shankara calls it *brahman*; it is the same thing. All these are positive terms. Only Buddha uses negative terms. He says anatman, which means "non-atman." It does not become the soul, it has perished. There is now no atman, no *brahman*, and what remains has no words.

He says the drop is not there, now let the subject go. When you say that the drop becomes the ocean, then too you are making it into a bigger drop, you give it a boundary. No matter how vast the ocean is, imagine, however vast it is, it has a boundary. Buddha says when you use positive words there will always be a boundary. Man's mind runs after the positive very quickly. If a man is asked to lose himself, he will ask, "Why should I lose myself; what will be the outcome?" If you reply, "You will become God," he will understand it quickly. If you say, "You will be *brahman*," he will understand it quickly. Hence Buddha's teaching did not take firm roots in this country. We are used to positive language.

Buddha used mostly negative language and this was the first time in the history of mankind. And the fact is that only negative statements concerning the ultimate truth can be made because all positive statements form boundaries.

So the Upanishads say, "Not this, not that." It is a negative statement: not this, not that. If you say that *brahman* is like this, it is not this. And if you say *brahman* is like that, it is not that either. If you ask the seer of the Upanishads, he would say, "*Neti-neti*, neither this nor that. Do not ask further: whatever else there is, that is it." Buddha also uses negative language. Buddha says it is nothing, void. The word he uses is *nirvana*. That word is very significant and meaningful. *Nirvana* means the extinguishing of a lamp. There is a lamp, and if you blow out the flame, it will be extinguished. If we ask where the light went, you say it is gone, lost. A drop is lost in the ocean. But where did the light go? Or if you want to, you can say that the light has become everything, it has become one with everything, now it has no limits.

Buddha and all those who want to be precise talk in negative terms. It is not that Mahavira or Shankara did not know this. But people want to know if the drop of water is willing to be lost, if it is willing to merge into the ocean. It will be willing only when it knows that there is no harm in being lost. The drop will disappear, but it will become the ocean. But Buddha says if a drop falls into the ocean with a desire to become the ocean, it will not be able to become the ocean because the desire will keep it as a drop of water. This greed, this desire, will keep its personality fastened on all sides.

That is why I use the word *void*. The ultimate has no limits at all, the individual simply vanishes. Gurdjieff says crystallization; I would say total de-crystallization, total dispersion, total surrender. Nothing is left – not even the lines on the water remain; the swans have flown away and no reflection stays on the lake. The drop has disappeared, and the light of the lamp is extinguished. In spite of searching for it in the endless space, no trace of it is found.

All the same, it is up to you to make your choice of words. If your mind is afraid of negative terms, use positive words. As you gather more and more courage, go on dropping the positive terms. One has to one day gather courage to jump into the negative. Only one who is willing to jump into the negative attains the whole. One who is willing to become the void is entitled to be the whole.

I am grateful that you listened to me with such love and silence. Now to end, I bow down to the godliness that dwells in you all. Please accept my *pranam*, my offering of respect.

About Osho

Osho's unique contribution to the understanding of who we are defies categorization. Mystic and scientist, a rebellious spirit whose sole interest is to alert humanity to the urgent need to discover a new way of living. To continue as before is to invite threats to our very survival on this unique and beautiful planet.

His essential point is that only by changing ourselves, one individual at a time, can the outcome of all our "selves" – our societies, our cultures, our beliefs, our world – also change. The doorway to that change is meditation.

Osho the scientist has experimented and scrutinized all the approaches of the past and examined their effects on the modern human being and responded to their shortcomings by creating a new starting point for the hyperactive twenty-first century mind: OSHO Active Meditations.

Once the agitation of a modern lifetime has started to settle, "activity" can melt into "passivity," a key starting point of real meditation. To support this next step, Osho has transformed the ancient "art of listening" into a subtle contemporary methodology: the OSHO Talks. Here words become music, the listener discovers who is listening, and the awareness moves from what is being heard to the individual doing the listening. Magically, as silence arises, what needs to be heard is understood directly, free from the distraction of a mind that can only interrupt and interfere with this delicate process.

These thousands of talks cover everything from the individual quest for meaning to the most urgent social and political issues facing society today. Osho's books are not written but are transcribed from audio and video recordings of these extemporaneous talks to international audiences. As he puts it, "So remember: whatever I am saying is not just for you... I am talking also for the future generations."

Osho has been described by *The Sunday Times* in London as one of the "1000 Makers of the 20th Century" and by American author Tom Robbins as "the most dangerous man since Jesus Christ." *Sunday Mid-Day* (India) has selected Osho as one of ten people – along with Gandhi, Nehru and Buddha – who have changed the destiny of India.

About his own work Osho has said that he is helping to create the conditions for the birth of a new kind of human being. He often characterizes this new human being as "Zorba the Buddha" – capable both of enjoying the earthy pleasures of a Zorba the Greek and the silent serenity of a Gautama the Buddha.

Running like a thread through all aspects of Osho's talks and meditations is a vision that encompasses both the timeless wisdom of all ages past and the highest potential of today's (and tomorrow's) science and technology.

Osho is known for his revolutionary contribution to the science of inner transformation, with an approach to meditation that acknowledges the accelerated pace of contemporary life. His unique OSHO Active Meditations™ are designed to first release the accumulated stresses of body and mind, so that it is then easier to take an experience of stillness and thought-free relaxation into daily life.

Two autobiographical works by the author are available:

Autobiography of a Spiritually Incorrect Mystic, St Martins Press, New York (book and eBook)

Glimpses of a Golden Childhood, OSHO Media International, Pune, India (book and eBook)

OSHO International Meditation Resort

Each year the Meditation Resort welcomes thousands of people from more than 100 countries. The unique campus provides an opportunity for a direct personal experience of a new way of living – with more awareness, relaxation, celebration and creativity. A great variety of around-the-clock and around-the-year program options are available. Doing nothing and just relaxing is one of them!

All of the programs are based on Osho's vision of "Zorba the Buddha" – a qualitatively new kind of human being who is able both to participate creatively in everyday life and to relax into silence and meditation.

Location

Located 100 miles southeast of Mumbai in the thriving modern city of Pune, India, the OSHO International Meditation Resort is a holiday destination with a difference. The Meditation Resort is spread over 28 acres of spectacular gardens in a beautiful tree-lined residential area.

OSHO Meditations

A full daily schedule of meditations for every type of person includes both traditional and revolutionary methods, and particularly the OSHO Active MeditationsTM. The daily meditation program takes place in what must be the world's largest meditation hall, the OSHO Auditorium.

OSHO Multiversity

Individual sessions, courses and workshops cover everything from creative arts to holistic health, personal transformation, relationship and life transition, transforming meditation into a lifestyle for life and work, esoteric sciences, and the "Zen" approach to sports and recreation. The secret of the OSHO Multiversity's success lies in the fact that all its programs are combined with meditation, supporting the understanding that as human beings we are far more than the sum of our parts.

OSHO Basho Spa

The luxurious Basho Spa provides for leisurely open-air swimming surrounded by trees and tropical green. The uniquely styled, spacious Jacuzzi, the saunas, gym, tennis courts… all these are enhanced by their stunningly beautiful setting.

Cuisine

A variety of different eating areas serve delicious Western, Asian and Indian vegetarian food – most of it organically grown especially for the Meditation Resort. Breads and cakes are baked in the resort's own bakery.

Night life

There are many evening events to choose from – dancing being at the top of the list! Other activities include fullmoon meditations beneath the stars, variety shows, music performances and meditations for daily life.

Facilities

You can buy all of your basic necessities and toiletries in the Galleria. The Multimedia Gallery sells a large range of OSHO media products. There is also a bank, a travel agency and a Cyber Café on-campus. For those who enjoy shopping, Pune provides all the options, ranging from traditional and ethnic Indian products to all of the global brand-name stores.

Accommodation

You can choose to stay in the elegant rooms of the OSHO Guesthouse, or for longer stays on campus you can select one of the OSHO Living-In programs. Additionally, there is a plentiful variety of nearby hotels and serviced apartments.

www.osho.com/meditationresort
www.osho.com/guesthouse
www.osho.com/livingin

Also by Osho

Early Discourses and Writings

The Art of Living
Astrology
Breaking All Boundaries
Compassion and Revolution
A Cup of Tea
Dimensions beyond the Known
Earthen Lamps
The Eternal Quest
Flowers of Love
From Sex to Superconsciousness
The Great Challenge
Hidden Mysteries
I Am the Gate
The Independent Mind
Into the Void
Keys to a New Life
Life Is a Soap Bubble
Love Letters to Life
New Dimensions of Yoga
The Path of Meditation
The Psychology of the Esoteric
Religion's Expiration Date
The Search for Peace
Seeds of Wisdom
Silence: The Message of Your Being
Work Is Love Made Visible
Three Steps to Awakening
Into the Void

Meditation

And Now and Here
In Search of the Miraculous
Meditation: The Art of Ecstasy
Meditation: The First and Last Freedom
The Inner Journey
The Perfect Way

Buddha and Buddhist Masters

The Book of Wisdom
The Dhammapada: The Way of the Buddha(Vols 1-12)
The Diamond Sutra
The Discipline of Transcendence (Vols 1-4)
The Heart Sutra

Indian Mystics
Bliss:Living beyond Happiness and Misery (Shiv Sutras)
Die O Yogi Die (Gorakh)
Enlightenment: The Only Revolution (Ashtavakra)
Krishna: The Man and His Philosophy
Showering without Clouds (Sahajo)
The True Name (Vols 1&2) (Nanak)
The Last Morning Star (Daya)
The Song of Ecstasy (Adi Shankara)

Baul Mystics
The Beloved (Vols 1 & 2)

Kabir
The Divine Melody
Ecstasy: The Forgotten Language
The Fabric of Life
The Fish in the Sea Is Not Thirsty
The Great Secret
The Guest
The Path of Love
The Revolution

Jesus and Christian Mystics
Come Follow to You (Vols 1-4)
I Say Unto You (Vols 1 & 2)
The Mustard Seed
Theologia Mystica

Jewish Mystics
The Art of Dying
The True Sage

Western Mystics
Guida Spirituale (*Desiderata*)
The Great Challenge (Treatise of St. Dionysius)
The Hidden Harmony (Heraclitus)
The New Alchemy: To Turn You On (Mabel Collins' Light on the Path)
Philosophia Perennis (Vols 1 & 2) (*The Golden Verses of Pythagoras*)
Reflections on Kahlil Gibran's The Prophet
Theologica Mystica
Zarathustra: A God That Can Dance (Nietzsche's *Thus Spake Zarathustra*)
Zarathustra: The Laughing Prophet (Nietzsche's *Thus Spake Zarathustra*)
The Voice of Silence (Mabel Collins' *Light on the Path*)

Sufism
Just Like That
The Perfect Master (Vols 1 & 2)

The Secret
Sufis: The People of the Path (Vols 1 & 2)
Unio Mystica (Vols 1 & 2)
Until You Die
The Wisdom of the Sands (Vols 1 & 2)

Tantra
Tantra: The Supreme Understanding
The Tantra Experience: The Royal Song of Saraha (same as Tantra Vision, Vol. 1)
Tantric Transformation: The Royal Song of Saraha (same as Tantra Vision, Vol. 2)
The Book of Secrets: Vigyan Bhairav
Tantra

The Upanishads
Behind a Thousand Names (Nirvana Upanishad)
Finger Pointing to the Moon (Adhyatma Upanishad)
Flight of the Alone to the Alone (Kaivalya Upanishad)
The Heartbeat of the Absolute (Ishavasya Upanishad)
I Am That (Isa Upanishad)
The Message beyond Words (Kathopanishad)
Philosophia Ultima (Mandukya Upanishad)
The Supreme Doctrine (Kenopanishad)
That Art Thou (Sarvasar Upanishad, Kaivalya Upanishad, Adhyatma Upanishad)
The Ultimate Alchemy (Vols 1 & 2)
(Atma Pooja Upanishad)
Vedanta: Seven Steps to Samadhi (Akshaya Upanishad)
The Way beyond Any Way (Sarvasar Upanishad)

Tao
The Empty Boat
The Secret of Secrets
Tao: The Golden Gate (Vols 1 & 2)
Tao: The Pathless Path (Vols 1 & 2)
Tao: The Three Treasures (Vols 1-4)
When the Shoe Fits

Yoga
Yoga: The Science of the Soul (Vols 1-10)
The Path of Yoga (Vol.1)
The Heart of Yoga (Vol.2)

Yoga: The Mystery beyond Mind (Vol.3)
The Alchemy of Yoga (Vol.4)
Yoga: A New Direction (Vol.5)
Essence of Yoga (Vol.6)
Yoga: The Science of Living (Vol.7)
Secrets of Yoga (Vol.8)
Yoga: The Path to Liberation (Vol.9)
Yoga: The Supreme Science (Vol.10)

Zen and Zen Masters
Ah, This!
Ancient Music in the Pines
And the Flowers Showered…
And the Grass Grows By Itself…
A Bird on the Wing
Bodhidharma: The Greatest Zen Master
The Buddha: The Emptiness of the Heart
Christianity, the Deadliest Poison and Zen, the Antidote to All Poisons
Communism and Zen Fire, Zen Wind
Dang Dang Doko Dang
The First Principle
God Is Dead: Now Zen Is the Only Living Truth
The Great Zen Master Ta Hui
Hsin Hsin Ming: The Book of Nothing
I Celebrate Myself: God Is No Where, Life Is Now Here
Kyozan: A True Man of Zen
The Language of Existence
Live Zen
The Miracle
Nirvana: The Last Nightmare
No Mind: The Flowers of Eternity
No Water, No Moon
One Seed Makes the Whole Earth Green
The Original Man
Returning to the Source
The Search: Talks on the 10 Bulls of Zen
A Sudden Clash of Thunder
The Sun Rises in the Evening
Take it Easy
This. This. A Thousand Times This
This Very Body the Buddha
Turning In
Walking in Zen, Sitting in Zen
The White Lotus
Yakusan: Straight to the Point of Enlightenment
The Zen Manifesto: Freedom from Oneself
Zen: The Diamond Thunderbolt
Zen: The Mystery and the Poetry of the Beyond

Zen: The Path of Paradox (Vols 1-3)
Zen: The Quantum Leap from Mind to No-Mind
Zen: The Solitary Bird, Cuckoo of the Forest
Zen: The Special Transmission
Osho: On the Ancient Masters of Zen
Dogen: The Zen Master
Hyakujo: The Everest of Zen – With Basho's haikus
Isan: No Footprints in the Blue Sky
Joshu: The Lion's Roar
Ma Tzu: The Empty Mirror
Nansen: The Point of Departure
Rinzai: Master of the Irrational

Responses to Questions

Be Still and Know
Beyond Enlightenment (Talks in Bombay)
Beyond Psychology (Talks in Uruguay)
Come, Come, Yet Again Come
From Bondage to Freedom
From Darkness to Light
From Death to Deathlessness
From Ignorance to Innocence
From Misery to Enlightenment
From Personality to Individuality
From the False to the Truth
From Unconsciousness to Consciousness
The Goose Is Out
The Great Pilgrimage: From Here to Here
The Invitation
Light on the Path (Talks in the Himalayas)
My Way: The Way of the White Clouds
Nowhere to Go but In
The Osho Upanishad (Talks in Bombay)
The Path of the Mystic (Talks in Uruguay)
The Razor's Edge
Sermons in Stones (Talks in Bombay)
Socrates Poisoned Again After 25 Centuries (Talks in Greece)
The Sword and the Lotus (Talks in the Himalayas)
Transmission of the Lamp (Talks in Uruguay)
Walk without Feet, Fly without Wings and Think without Mind
The Wild Geese and the Water
Yaa-Hoo! The Mystic Rose
Zen: Zest, Zip, Zap and Zing

Osho's Vision for the World

The Golden Future
The Hidden Splendor

The New Dawn
The Rebel
The Rebellious Spirit

The Mantra Series
Hari Om Tat Sat
Om Mani Padme Hum
Om Shantih Shantih Shantih
Sat Chit Anand
Satyam Shivam Sundaram

Personal Glimpses
Books I Have Loved
Glimpses of a Golden Childhood
Notes of a Madman

Interviews with the World Press
The Man of Truth: A Majority of One

For any information about OSHO Books, please contact:

OSHO Media International
17 Koregaon Park, Pune – 411001, MS, India
Phone: +91-20-66019999 Fax: +91-20-66019990
E-mail: distribution@osho.net
Website: http://www.osho.com

For More Information

For a full selection of OSHO multilingual online destinations, see osho.com/allaboutosho

The official and comprehensive website of OSHO International is osho.com

For more OSHO unique content and formats see:

- OSHO Active Meditations: osho.com/meditate
- iOsho, a bouquet of digital OSHO experiences featuring OSHO Zen Tarot, TV, Library, Horoscope, eGreetings and Radio. Please take a moment to do a one time registration which will allow you a universal login. Registration is free and open to anyone with a valid email address: osho.com/iosho
- The OSHO online shop: osho.com/shop
- Visit the OSHO International Meditation Resort: osho.com/visit
- Contribute in the OSHO Translation Project:oshotalks.com
- Read the OSHO Newsletters: osho.com/NewsLetters
- Watch OSHO on YouTube: youtube.com/user/OSHOInternational
- Follow OSHO on Facebook: facebook.com/osho.international.meditation.resort
- and Twitter: twitter.com/OSHO

Thank you for buying this OSHO book.